ADVENTURE EXPEDITION ONE

ADVENTURE EXPEDITION ONE

Plan & Execute Your First Successful Expedition

Aaron Linsdau, M.S.
Terry M. Williams, M.D.

SASTRUGI PRESS

©2019 Aaron Linsdau, Terry M. Williams
Interior image copyrights © Aaron Linsdau and © Terry Williams
Email transcripts © Jason Thompson

All rights reserved. No part of this book may be reproduced or transmitted in any form or by any means, electronic or mechanical, including photocopying, recording, or by any information storage and retrieval system without the written permission of the author, except where permitted by law.

Sastrugi Press / Published by arrangement with the author
Sastrugi Press: PO Box 1297, Jackson, WY 83001, United States www.sastrugipress.com

Adventure Expedition One: Plan & Execute Your First Successful Expedition

The activities described in this book are inherently dangerous. The publisher does not have any control over and does not assume any responsibility for author or third-party websites or their content.

Modern medical treatment is a constantly evolving field—recommended treatment and drug therapy are always changing. All medical treatment discussed in this book must be evaluated using the most current product information provided by the manufacturer to verify the recommended dose, the proper administration, and contraindications. It is always the responsibility of the licensed practitioner, relying on training and knowledge of the patient, to determine the best treatment and proper dosages for each individual. Neither the publisher nor the authors assume any liability for any injury or illness related to the medical discussions in this publication.

Any person participating in the activities described in this work is personally responsible for learning the proper techniques and using good judgment. You are responsible for your own actions and decisions. The information contained in this work is subjective and based solely on opinions. No book can advise you of all potential hazards or anticipate the limitations of any reader. Participation in the described activities can result in severe injury or death. Neither the publisher nor the authors assume any liability for anyone participating in the activities described in this work.

Library of Congress Catalog-in-Publication Data
Library of Congress Control Number: 2018912634
Linsdau, Aaron and Williams, Terry M.
Adventure Expedition One / Aaron Linsdau and Terry M. Williams—1st U.S. ed.
p. cm.
1. Travel 2. Exploration 3. Adventure 4. Polar Regions 5. Mountaineering
Summary: Master the fundamentals of an expedition so you can create a successful, enjoyable, and safe first expedition experience.

ISBN-13: 978-1-944986-51-3 (hardback), 978-1-944986-52-0 (paperback)
613.6—dc23

Printed in the United States of America
10 9 8 7 6 5 4 3 2 1

Interior graphics courtesy of all-free-download.com

*To Dad and Mom for all the sleepless nights you
have endured while I was away.*

—AL

*To Diane, my wife and best friend, who has always encouraged me to
make space in my life for adventure.*

—TW

Table of Contents

Part One: Your Own Expedition   **1**

    It's a process   2
    Overview of steps to your expedition   3
    Where to start?   4
    Inspiration   6
    Why an expedition?   7
    Emotions   10
    Safety   12

Part Two: Create an Expedition   **15**

    Identify and define the expedition   15
    What is an expedition?   16
    Expedition ideas   19
    Purpose   22
    Documentation   22

Part Three: Planning   **25**

    Overview   25
    Expedition goal creation   26
    Fallback Plan   28
    Injury or illness   31
    Equipment damage   32
    Equipment loss   32
    Navigation errors   32
    Technology failure   33
    Weather   33
    Human factors (inexperience, conflict,
       morale) inside a team   33
    Human factors (culture, criminals, terrorism)
       outside the team   34
    Contingencies   34
    Project management   35
    Roadblocks   36
    Timetable   37

Crisis planning	38
Discipline	39
Training plan	40
Go fast, go slow	41
Flight and travel planning	44
Planning for team dynamics	45
Travel and expedition insurance	47
People	48
Equipment	49
Conflict	52
Mini-expeditions	52

Part Four: Financing — **54**

Adventure resumé	54
How do I get the money?	55
Self-funding	55
Non-profit funding	58
Crowdfunding	60
Traditional sponsors	62

Part Five: Physical Training — **67**

Physical preparation	67
Supported expedition training	68
Extreme or long-range unsupported expedition training	70
Great nutrition overview	71
Adventure-specific training	73

Part Six: Skills — **75**

Overview	75
Skills for success	77
Expedition manager	79
Rescue mentality	85
Teamwork	92
Certified outdoor education	92
Self-sufficiency	93
Discipline	93

Social courtesy	95
Patience	96
Survival Skills	96
Survival Essentials	98
First aid	101
Field diagnosis tricks	102
Cold climates and solar radiation	103
Personal hygiene	104
Hot climates	111
Hydration	111
Nutrition	113
Salt intake	115
Trace mineral intake	116
Logistics	117
Navigation	120
Weather and the Elements	124
Rescue and medical insurance	124
Part Seven: Equipment	**127**
Ten essentials	127
Gear minimalism	132
Clothing	138
Shelter	142
Sleep system	144
Cooking	147
Stoves	147
Food Storage	151
Communication	151
Recording the experience of the expedition	157
Part Eight: Medical	**160**
Expedition medical issues	160
Introduction	160
Planning for medical issues	161
Pre-existing chronic illness	163
Traveler's diarrhea	164

Serious illness or injury in the field	173
Mental preparation	175
Special considerations for women	176
Special considerations for children	179
Special considerations for elderly expedition members	182
Common illnesses: colds and other respiratory symptoms	187
Treatment of pain	191
Insomnia	192
Common skin problems	193
Serious venomous injuries	195
Exotic diseases	199
High altitude	211
Cold injuries	229
Heat illness	238
Injuries in remote areas	242
ABCDE trauma management	251
Part Nine: A Full Expedition Day	**264**
Antarctica	264
Electronics	278
The Nightly Routine	279
Other notes	282
Part Ten: Return and Recover	**287**
Closing	289
Part Eleven: Survival List	**291**
Part Twelve: Selected Resources	**294**
About the Authors	**296**

Terry on the summit of Aconcagua. (22,841 ft / 6,960 m)

PART ONE

Your Own Expedition

WELCOME TO ADVENTURE EXPEDITION ONE!
In this book, you're going to learn the fundamentals of putting together an expedition. Whether you are planning to sail around the world solo, climb to the top of K2, or trek across the Gobi Desert, you need to know the essentials of assembling an expedition. Some journeys are easy to put together. Others may take a decade of planning, saving, and training. Whatever you are planning to do, you need certain skills. Those abilities can be learned and applied to make your expedition rewarding, enjoyable, and successful.

This book assumes you're the one putting together your own adventure, whatever it may be. You may be looking for guidance on how to put it together. Or, you may be looking for inspiration. Whatever the case, this work is written for you.

There are concepts, ideas, and information contained in this book that every expedition member needs to know. If you don't use every piece of it, that's okay. There's always something new to learn. And what you find in this book might inspire your next great adventure.

This book is based on the process the author used for his expeditions around the world: Patagonia, Greenland, Yellowstone, Antarctica. Notice the windy and cold themes? Expeditions are all about going to unexplored or remote locations.

ADVENTURE EXPEDITION ONE

There are myriads of reasons why people go on these treks. There are as many ways to explore as there are places to explore. This book provides you with the overall knowledge you'll need to be successful. It is also meant to give you ideas for things you might not have thought about before.

The best part: adventures can be undertaken by anyone, of any age, of any gender. An eighty-year-old Japanese man summited Everest in 2013. A fourteen-year-old Dutch girl sailed around the world by herself, completing the voyage in 2012. Attempts to set records and be the first, youngest, or oldest are not without their risks. These successes illustrate that the possibilities are nearly limitless. What is your vision for your own unlimited potential?

Encouraging your dreams and making your expedition successful is what this book sets out to accomplish.

It's a process

Welcome to the book that focuses on preparing you, the reader, for an adventure or expedition. This book is targeted at those who want to expand their knowledge of the semi-closed world of exploration. In this book, you'll learn hard-won secrets. And the best part is, they're all in one place. You don't have to spend countless hours scouring the Internet trying to put this information together. There are many resources to consider, this book being one of them.

The goal is to provide you with all the fundamentals you'll need. There are many things you will need to know to be successful. Every expedition is different. The varieties of adventures on Earth are endless. Transportation and how to get there are also variables unique to your trip. For all the variety of options, there are fundamentals that every explorer needs to know. Without this knowledge, you may find yourself in the difficult situation of wishing you had learned a critical skill before leaving.

It's impossible to provide the specifics for each type and style of an expedition in one volume. The tribal knowledge amassed by explorers in your particular field of interest exceeds the practical limit of this book. And each adventure goal, whether it be mountains, oceans, jungles, or polar, requires that much more knowledge. To contain this knowledge would require an encyclopedia set. With today's rapidly advancing technology, this theoretical set would be outdated in short order.

What this book does for you is to compile the core of what you'll need for *any* expedition. All treks have certain aspects in common. You need to know these in order to succeed and, perhaps, survive. The foundation of exploration is universal: knowledge, adaptability, strength, endurance, and perseverance. You'll need all of these to succeed.

This book shares the secrets of what you need to know for any adventure.

Once you understand the knowledge contained in this volume, you'll be better prepared to venture out. You'll understand the language of the outdoors. The chapters of this book will open a window to a way of thinking. It's not only knowledge you need. Your mind needs to be retrained for success in exploration. With this knowledge, you'll have the confidence to move forward and search out expedition-specific information with a solid foundation.

Overview of steps to your expedition

The goal of this book is to provide you with a step-by-step process for envisioning, planning, and executing your first or next expedition. Figuring out what to do first is the biggest challenge. Once you understand everything you need to know and do, your confidence will improve and you will be more likely to successfully plan and execute your expedition.

Below is an overview of the steps you'll need to follow in order to plan, train, and make your expedition happen:

1. Originate idea
2. Research
3. Recruit team
4. Planning
5. Fundraising
6. Skill building

Adventure Expedition One

7. Training (physical, mental, emotional)
8. Mini-expeditions and training trips (shakedown)
9. Actually do the expedition
10. Return to "real" life

Many of these steps are often performed in parallel. In order to take care of everything you need to manage, you'll need to become an expert at juggling multiple tasks at once. This is the nature of preparing for any major trek. You'll find that once on the expedition, you only need to be concerned with enjoying yourself, moving toward your objective, and returning safely. However, an ongoing challenge can be keeping sponsors updated and fulfilling obligations to them. The financing chapter expands on effectively raising funds.

Two additional steps are covered in this book, beyond the run-up to the expedition: the doing and the return.

Although step 9 isn't part of the preparation, it is the entire focus of this book. How do you keep yourself going when your time is running out, rations are short, and morale is flagging? The chapter on skill building and training helps prepare you for such eventualities. You'll want to ensure that you and your team are able to work under duress while still keeping a positive outlook during the mini-expedition phase. It's advantageous and safer to discover problems well before traveling to a far-off location.

Step 10 appears to be simple enough—return to your normal life and move on. However, if you enjoyed an extended expedition, you'll find your life perspective changed. Also, you and your teammates may experience unexpected psychological effects after returning from a stressful and challenging trek. Handling this step correctly ensures your recovery from the experience is positive and helps you look forward to the next trip.

Where to start?

The variety of expeditions is endless. Attempting to define how to go about specific tasks for a specific expedition is beyond this book. What this book does for you is help you understand the overall

YOUR OWN EXPEDITION

concept of how to create, plan, and execute your expedition. We want to dispel the myth of a secret society of explorers.

If you have ever taken a trip with the purpose of seeing, doing, or discovering something, you have participated in your first expedition, even if it was a car trip across the country. There is a threshold everyone must cross when preparing a major trek. Once you understand how to cross it, your life will never be the same. Even if you only partake in one expedition, you will join the few who have left home and discovered the world beyond their home. And, there is a good chance you will discover something inside yourself.

The next chapter focuses on how to come up with your expedition idea if you don't have one. And, if you do, it will help you refine the idea. It's important to have clarity about your expedition. It makes planning, team building, and decision-making far easier. A fuzzy goal makes everything more difficult on a significant trek. Should you wish to go somewhere and figure it out, you'll have a corresponding learning curve in the field. The consequences of poor preparation will happily greet you.

This book provides a process to follow. Each chapter and section will touch on a key point, a piece of information, something you'll need to know in order to move on. Once you understand one concept, you will be ready to learn the next. Even if you don't fully grasp the subject, your exploration understanding will improve.

Is there one real path to expedition success? No. There are as many paths to succeeding as there are to failure. What works well once may bomb the next time. Adaptability and ingenuity are keys to success. Additionally, training hard and consistently is critical to your success. If you're not fit, knowledge and desire will not be enough to take you to the top of that far-flung peak.

Stories are also sprinkled into the text to illustrate points. They also serve as memory aids. You may not remember a specific idea, but you'll remember the story. And remembering what someone else did (or didn't do!) can keep you alive and moving forward.

Other books on exploration are also recommended in the text. There are references in the appendix. As always, avoid relying solely on one resource. Learn everything you can to better prepare yourself.

ADVENTURE EXPEDITION ONE

This book is loaded with how-tos and earned wisdom. Use it for all it's worth to make your experience valuable and more enjoyable. Many of the tips in this book are derived from the "I wish I would have known..." stories. The author shares his education from the school of hard knocks to save you from the same mistakes.

A word of caution about using the Internet as your only resource: anyone can write about anything online. Even if someone sounds authoritative, it doesn't mean anything. Many online writers regurgitate information without any experience. The standard opening is, "Well, I've never done/read/owned one, but here's my opinion..." Read these words with extreme caution. There is no guarantee of vetting, editing, or verification of any blog, article, or remark online. You never know who is really behind those words.

Sharing outdoor knowledge is part of the impetus of this book. It's based on experience and what real people have done in the field. If you are planning a "first", the author hopes you'll share your experience with the world, so that others may follow.

Real experience. There is no substitute.

Inspiration

This book is also meant to inspire those thinking about an expedition but not sure where to start. There are stories meant to encourage and inform the beginning explorer. And for those with more experience, the book aims to expand your understanding and skills. Armed with more information, you will be able to go higher, faster, and farther. More importantly, you will be safer, too.

As a motivational speaker, the author wants to convince you, the reader, that incredible adventures are within your reach. The only thing standing in your way is believing you can succeed. Concepts in this book need to be practiced so they become second nature. You do not want to attempt learning to tie yourself into a belay line while at 20,000 feet (6,000 meters) in the dark at minus forty degrees.

For all the things the author wished he had prior to his first expedition, it was this book. Learning the nuances of expedition life is much easier in the comfort of home. That said, certain aspects of outdoor

Your Own Expedition

living can only be discovered by doing. The author wants to prepare readers to be confident and knowledgeable under pressure situations.

Reading a book can't teach you everything, though. Patience to wait out a storm for a safe weather window cannot be learned. That's why this book includes stories—to illustrate the principles that will help your expedition to be successful and safe. Thinking "it won't happen to me" is the safety mistake that can lead to an emergency.

Learning to be patient and wait out a storm is a difficult skill to learn or teach. Some people are naturally impatient. This is where clear objectives, risk management, and knowing personalities can make the difference between life and death. The chapters on planning and skills expand on these points.

Read classic expedition books. Watch documentaries on exploration. These will build excitement. They show that you, too, can achieve something great. You may discover a tidbit that makes all the difference on your trek. Though something can be learned from all material, focus your efforts on your specific genre of adventure. Find material that is honest and deep. You want to know what the experience is really like. Delve into the mental aspect of the trek. It's as important as the physical aspect.

Why an expedition?

Ask a fundamental question—why participate in an expedition in the first place? It appears to be a great deal of work, effort, and risk. Yes, expeditions have those challenges and more. The personal value of participating in a trek to a far-flung corner of the planet can't be overstated. If you can create an expedition with cultural, scientific or historic value, then your efforts have even more value.

You might ask if there's anything left to be discovered. Do Internet searches provide all the answers? In a word—no. An online search engine cannot endow the satisfaction of standing on top of a high peak after weeks or months of effort. No one can do your push-ups for you. Every year there are incredible discoveries being made. The edge of human endurance is being pushed constantly. New species are being found constantly. And you can be the person to make the new discovery.

ADVENTURE EXPEDITION ONE

Sometimes, the greatest discoveries come together through a mix of perseverance and chance. In 2013, a team led by paleoanthropologist Lee Berger identified a whole new humanoid. His team of lanky female scientists, the only ones able to crawl through an opening one-foot tall, unearthed hundreds of human-like fossils.

These were hidden in South Africa's Rising Star cave. It's only 240 feet (73 meters) long and heavily visited. Only because two people pushed their boundaries was the discovery made. Scientists are unsure of how the bones came to be so deep in the cave. What these explorers found in fact raised more questions than were answered.

Perhaps another explorer will make a new discovery, connecting the disjointed fossil record. Or, maybe she will find something that upends our entire body of knowledge. Wouldn't that be exciting?

There are so many new species, geologies, and human boundaries waiting to be explored. The recent crop of super-runner endurance athletes has radically altered what was thought impossible prior to the 21st century. Attempting to recreate expeditions of old has become popular, too. Thor Heyerdahl's 1947 expedition suggested South American sailors could have traversed the mighty Pacific to reach South Pacific islands. It was a stunning success for a historic re-creation.

Rules-enforced expeditions are also compelling. Perhaps you want to try navigating across Antarctica with only a compass and sextant like Amundsen did, using no electronics. Your goal might be to solve the Peary versus Cook debate of who reached the North Pole first, using old records. Whatever your motivations are, using pre-electronics technology to travel can be a rewarding challenge. With only a compass, explorers have traversed vast and unmapped regions.

YOUR OWN EXPEDITION

> A professor from Southwestern College in San Diego, CA, set out to discover what was hidden in the southern California desert. He chose an ambitious approach to his expeditions. He and his team did not follow trails. They ignored the path of least resistance. Instead, they took a compass bearing. And then they followed it. No matter what the obstacle.
>
> Using this difficult technique, his team made multiple discoveries. They were willing to go where others wouldn't. They ignored convenience. Instead, they set out on a mission. And, though travel was difficult and dangerous, their effort was rewarded.

Purely recreational expeditions are just as satisfying, too. Climbing Denali or Everest are irresistible draws for many. Are there great discoveries to be made while being guided up either? Probably not. But is there value in the personal satisfaction of summiting and returning safely? Absolutely. Finding and smashing your personal limits is undeniably satisfying. For this reason alone, undertaking the effort of an expedition is worth every drop of sweat and every dollar.

That said, being scrupulously honest about what happened during your expedition and how you did it is crucial. Living with a lie will wear you out. And, when discovered, it will ruin your reputation. Misrepresentation casts all you have done and what you will do into doubt. The list of those who forever damaged their reputation is long. If you had to turn back three hundred feet from the top, avoid claiming the summit. Turning around for good reason tells a compelling story, one of wisdom and survival.

> The great climber Ed Viesturs is highly respected for his willingness to turn back from the summit because conditions have been too risky, even when the top has been tantalizingly close. He once turned back 300 feet from the summit of Everest. His motto: "Reaching the summit is optional. Getting down is mandatory."
> (see *No Shortcuts to the Top*, Ed Viesturs with David Roberts)

Adventure Expedition One

Emotions

Personal dynamics is the number one factor that makes or breaks expeditions. Positive human interaction is more important than finance, technical considerations, or physical challenges. The only thing more important is health maintenance. Illness or injury, personal hygiene, food, and water issues can all erode emotional resilience and wipe out an expedition.

Keeping the team together can be the most challenging part of any trek. People are unpredictable under duress. They may rise to the occasion or they may go down in flames. Discovering that someone, or yourself, becomes completely unmanageable after a few weeks of difficult travel can bring your dream expedition to a sudden end.

Minor annoyances in the comfortable city can become unlivable when trapped in a tent for a week. The expedition literature is rife with stories of lifelong friends who are reduced to near-hatred by minor annoyances, such as the way they chew their food while tent-bound in a storm.

Make sure you can live with the personalities you invite on your expedition. Every person has quirks and foibles, even you. Knowing what you can and can't live with will determine your choice of partners. Sometimes you'll be forced to accept a difficult person to achieve your objectives, too.

The most successful teams are usually made up of individuals who enter the project with an attitude of patience, consideration, and forgiveness toward their teammates and a willingness to subordinate their personal desires for the success of the overall team.

Emotional maturity can make the difference between life and death on an expedition. Often, your life is in the hands of someone else. If a teammate freezes up or makes a rash decision, everyone on the team is in jeopardy. This is why test trips are critical to your success.

Completing an expedition

Greenland, four miles east of Sisimiut.

The last crossing of an ice-choked river was one of the most treacherous. Both banks were loaded with shelf ice. The river

YOUR OWN EXPEDITION

undercut the six-inch-thick shore ice. The water level was one foot below the top of the ice edge. If I was in the deep rushing water, I'd be in trouble. The overhanging shelf was smooth, almost glassy. There was nothing to hold on to. I would be trapped.

Scanning up and down the river, I could see the situation didn't improve at all. The point where the trail led had the only visible crossing for a quarter mile either way. I investigated one other promising point on the river. Though there was ice all the way across, it was thin and rocks protruded through it. No help there.

Several large rocks offered potential leaping pads. It looked relatively easy to gain the large boulder in the middle of the river. However, there was a five-foot leap past that to gain the opposite shore. The middle boulder offered no runway to build up speed for the leap. And its surface was wet. Five feet isn't far until you have to make a leap across a chasm.

The river was particularly deep at this point. In Greenland's warmer months, this would be a fun splash and I could dry myself in the sun. But it was −26 degrees C (−15 degrees F) and windy. And it was late in the day. I was cold, worn out, my feet were sore, and I only had my emergency rations remaining. I needed to reach Sisimiut today.

My pack weighed thirty-five pounds at this point. With it, I had no confidence that I could make the leap off the wet boulder without slipping. There was the option to take my pack off and throw it. However, the far snow-covered bank sloped back into the river. There was a good chance my pack would slide back into the river and be washed away.

As I was weakened from the journey, the pack throw seemed impossible. I decided to take it off and try a practice throw. The throw was pitiful, maybe three feet. There was no way I would clear the far riverbank so my pack wouldn't slide back.

I was in a quandary.

11

ADVENTURE EXPEDITION ONE

Then the solution occurred to me. Make the leap to the middle rock. Then unload the pack and toss each item beyond the far bank. That way there was no chance anything could roll back to the river. The plan was risky but far less so than risking the loss of my entire pack.

I was cautious, slowly taking out each item and clipping my pack shut after. This prevented the pack from tipping and spilling its contents while tossing each item. Minimizing the risk made the process laborious.

After tossing the sleeping bag and finally the pack itself, I laughed out loud to the wind at the absurd scene. Gear was strewn beyond the far bank and I was perched in the middle of the river. It looked like a cruel joke. An icy landing with fatigued legs and no running start was dicey. I opted for the full body approach. Steeling myself, I launched toward the far bank with everything I had left.

Landing outstretched, as though jumping for a touchdown, I clawed at the snow. I didn't want to slip back into the river. After army-crawling up the embankment, I rolled over, stared at the darkening sky, and laughed. I had conquered the last obstacle to reaching Sisimiut. —*AL*

Safety

The entire purpose of this book is to provide a good basis of knowledge for you to return home safely. The authors want you to come home in one piece, with all of your team members. Expeditions are, by nature, hazardous. Overcoming those challenges safely is a big part of why expeditions are exciting and valuable.

This said, the authors, publisher, printer, and whoever sold you this book are not responsible for your actions or life. You are solely responsible for your actions, decisions, and the outcome of any and all of your activities. Expeditions involve risk. People may be injured or, sadly, may perish. Paying attention to safety at all times cannot be

Your Own Expedition

emphasized enough. Sure, it's dangerous to dangle off a 3,000-foot (914 meter) cliff in Yosemite. But, with proper tools and training, the danger can be substantially mitigated.

The goal is not to eliminate danger. That's impossible. Have you witnessed a car crash? Did either driver start out their day saying, "I'm going to crash my car today." No. The same thing goes for trekking anywhere. The goal is to be prepared for any eventuality and to return alive.

As the disclaimer on the copyright page makes clear: this book is to be used as a guide and not your only resource. When you need help, consult a professional. What you do with this information is up to you. In no way, shape, or form should this book be construed as guaranteeing it will keep you alive and out of harm's way. Even with the best knowledge, people perish every year on expeditions.

THE AUTHORS, PUBLISHER, PRINTER, DISTRIBUTOR, AND SELLER OF THIS BOOK ARE NOT RESPONSIBLE FOR YOU. YOU ARE FULLY RESPONSIBLE FOR YOURSELF AND YOUR ACTIONS. This cannot be over-emphasized. Don't jump off a cliff and point an accusing finger complaining that someone else told you to do it. Stay safe. Stay alive. Come home in one piece.

Let's go exploring!

Polar storms will bury gear quickly.

Aaron at the South Pole after 81 days alone. (9,301 ft / 2,700m)

PART TWO

Create an Expedition

Identify and define the expedition

Once the bug of exploration bites a person, it often becomes part of their life. Even though such thoughts might float away for a while, they'll come roaring back. For anyone who thinks it might be, was, or is fun, one of the foremost thoughts will be, "Where am I going next and how can I make it happen?"

What's the process for identifying, selecting, and defining an expedition? Are there unexplored places in the world? There are but there are fewer every day. With disposable income in the modern western world, more and more people are venturing out into the unknown. Many people look for new challenges. Saber-tooth cats do not threaten us anymore, yet we're still programmed with the need for an adversary. There is something in the human psyche that compels us to have some sort of challenge. Going on an expedition can feed that need.

What ways are there to capture a fleeting idea when it comes? Keep a notebook and pen next to your bed. Sometimes stunning revelations pop into your head only once. Purchase a journal or composition book from your local office supply store. They're inexpensive but do wonders for getting ideas onto paper and out of your head. As an added bonus, doing this will help you sleep, so you stay refreshed.

ADVENTURE EXPEDITION ONE

This habit will help you on your expedition, too. Do not end up with a bunch of post-it notes. They're easy to lose.

Break your ideas down into bite-sized chunks. Think about all the different places you can find on the globe. What is there? Simply because someone has already gone there doesn't mean you can't. It will be a first for you and that's perfectly fine.

Some expeditions are so extreme that few if any people succeed. Some have a high casualty rate, like climbing Annapurna, the world's 10th highest peak. Climbing Annapurna has a fatality rate of about 33%, highest among the world's fourteen 8,000 meter peaks. Though challenges like this aren't a good choice for a first expedition, you can start with less ambitious projects as a starting point for something more extreme. Or, you may discover that whatever you find is already at the edge of your comfort zone. Avoid stepping too far out. You may be emotionally or physically burned and will never want to try again. Few if any people can tolerate going from nothing to the extreme.

The goal of this chapter is to help you explore yourself. We want to help you discover what adventure or expedition you want to undertake. This chapter will guide you through sources and ideas that may inspire you to something new, something you never would have imagined.

What is an expedition?

What do you envision when you read the word "expedition"? Do you think of climbing Everest or of Ernest Shackleton's failed voyage to the South Pole? Using the word in modern conversation often conjures visions of distant lands, dense jungles, and high mountain peaks. Sometime in the 21st-century humans will likely mount their first expedition to the planet Mars.

A typical dictionary definition of the word "expedition" might be:

A journey or voyage undertaken by a single person or group of people with a particular purpose, especially that of discovery, scientific research, or exploration.

CREATE AN EXPEDITION

Often, climbing a well-known summit or rowing across the Atlantic isn't a journey of scientific discovery, as it has been completed many times. Instead, these treks are often for the purpose of discovering the limits of human endurance on an individual basis. What may be relatively straightforward for one person may be a near death-defying journey for another.

For someone who has never traveled more than twenty miles from their childhood home, the thought of being the first woman to summit Everest twice in a five-day span on a single expedition, like Anshu Jamsenpa from India did, is beyond comprehension. People questioned Anshu about her motivations and, indeed, her sanity for attempting such a record. She was peppered with questions like these:

"Why waste the money?"

"Aren't you afraid you're going to die?"

"Can't you do something more family oriented?"

For someone of this caliber, an expedition may well be a difficult, potentially lethal, trek to a far-flung location. She was not the first woman to the summit, incidentally. That honor goes to Junko Tabei, who became the first woman to summit Everest on May 16, 1975. She was a pioneering explorer, traveling at a time when reaching Nepal was far more difficult than it is today.

Are there any particular rules for defining what an expedition really is? For those who have been on expeditions, the dictionary answer is vague at best. No one will (likely) argue that climbing Denali in Alaska is anything but an expedition. It takes months of physical training, the climb traditionally takes two to four weeks, and climbers statistically only have a fifty percent chance of success.

With the advent of ultra-running, significant distances and elevation gains are now being covered in twenty-four hours. Extreme endurance athlete Kílian Jornet Burgada climbed Denali by starting from base camp, reaching the summit, and returning in less than twelve hours. Does this mean that Denali is no longer an expedition? Not at all.

However, there are other examples of long treks that wouldn't be considered expeditions by people who backpack regularly. Take the example of an eighty-mile circuit trek around the Golden Trout Wilderness in California. Suzanne Swedo's book *Hiking the Golden Trout Wilderness* describes this eighty-mile route circumnavigating the wilderness area as a real expedition. For hikers who like to take their time or carry a heavy load, it may take five to eight days to complete the backpacking trip. The author completed the trek in four days with a light backpack. An ultra-distance runner like Pete Kostelnick might complete the circuit in fourteen hours at a nine to ten minute per mile pace.

How about the John Muir, Pacific Crest, Continental Divide, or the Appalachian Trails? Do these qualify as expeditions? Does driving from Mexico to Canada without traveling on a paved road? Perhaps floating the Amazon River on a raft or walking the length of that river?

Interestingly, hiking the Appalachian, Continental Divide, or the Pacific Crest Trails are not considered expeditions, even though it takes months to walk thousands of miles to complete any of these trails. The ease of resupplying, ability to visit towns every few days, and the simplicity of access eliminates these major undertakings from the expedition realm. However, ask someone who lives in a city, has never walked a mile in boots with a backpack, or slept outside, and they may have a different opinion.

So what, then, is an expedition? It is a combination of remoteness, difficulty, expense, and time that differentiates an expedition from a backpacking trip or the like. The modern definition hinges on a combination of:

- Traveling somewhere out of the normal tourism circuit
- Participating in a potentially risky activity
- Something that requires camping or sailing in remote locations for extended periods of time
- Attempting to climb, hike, ski, row, sail, etc., over an extended period of time
- Climbing a high-altitude mountain that requires a significant investment of time and finances
- An activity that requires significant physical, mental, and skill training
- A group of people (or a soloist) working together to reach a remote destination
- Requiring logistics well beyond a normal backpacking trip

Create an Expedition

Climbing Denali is a serious and dangerous undertaking. It requires concentrated effort, training, and time to attempt the summit. Climbing Kilimanjaro isn't a particularly dangerous undertaking and only takes five days, yet it requires a large support staff to complete. Even though climbing Mt. Elbrus (another of the seven summits) typically takes four to five days, it is still considered a small expedition. Traveling to Russia and navigating cultural challenges is an expedition in itself.

Expedition ideas

If you have not figured out an idea for your expedition, this section is for you. Even if you have the idea for your expedition set, reviewing this section won't hurt. In fact, it may give you ideas to add to what you're already doing or help you make plans for the next one.

There are multiple ways to figure out what you want to do and where you want to go for an expedition. The process is as simple or as complex as you want it to be. With the Internet, you can find yourself spending months searching for the "right" activity and coming to no valuable conclusion. One of the big dangers of web surfing is you can waste weeks of valuable time with no solid results.

Instead, promise to yourself that you'll spend no more than a single day researching what you might want to do. Make a list on paper or on the computer. Then, using only that list, begin sorting your ideas into the most exciting, interesting, valuable, difficult, or whatever might be your criterion.

At first, you may think that an expedition that's too extreme may not be the best choice. On the contrary, it might be the best choice for you. However, you may need to go on one or more training trips or mini-expeditions before you're ready for the big trip. Avoid selling yourself short. If you want to sail around the world, climb Everest, ski to the North Pole, or kayak solo across the Indian Ocean, then perfect. Just know that you will need to beef up your skills before you head out alone or with a team.

ADVENTURE EXPEDITION ONE

Some people start off by going big and hiring a guiding company for a climbing expedition. That is an excellent way to go if that's what you want. Thousands do this every year with great success. However, if your desire is to put together your own expedition, then there are more things you'll need to consider. That's the whole purpose of this book, to take you from sitting at home on the couch to achieving whatever your ultimate goal might be.

Doing something completely new or repeating what someone has done before are both valid approaches. Simply because someone else has done what you're planning to do does not take away your merit. Having an established path to follow is a judicious way to proceed. You can always follow the classic route up the mountain and put your own spin on it.

Below is a tiny list of ideas for expeditions around the world. Some ideas are not necessarily expeditions, but they'll start the flow of ideas. Some of these names may be unfamiliar. The goal is to coax the reader into discovering ideas and people they may never have heard of.

Pursue the Adventure Grand Slam
Climb any or all of the Seven Summits
Hike the Triple Crown in the US
Kite-ski the north-south length of Greenland
Cross the Atacama Desert
Walk the length of the Volga River
Climb some of the many unnamed peaks in the Trans-Antarctic range
Bike from Point Barrow, Alaska to Ushuaia, Argentina
Hit a golf ball all the way across the Gobi Desert
Repeat the feat of the book *The Long Walk*
Explore and document little-known cave systems
Ski across Antarctica
Map newly discovered underwater caves
Kayak from Los Angeles to New York via the Panama Canal
Circumnavigate the Arctic
Navigate the Zambezi River
Complete the Camino de Compostella
Find a lost shipwreck

Create an Expedition

Repeat one of Thor Heyerdahl's sailing trips
Recreate Amelia Earhart's circumnavigation flight
Bike Baja California, Mexico
Search for a lost WWII plane
Repeat any of Wilfred Thesiger's expeditions
Walk across central Africa
Pursue an old or ancient family story
Repeat the climb in the book *Touching the Void* without the tragedy
Document Siberian reindeer herders for a season
Recreate the expedition of Stanley searching for Dr. Livingstone

Note that some of these ideas or locations are incredibly dangerous or inaccessible for any number of reasons. Terrorism, geopolitical tensions, weather, and geography may render some of these ideas nearly impossible. Risk management is a critical part of expedition planning and execution—you have to know when to change your plan and have the flexibility, prudence, and wisdom to make those changes.

Other sources for expedition ideas:

<u>General</u>
Local library and librarian
Natural and history museums
Historical societies
History professors
Boy Scouts
Outdoor shows
Local outfitters
Explorersweb.com
This book's webpage
Expedition and guide companies
Expedition news websites
Famous and infamous explorers
Explorers Club
Explorers in the news

ADVENTURE EXPEDITION ONE

<u>Media</u>
  Walter Mitty
  Into the Wild
  Lord of the Flies
  Lost City of Z
  Roughing It by Mark Twain
  Bear Grylls television show
  National Geographic
  National Geographic Adventure
  Outside
  Backpacker
  Off-road magazines
  Vanity Fair

<u>Maps</u>
  Library, map stores, bookstores
  Historic recreation
  In other adventure books
  World map
  Individual country map
  Globe, physical

Purpose

What is the purpose of your expedition? If you can identify the purpose, the *why*, it's easier to struggle through the challenges of planning and executing the trek. There doesn't always have to be a grand, scientific, or world-changing purpose. Instead, your trip may be an exploration of what you're capable of. How much can you physically and mentally handle? As you develop your idea and read this book, keep in mind that people will always ask, "Why would you put yourself through this?" or simply, "Why?" Be prepared to answer this question many times.

Documentation

Give serious thought to how you will, if at all, document your expedition. Even if you plan to film the trip with a GoPro, consider how

Create an Expedition

you want to capture your experience. Not every expedition is worth a movie or book. Years later, you may want to share your experience with coworkers, friends, and loved ones. Keeping a written journal, taking pictures, and creating a video will help you do that. Although the expedition is dramatic while it's happening, details will slip your mind after a short time.

Aaron prepares to cross an icy river barefoot to keep his boots dry while on an expedition in Greenland.

Aaron climbing a sand dune in the Sahara Desert, Morocco.

PART THREE

Planning

Overview

Planning an expedition is everything. Success is far more likely when you and your team plan, discuss, analyze, and train for the expedition. Creating a clear, defined plan will make the difference between success and failure. Starting with a well-developed plan is key.

Your plan needs to be adaptable, too. Unexpected conditions occur. Injuries and illness happen. Equipment fails. Weather changes. All of the research in the world will not guarantee the conditions when you arrive. If your plan considers these factors, you will be ready.

The idea is to consider every contingency. Every failure. Every possibility. But just as important is avoiding "analysis paralysis." It's easy to over-focus on the negative. This can easily destroy the expedition morale before anyone steps outside his or her door. A delicate balance must be maintained. Remaining positive while being realistic about difficulties is the job of everyone on the expedition. Keeping the team positive, healthy, and moving forward is the job of the expedition leader.

ADVENTURE EXPEDITION ONE

Expedition goal creation

What are the goals of the expedition? Is it to reach the top of a distant peak in record time? Row across the Indian Ocean? Fly around the world using only pedal power?

Once the idea for an expedition is established, the primary goal is apparent. However, there are other considerations. Below are some questions to consider. These will help direct you to focus on a multitude of possible goals. Sometimes an expedition can even have multiple goals, such as documenting weather, performing high-altitude physiological research, or measuring long-term environmental trends. Though this may take some more work, these added activities could bring in additional sponsorship. Often, a team also needs to return with photographic or video footage, provide field updates, write a book, etc.

Potential list of expedition goals

- What about the style of the expedition? Travel in 17th-century style, using only a sextant and compass?
- How will you and your team arrive at the start? Will they fly, walk, bicycle, swim, cartwheel?
- Will it be a "carbon-neutral" expedition, where other objectives have to be met before or after the expedition?
- Does the expedition involve a traditional sport? Driving golf balls across the Gobi Desert?
- Have a team of physically impaired individuals cross the Greenland icecap? Is everyone on the team handicapped in some way: blind, missing limbs, military wounded, etc?

It's valuable to write out ALL of the goals of the expedition with the leaders and team. After examining all objectives, conflicts may arise. Perhaps there are two (or more) goals that are mutually exclusive of each other. This is important to determine as early in the process as possible. Don't make the mistake of ignoring this until later and then discover that one objective makes the other impractical or impossible well into the preparation phase. This can wound or ruin camaraderie, sponsorship support, and media relations.

26

PLANNING

Clarity is key. Ensure all involved are perfectly clear on what the mission is, what is at stake, and what the fallback plans are. When everyone understands what all of the objectives are, misunderstandings are significantly reduced. The most challenging aspect of human expeditions is not how high, far, or cold the trip is.

It's communication.

Failure to honestly communicate has led to an unending list of man-made disasters. The temptation will be to assume everyone understands. Rarely is that the case. Team members may envision a complete polar opposite of what you're thinking. This is especially true when things fail to go according to plan.

> Randall Peeters had this happen on his guided expedition to Mt. McKinley (Denali) in 1988. In his book *Journeys to the Edge*, he recounts the communication and skill difficulties encountered on a major mountain. His team was able to climb agonizingly close to the peak. They were within four hours of the summit. Twice.
>
> His team became trapped at high camp for a week due to a powerful weather system. (Does your plan include being stuck on a mountain for a weeklong storm?) Ultimately his team failed to reach the summit.
>
> "Some members of the group were due back at work and simply wouldn't change their flight schedules."
>
> Summiting after the weather cleared may have been possible. Becoming stuck at High Camp for a week wiped out the team's available time. Some members wished to push on. Others didn't. Goal conflicts dictated that the entire team abandon their summit attempt.

Is everyone under pressure to catch a plane back to civilization next Tuesday? This happens to climbing teams routinely. One member may be ready to stick it out for the duration, but all other team members have obligations to leave and return to work. This is a perfect formula for resentment.

ADVENTURE EXPEDITION ONE

Return times are one of the challenges of guided climbing. Unless the group is big enough to split, the team will only move as fast as its weakest member. The concept of a guided expedition is that everyone returns safely, regardless of achieving the primary objective. It's more important to return alive. The weakest member always determines the risk level.

Fallback Plan

When planning an expedition, both the successes and challenges must be considered. Plans are usually made in the comfort of a home or office. It's easy to be absorbed in the excitement of a trip. The camaraderie, glory, and thrill of the experience will permeate the air. But what happens when something goes wrong?

Considering all the what-if's is important to the team's safety and the expedition's success. It's of paramount importance to have everyone return home in one piece. Although achieving the expedition goal is desirable, an injury or death will overshadow any success.

When discussing the potential challenges, it's important not to become absorbed in the negative. Complete preoccupation with dark possibilities may even cause a failure to launch. Understanding what can happen up front, being honest, and having a plan is imperative.

Is it possible to anticipate everything that can go wrong? It's impossible. No one, however clairvoyant, can see the future. But take heart. It is possible to anticipate most problems. The team will have to work through three categories of risk and difficulties:

Categories of challenges:

- Knowns
- Unknown knowns
- Unknown unknowns

Knowns

These are generally apparent from the obstacles facing the expedition. The distance, altitude, or terrain may be known perfectly. Some

Planning

expeditions know these details precisely. They are measurable and quantifiable. They can be calculated for. Knowns hold few surprises.

Known challenges are a pleasure. Even if they seem daunting, it's possible to find solutions, given enough time. If there is no world expert on the challenge, you have the opportunity to become the expert. There is value in this, as you can contribute to the world body of knowledge, further increasing the value of your expedition.

Few challenges are truly insurmountable. Humans have stood on the moon. Spacecraft have now left the solar system. Someone has skydived from above one hundred thousand feet above the Earth. With enough ingenuity and work, most any known expedition problem can be overcome.

Unknown knowns

A more nebulous but just as important category of challenges are the unknown knowns. This might be precisely how long an expedition might take. Or it could be weather variables.

Unknown knowns are items where you can place a blank next to something yet still make a good guess about it. But you won't have an exact answer. Estimating within a certain tolerance will help you anticipate these factors.

These factors must be considered carefully, as they will have a significant impact on an expedition. If overestimated, too much effort may be expended on conquering the unknown knowns.

One example is taking *too much* food. Overloading food means the team will be traveling unnecessarily slowly. In turn, this may cause a team to miss a connection. The food may rot before it's consumed. Disposing of extra food may even be impossible, as on Denali (where it's illegal to "pitch" supplies).

Unknown unknowns

The most difficult challenges to deal with are unknown unknowns. They add the most risk, stress, and difficulty to an expedition. The most challenging part is that they're rarely easy to anticipate. How is it even possible to plan for something unforeseeable? Unknown unknowns are those things that catch the unwary off-guard. This is where

ADVENTURE EXPEDITION ONE

having previous experience pays off. The more experience you have, the more likely you are to survive a completely unexpected setback.

An example of an unknown unknown is a map error. Outside of the United States and Western Europe, maps can be suspect. This is common for water navigation of rarely visited islands. Inlets, shoals, and reefs may be inaccurately marked. They may not be marked at all. There is rarely any way to know this beforehand.

The Internet is an invaluable resource for ferreting out unknown unknowns. It's worth reading discussion boards and reviews of the area you are traveling to. Often, gems can be found. Much garbage may impede this search, too. All Internet discussions are tribal knowledge. The source is *always* suspect. As in, "A cousin of someone who worked with my sister knew this person who read about someone who went there in the 1950s." The cliché "old wives tale" comes to mind.

All web information must be used with caution. Remember—anyone can write anything online without consequence and it's nearly all anonymous. That means that an armchair adventurer can write as though they've been there, and you'll have a difficult time verifying the truth of their words.

You and your team alone are responsible for relying on unverifiable Internet information.

In the movie *Space Cowboys*, the character William "Hawk" Hawkins debates with the NASA shuttle simulation leader Ethan Glance. Hawk wants to know what the flight crew would need to do if the flight computer failed. Glance replied that there has never been a computer failure.

Although not *probable*, flight computer failure is still *possible*. In a worst-case scenario, it could happen. If the crew was not trained to deal with such a situation, and the computer failed, what would happen? Would they be able to land the shuttle safely? Or at all?

The difference between *probable* and *possible* is what every trekker must be aware of. Is it probable that a shovel will break on an expedition? No. But is it possible? Yes. The author had exactly this happen, documented in *Antarctic Tears*. —AL

PLANNING

It's not impossible to train or plan for unknown factors. To manage these effectively, creative problem-solving skills are a must. It does not have to be you. Someone on the team may save the day. People with mechanical or engineering skills can turn a disaster into a miraculous recovery. They may render a problem moot. These are the best stories.

The phrase "repaired it with bailing wire and chewing gum" comes from people overcoming unexpected issues. Carrying enough equipment to deal with every possible challenge is often impossible. A failed piece of gear may require a machine shop to repair. There are few if any in remote locations. Luck and preparation will save you here.

There are common unknowns you will need to have contingency plans for. Each root category can branch out to infinite possibilities. Understanding that preparing for a general failure of any of the below will likely enable you to overcome a specific problem. It's impossible to enumerate all of the unknown unknowns. But it is possible to formulate a matrix of contingency plans based on common failures.

In no particular order, the unknown unknowns are:

- Injury or illness
- Equipment damage
- Equipment loss
- Navigation errors
- Technology failure
- Weather
- Human factors (inexperience, conflict, morale) inside the team
- Human factors (culture, criminal activity, terrorism) outside the team

Injury or illness

Field injuries are the most troublesome of all difficulties on an expedition. Once someone is injured, however seriously, the damage must be dealt with. Physical problems require immediate attention. The longer they're ignored or hidden, the greater the risk is to the team.

Dealing with diseased team members is more challenging. The onset of symptoms may be immediate or take months. Your preparatory planning will involve researching infectious diseases that are unique to the area your team will be exploring and learning how to mitigate that risk. Clean (purified) water sources, good food safety, personal hygiene, and using medications to prevent or treat common infections all need to be part of your planning. Educating every team member about the most likely ailments and their prevention and treatment is helpful. It makes everyone aware of what they're exposing themselves to and how to avoid or minimize exposure in the first place.

Equipment damage

Assume every possible piece will fail. What is your plan when XYZ breaks? The author never anticipated a shovel, boot, or sled failure on his Antarctic expedition. Each failure nearly ended his adventure. The most mundane gear failure can terminate a trek. Examine the complete equipment list. Write out how you will deal with this failure. Have everyone participate in this exercise. It may save your lives in the field. Do you have the necessary tools to make a repair?

Equipment loss

Lost equipment has greater consequences than damaged equipment. Damaged equipment may be repairable. But lost equipment is just that. Gone. What will you do when XYZ is lost? Will everyone survive until help can be summoned? Never assume something important can't be lost. Gloves have been lost in high mountains and in windy polar regions. Fingers will freeze in minutes in poor weather. What will you do?

Navigation errors

You think you're on the right path. Then you come over a ridge expecting to see a lake. Except it isn't there. You're lost. How will you and your team find where you need to be? Where and when was the

PLANNING

last known navigation point? What tools will you take to keep this from happening? Even the best have run into this problem.

Technology failure

Modern expeditions are dependent on modern technology. Time keeping, navigation, and communication are all electronic. Some expeditions may opt to use ancient navigation techniques, say using only a compass, chronometer, and sextant. These old technologies require no batteries. But lack of electricity doesn't preclude them breaking.

What happens when one, or more, or all of your gadgets fail? Impossible, you say? Consider this example. Your sled tips over on the mountain. One of the fuel bottles breaks. And, you don't notice. White gas spills into every piece of electronics you have.

How will you avoid these problems? What level of redundancy will you need to maintain? Take into consideration the difficulty, remoteness, and likelihood of rescue on the trek.

Weather

Nature is the great unknown unknown. You know you'll have some type of weather on an expedition. Even a gale or hurricane-force storm. But are you prepared for a five day storm? Long storms are commonplace on Denali. Weather forecasts are still guesses. What is predicted and what actually happens may be worlds apart. Be prepared for *anything*.

Human factors (inexperience, conflict, morale) inside a team

Internal team problems may be the most difficult to deal with. Rallying around an injured teammate—that's easy. Keeping a team going when there are big arguments—that's more difficult. If the team has not worked together on prior challenging treks, you may be in for a mean unknown unknown. Here's where a "shakedown" mini-expedition is an invaluable part of your preparation. Previous experience is one of the only ways to uncover problem issues.

33

ADVENTURE EXPEDITION ONE

Human factors (culture, criminals, terrorism) outside the team

Cultural blunders can be avoided by using a local guide. Even then, misunderstandings happen. No amount of book reading will prepare you for every nuance you will encounter.

Criminal and terrorist activity are real problems today. You must remain alert and wary of developing situations in your region. What was a calm expedition can turn into the next thriller movie instantly. It's impossible to completely avoid crime anywhere on the planet.

Terrorism is a growing global problem. Carefully consider the safety of your team before venturing into a known terrorist region. Even then, the unexpected can happen in the most unexpected of places. A tragic example of this happened in Paris on November 13, 2015, when a series of coordinated attacks occurred, starting with suicide bombers detonating their explosives at a stadium. This was followed by mass shootings and another suicide bombing at several cafés and restaurants. Another mass shooting and hostage taking happened at a concert venue at the same time, ultimately causing 130 deaths with another 413 wounded.

Contingencies

How far will you tolerate deteriorating conditions or team members before evacuating? An example is sticking with the agreed upon turn-around time on high mountains. There are countless stories of teams pushing far past their time, resulting in disastrous consequences.

Questions to ask yourself and the team:

- How many team members can you lose before the situation is untenable?
- How will you deal with the debilitation of any one team member? (Consider everyone, including a guide!)
- Will others be able to keep moving forward?
- How many will be needed to tend to the disabled person?

PLANNING

- Will the reduction in manpower terminate the expedition?
- If you lose one particular person, will the expedition end?
- Is there a way to build in redundant skill sets for each person?

Although this discussion reads like a doomsday scenario, consider this example:

You are on an expedition to the North Pole. Moments ago, a team member fell through the ice. She sprained her ankle during the fall. And, a storm has built up seemingly out of nowhere. And you injured your shoulder on an ice fall earlier in the day, slowing you down. You have lost sight of the other members of the team.

Are you prepared for a worst-case scenario? A string of disasters can rapidly turn a minor annoyance into a life-threatening situation.

Will you call in for an expensive rescue? How long can you hold out? In stormy, remote locations, help may be a long time in coming or may be impossible. Complacency is created by modern cities, transport, and communication. Explorers must be self-contained and prepared for anything.

Project management

For an experienced backpacker, an overnight trip may only require a few hours of planning. Sailing around the world to win the Vendée Globe race may take years. The scale of an expedition will determine the level and complexity of the planning process. For small trips, a simple hand-written list may suffice. But for a major trek, lists, lists of lists, spreadsheets, and even project management software may be required. Regardless of the trip scale, some planning is always required.

Some people plan an entire trip on a cocktail napkin. Others will use Microsoft Project to outline every detail. Experience, difficulty, and complexity will determine what level of project management will be required. Planning is one of the least thrilling aspects of trekking. What it lacks in appeal it makes up for later on. To have a safer, more enjoyable expedition, plan extensively. And then map out contingencies.

35

ADVENTURE EXPEDITION ONE

This is not to say everything needs to be micromanaged. The risk tolerance of the team must be taken into account. Remote and inhospitable locations demand organization. No experienced polar explorer would arrive in Greenland without testing equipment beforehand. Don't believe you can get away without doing the same.

Whatever method of planning you use, be adaptable. And keep everything together. Nothing is worse than losing a critical note in a pile of scrap paper. Invest a few dollars in a bound notebook and calendar. Organize your expedition computer files in a single place. And back them up! Countless hours are wasted looking for lost things, all for want of organization.

Social media sites go down. File-sharing services fail. Be paranoid. Losing 200 hours of research and planning for the want of an inexpensive backup device is not worth it. Your expedition is likely expensive. High-capacity memory sticks are not.

Create a checklist that everyone can see. Someone else might notice an important missing task. Discovering an omission early will save everyone trouble later. An initial checklist may feel overwhelming, but it's good mental training for what's to come. Plus, checking off items creates an emotional boost. This will help soften the sting of your twentieth sponsor rejection letter.

Roadblocks

- Unexpected problems—they will happen
- Surprises out of nowhere—they will happen
- Team members dropping out—count on it
- Funding falling short—guaranteed

Impediments can actually be valuable. You want to uncover what isn't going to work well before embarking on the trek. Discovering your newly built sea kayak doesn't float properly three weeks before launch is not where you want to be. The longer the trip is, the earlier you need everything prepared. Ideally, you will have tested everything well in advance.

PLANNING

If the trip is limited by the seasons, try everything out an entire year before. It's impossible to test snow gear in cool October temperatures, especially when you're headed for –50-degree temperatures in Antarctic November. There are no outdoor stores at Union Glacier.

Does your expedition rely primarily on a vehicle (boat, car, aircraft)? Have everything tested months in advance of launch. This will save sleepless nights making last-minute preparations. Should you procrastinate on a critical item, your expedition may be scrubbed. The easiest way to avoid this is to prepare everything well in advance.

Have a plan to reroute or make adjustments to your goal, too. Conditions, equipment, or team members may not work out. Prepare sponsors and the support team for this. Early identification of problems reduces stress on everyone involved.

Sometimes funding doesn't come through. What will you be able to do if you only have 80 percent of your funding? 50 percent? 20 percent? Can you still do something worthwhile? There are minimum entry costs for some locations like Antarctica. Sometimes only 100 percent funding will work. How will you manage a funding shortfall?

Remember, too, that you're going to be gone for the duration. What will happen to your life back home? Family, home, and job obligations are important and can't be ignored as you develop your plan. How will you pay the bills during your absence? Returning home to massive debt adds stress to an already tough expedition.

Timetable

You need to prepare things months or years in advance for a major expedition. Here's a list of things you need to do well in advance.

14 months

Gather all seasonal gear and test it under as similar conditions to your trek as possible, ideally with other team members in a training trip or mini-expedition. If you've already been training and preparing, you've completed this step.

37

ADVENTURE EXPEDITION ONE

<u>6 months</u>
Vaccinations
Test out vitamin/supplement regimen, make sure they all help.

<u>2 months</u>
Obtain medications specific to your expedition (such as antibiotics, antiparasitics, etc.) and make sure you have adequate supplies of all of your personal medications.

Check ALL gear for tears, fraying, etc. Order duplicates or repair. Note that seasonal gear may need to be ordered at least six to twelve months in advance. Specialized winter gear can be difficult to purchase in spring/summer for Antarctic, Himalayan, or southern hemisphere travel.

Crisis planning

As a leader, it's important to know the plan backward and forward. Commit it to memory. In a crisis situation, your brain looks for answers. Do you and your team know what they are supposed to do in a crisis situation? If so, stress and conflict will be much lower. If not, a grim outcome may be the result.

If everyone can confidently recite all aspects of the expedition, problems will be fewer. Have everyone trained with basic safety, communication, and rescue equipment. For instance, what if the rescue equipment operator is the one needing rescue? Maybe he or she is knocked unconscious. Will any one of the team be able to step up and competently operate the equipment? This may never happen.

But it might.

An emergency is not the time to learn. There is only time to act. When stress skyrockets, human ability deteriorates. People develop tunnel vision. They may not see what is right in front of them. A high pulse rate will impair a person's fine motor skills. What was relatively easy when calm and relaxed will become difficult, if not impossible.

Training under duress can make the difference between life and death. That's why emergency personnel and the military train constantly. They need to practice until essential tasks become automatic.

PLANNING

In a disaster, the brain is operating at maximum capacity. There is little spare ability to think about normally routine actions.

Part of expedition planning must incorporate training for potential disasters. Think of the worst-case scenarios. Plan them out with the team. Use the power of their collective minds to create solutions. Do this when everyone is relaxed.

Once everyone agrees upon the proper response, test it out in the worst weather and in the dark. For example, simulate an accident during which a teammate suffers a broken limb. Can half the team accomplish the rescue or disaster response? What is the bare minimum of people needed? Now suppose half the team is injured or becomes incapacitated. All team members need to practice stabilizing the injured until help comes or until an evacuation can be accomplished.

This may sound overly negative. But these scenarios occur on expeditions. Planning an expedition to a remote location means help is far away and long in coming, or not coming at all. You and your team may need to be self-contained for an extended time—days to a week or more. Or, it may be impossible to communicate with the outside world. For the safety of the team, all of these considerations must be discussed, understood and practiced.

Discipline

Putting together a significant expedition requires loads of discipline. For the inexperienced, the time required to plan, train, and gear up will be daunting. It's amazing to read how trekkers are assembling gear hours before a flight. Avoid being that person.

Ways to ruin an expedition

- Ignore a workout
- Ignore a lot of workouts
- Delay buying decisions
- Wait too long to contact media
- Try to raise last-second funding

ADVENTURE EXPEDITION ONE

Training for physically demanding treks takes time. A lot of it. All high-altitude mountains require *six* months of prior training. Every workout is cumulative.

If your workouts don't add up to enough, you will not step foot on the peak. Fail to tow a tire for innumerable miles and you won't reach the North Pole. Not enough practice navigating? Forget sailing the world safely.

It's easy to put things off until the last moment. Next-day air shipping can quickly ruin a budget and add stress. Expenses add up. Modern gear is expensive enough. Waste none of your budget on rush shipping. The author writes from experience...

Ways to succeed on an expedition

- Announce your plans to the world early
- Keep an online log of your plans
- Make yourself accountable to people

Peer pressure is incredibly powerful. Avoid overdoing it, as you can lose heart. Announcing your plans to the world is a powerful motivator. Broadcast your plans to everyone you know. The question, "How's the expedition planning going?" will keep you on track even when you don't feel like working out.

Create an advisory committee for your expedition. Enlist the help of others experienced in your planned arena. They can be a great boon to your efforts. Let them know you want an honest evaluation. Their realistic feedback will be invaluable in improving your planning and preparation.

Some have come through against seemingly impossible odds. But do you want to set yourself up for a crisis situation? Being the first to do something increases the challenge. You must balance recommendations, risk, criticism, and chances. You never know until you try.

Training plan

Outline a serious training plan. Make sure it's at least as difficult as what you expect to be up against. If you and your team are only

PLANNING

tested at 80 percent of capacity, what will happen when 100 percent is required? It's important to know what will happen at full capacity. Once you are in the field, discovering that physical and mental training was inadequate is a terrible mistake.

Classic training programs suggest a ramp-up approach. This is where you start easy and slowly work your way up to what you expect during the expedition. This works well when you have had previous expedition experience. Have you worked out at the level the expedition requires? Do the conditions closely mimic what you're going to encounter? If not, you may be in for a difficult surprise.

Taking a full simulation trip is critically important. You may discover you or your gear is not fully ready for what you will encounter. Granted, it's difficult to simulate being at 28,000 feet (8,500 meters) or in the middle of Antarctica. But, you want to uncover every weakness prior to departure. Discovering you and your team aren't quite prepared for conditions is demoralizing at best.

Find out everything you can as early as possible. Two weeks before the expedition is not the time to realize your training is inadequate.

The worst planning admission on an expedition:

"I wish I'd trained harder."

Go fast, go slow

There are two competing philosophies to speed on expeditions. The first approach is to go slowly, enjoy the experience, and take in the sights. The second is to go as fast as possible while keeping safety in mind.

When traveling in the mountains or in polar regions, there's a saying:

"Speed is safety in the mountains."

41

Adventure Expedition One

If the goal of the expedition is immersion, exposure, and media capture, slow may be the way to go. Often, speed causes people to miss subtle details. Rarely is it possible to delve into the nuances of a location when the only vision is completing the expedition. Perhaps extra time spent in a location may generate lasting benefits.

Speed has numerous advantages, though. Often, time in the field is limited by budget, season, travel permits, or otherwise. At extreme altitude, it's simply impossible to survive for prolonged periods. Relatively stable Arctic sea ice only lasts for so long. If an avalanche-prone area cannot be avoided, then moving through the zone quickly may be the best way to mitigate the danger. Many conditions dictate a limited calendar window. Limiting time away from family and work reduces stress, too.

What is to be done on the expedition will dictate how fast everyone needs to travel. If you are planning a high-mountain expedition, you want to travel quickly. But you can't travel too fast, as altitude sickness can be caused by too much elevation gain too quickly. If you are traveling for scientific purposes, you may need as much time as possible to collect data.

Below is a short list of pros and cons of each approach:

Slow advantages
    Opportunity for acclimatization
    Increased cultural experiences
    Time for photography and filming
    Allowance for slower team members
    Schedule accommodates the collection of scientific data

Slow disadvantages
    Increased travel costs
    More time away from family/home/work
    Heavier loads due to increased food and supplies
    Longer exposure to extreme conditions, other objective hazards, and workload

PLANNING

<u>Speed advantages</u>
Reduced time away from family/home/work
Lighter loads from decreased supply needs
Limited exposure to weather
Less exposure to extreme conditions, other objective hazards, and workload

<u>Speed disadvantages</u>
The entire team must be highly fit
Less time for acclimatization
Tension between slowest and fastest team members
Increased risk of taking chances to move quicker
Food and fuel supplies may be inadequate if unexpected delays occur
Decreased opportunity for a cultural experience, photography, or the collection of scientific data, etc.

Consider safety, goals, enjoyment, human factors, and the environment when determining speed. It would be a rare case for someone to say they wish they'd taken longer to cross Greenland. Records are usually for speed. Toughing out slow travel makes for good stories, though.

Having completed several expeditions, my thought on speed derives from the need for safety and enjoyment. A slower pace makes trekking more enjoyable. Taking the time to experience local cultures, landscape, and animals is worth the time. But when you're faced with a weather or calendar window, there is a definite advantage to more speed. If unexpected weather moves in on your team, having the ability to move rapidly can mean the difference between life and death.

"No matter how fast I am, I always wish I could be faster."

ADVENTURE EXPEDITION ONE

Flight and travel planning

Ensure that your travel plan allows for resting from travel and time zone differences. Do not underestimate how much long-distance flights and little sleep will affect your mind and body. Although it's tempting to believe you can tough through it, avoid it if possible.

> **First Time on Denali**
> Climber Jason Thompson of Australia emailed us about his travel to Denali.
>
> "One of my lessons was that it pays to travel and give yourself time to adjust and relax before starting your expedition. I understand that sometimes it is difficult to allow time but if you can it's best practice. An example of my recent Denali expedition is I left Australia and flew directly to Los Angeles for 16 hours. I arrived at six a.m. I then had the day in Los Angeles and flew the red-eye to Anchorage, arriving at four a.m.
> I only had two hours of sleep in a hotel before spending the day collecting my supplies before driving to Talkeetna that afternoon. I spent the night in the hanger in Talkeetna then flew to Denali base camp the next afternoon to start my expedition.
> From home in Australia to Denali base camp took two and a half days. I was exhausted just from that which did not help me adjust to the altitude. I felt bad almost the entire time on the mountain. Next time I will allow a few days at my final destination to unwind, sort my gear, and mentally prepare for what I am undertaking."

The farther you are traveling from your starting point, the more important it is to plan for delays. If you are traveling across continents, consider arriving an extra day or two before the expedition. Although modern travel is reliable, it is not infallible. You do not want to train for months and have a lot of money invested in an expedition only to miss the starting date.

PLANNING

International Flight Delay

The authors of this book met for the first time in the San Francisco airport when our flight was canceled due to a plane mechanical problem. We had both planned to arrive in Africa one day earlier than our Kilimanjaro expedition date. The gate agent quickly surmised that we were both headed to the same location, an amazing coincidence. The agent asked if we wanted to stay the night in San Francisco and catch the next day's flight. We instead asked to be flown to Amsterdam, the halfway point. We reasoned it was better to be one continent closer to our destination.

This proved to work quite well. The airline put us up in comfortable rooms in Amsterdam for the inconvenience and we enjoyed some unexpected time there. It also gave us time to adjust to the eight-hour time zone difference between the western United States and East Africa. This extra day allowed us to arrive somewhat fresh. Our flight landed at midnight in Tanzania, so the extra night's sleep was appreciated.

Planning for team dynamics

There are countless books written about leadership and team dynamics. Instead of rehashing that material, a story from a first-time climber illustrates some of the issues you need to be prepared for. He also discusses plans for the mental shock of the experience, another factor that will affect team dynamics.

Climber Jason Thompson of Australia wrote this about his team experience on Denali:

"From the beginning, the biggest lesson I learned from this experience was to make sure you know, have traveled, or

ADVENTURE EXPEDITION ONE

camped with or have spent time doing similar things with the people you choose to attempt serious expeditions with. I made the mistake of allowing someone to join my expedition without meeting them directly, been camping with them or done anything with them at all.

Now the person in question is in no way a bad person at all. He is a very nice guy and very motivated. However, his attitude towards our climb was such that he was not interested in listening to the group and how the group was feeling. This was probably the biggest issue as he was pushing the team along quicker than was needed and outside our original plan.

This behavior led to smaller things becoming an issue that otherwise may have gone unnoticed. Things like him bringing double the amount of gear as myself. I ended having to help carry some of his kit. He left dirty pots full of food for days, really bugging me.

An example of this is we flew into Denali base camp, lower Kahiltna Glacier, and we had discussed and agreed that it would be a rest day and night at base camp to adjust, as it would be the biggest altitude gain. We arrived in the afternoon. As I was unpacking tent gear, he was directing our other team member and packing up his sled himself and making ready to move to Camp One.

I didn't plan to leave so soon and was caught by surprise. All of us did not arrive into Talkeetna until midnight and were exhausted. This fatigue contributed to me feeling unwell due to moving higher too quickly. It caused me to start my climb off with acute mountain sickness (AMS). You need to be sure of the people you are with. You will fully rely on them in the event you are in trouble high on the mountain. It will be them that you must trust to get you down. As a result, I did not complete the trip with him as I felt I could not trust this person to help me in the event I needed it. This was my biggest lesson.

PLANNING

Next lesson would be to be mentally prepared. Although I was mentally prepared for an expedition, I was not fully aware of the severity of extremes I would encounter. I had spent two years prepping for this expedition to Denali and overall I feel pretty good about how I organized it. I knew that it was going to be cold; however, where I fell short was in underestimating how cold it would actually be.

In my defense, it is very hard to train for this type of weather and conditions here in Australia. But I will be sure to apply what I have learned next time and think long and hard about what it will involve. I found the cold, well, just very cold. It was hard to warm up at altitude once you were already cold. That was a very big kick in the arse for me and I will not make that same mistake again."

Travel and expedition insurance

What type of health and accident insurance do you currently have? Do you have medical insurance through your employer, pay for your own, or have no insurance at all? Although many expeditions unfold without a single incident, the chance of injury is far higher than during your normal activities. It is the nature of expeditions that you subject yourself to a higher physical and emotional risk. Should anything happen, you will need coverage to take care of your recovery.

Some expedition companies will require you to carry a significant amount of emergency evacuation insurance. In the case of a trip to Antarctica, you will be required to have $300,000 or more of accident and evacuation insurance. If you don't have this insurance, some companies will refuse to transport you.

Recovering someone and transporting him or her back to their home country can be incredibly expensive. Flying someone out of a remote region with a broken leg or serious illness can cost tens to hundreds of thousands of dollars. Medical helicopters and jets can easily cost ten times the amount of a regular flight.

If you leave your job, plan to have some type of basic medical insurance. What about your team? Does everyone have coverage? If not, you may be subjecting yourself to financial liability. Even though you may not officially be a guide, because of your leadership of the expedition, an injured person, their family, or their lawyer may claim that you bear financial responsibility. At the outset, people start with smiles and handshakes. When things go wrong, that can all be forgotten. It is better to sweat the details before leaving rather than sweating lawsuits afterward.

People

It is important to make sure all of your team is field-tested. It's critical to the safety, enjoyment, and success of your team. Ideally, you want to have lived with each other in the field before your expedition. There are some expeditions, like climbing trips on Kilimanjaro, where you can get by without testing your team. But, on a more serious and dangerous mountain like Denali, making sure you know how your team operates under duress is key.

Do all teams who haven't traveled together fail? No, they often succeed. Guided groups on Denali have a team that's never met or climbed together. And every year scores of these climbers successfully reach the summit. Teams come together that haven't ever met and successfully pull off a summit attempt.

The question you have to answer as an expedition leader or member is:

What's the safety and success risk if one or more team members aren't prepared?

Both authors have been on trips where someone has said:

"I should have tested out my knee better. I can't go on."
"I don't really like the cold. I want to turn around."
"We just didn't have time to train."
"I didn't think it would be this hard."
"I was talked into this by a spouse/friend/etc., but I'm not really into this."

48

PLANNING

These statements are demoralizing and set the team up for failure. It's nearly impossible to avoid bad feelings. Some teams can work through this, others cannot. Besides the physical challenge, the most difficult obstacle to overcome is human conflict. What can be ignored at home may become impossible to deal with during the challenges of your expedition.

Consider this scenario:

Imagine being trapped inside a tent for a week in a blizzard. Every three hours you have to shovel out your tent to prevent its collapse. The temperature has not risen above negative thirty in days. The forty-mile-per-hour wind noise has made sleep nearly impossible. Your cough has become worse. Your tent mate decides to quit helping with the shoveling chores.

"It'll be fine," she says. "The tent can handle it and I'm too cold to go out."

You believe otherwise. You're now in a dangerous situation. If your tent fails, what are you going to do? Will you be able to dig a snow cave in a raging storm? More importantly, why should you risk being buried in your tent?

Under the stress of the situation, small irritations can become huge issues.

"You drive me nuts every time you roll over. Your sleeping pad crinkles. I can't stand that sound," she says.

"Your habit of smacking your gums every time you take a drink drives me up the wall," you retort.

Even worse, the storm may last for three more days. These examples are low-grade irritations. If the leader's risk tolerance is higher than the team's, many a mutiny can occur. Teams have even decided to split up, making camping, cooking, travel, even survival more risky for everyone.

Equipment

In the film *Ghost in the Darkness*, one character borrows another's rifle. At a critical moment, it fails to fire. The main character saves

ADVENTURE EXPEDITION ONE

another with a miraculous shot. After a bit of dialogue, the main character discovers the failed weapon wasn't tested. And this failure nearly cost someone his or her life. The main character chides the other's failure by saying,

"Never take an untested weapon into the field."

The same is true of your expedition. Though you may not need firearms, you will certainly need some equipment. And you'll have teammates you're relying on who have their own equipment. Has every piece of gear been field-tested? If something critical fails, how will you adapt? On smaller-scale expeditions, you can often improvise. In more remote locations, like in the middle of the Arctic Ocean, there may be zero physical resources to build from.

Creating a risk mitigation plan can be exhausting and focuses on the negative. You want to do everything you can to be positive but realistic. If something breaks, is it an inconvenience, a major problem, or will someone be seriously injured or die from the failure? The more you think about what you'll do before you leave, the less stressful it'll be in the field when failures happen.

If you already have a plan and simply have to execute it, both risk and conflict are reduced. You won't have to formulate a plan when you're fatigued, hungry, and dehydrated. You'll have the satisfaction of knowing you saw this coming and know what to do.

Be assured that something will fail. Having a repair or rescue already planned will improve your chance of survival. Your plan will keep you alive. It's impossible to foresee every contingency, though. Creativity and teamwork are key factors to recovering from a failure.

You don't plan to fail.
You simply fail to plan.

PLANNING

When you write your equipment list, create a column for risk. Try categorizing equipment failure in the following way:

Annoying
Important
Critical

Make sure everyone on your team agrees with your assessment. What one person thinks is an annoying failure may be important to another. And it might be life-and-death to another. Everyone has a different tolerance level for problems. This is also a good time to evaluate the risk tolerance of your teammates. If you think something is only annoying and another person thinks it's critical, you may have discovered a looming personal conflict. A differing point of view like this can cause large problems down the line.

If you really want to test to see if your team's risk personalities match, bring an equipment printout to a team meeting. Have each person independently rank each piece of equipment using the above three levels. Once everyone is done, collect the papers and have an open discussion about each. Someone may feel pressured to change their ranking based on other people's opinions. Even if the dissenting person doesn't voice their honest opinion, they might surprise you with their true feelings in the field. Honesty is the best policy here.

The fun part of the process comes after you've gone through the ranking process. Have everyone contribute ideas for how to overcome a failure. You have a team (unless you're solo) and you never know who might have a solution. It might surprise you who this solution comes from—you may have just uncovered a great problem-solving teammate!

Does this process seem like overkill? Perhaps. Highly experienced trekkers likely won't need this process. If you're planning a weeklong trip into the Rockies, you might not do this. But if you're headed off for a three-month trip into northern Greenland, the few hours you spend on this may save your expedition or even a teammate's life.

Conflict

Conflict is bound to happen on a trip. It may be minor or major. When people are under stress, both their best and worst can come out. How will you handle this when it happens? Will you be able to defuse the situation before the interpersonal damage becomes permanent?

There are many significant texts on the subject and more are published every year. Find one that works for your style and read it through. It is your responsibility to be aware of people's feelings. Everyone has a different leadership style and this may not work for all. Honesty while being considerate is key to keeping hurt feelings and anger at bay. You want to come home happy and smiling rather than never speaking with your teammates again.

Mini-expeditions

How will you be sure that your equipment and people are really ready for the expedition? One of the best ways is to take a mini-expedition together. This will be your chance to see if everything you purchased can stand up to conditions. You'll find out the real strengths and weaknesses of yourself and your teammates.

If you are planning a major ocean crossing or a trip where you'll spend significant time in cramped quarters with someone, find out if you can tolerate each other early. Someone might find one of your habits to be maddening. You need to be honest about yourself and with others.

Plan for a few shakedown expeditions. The bigger and longer your trip, the more training you'll need. If you are going to a polar region solo, have you camped in extremely cold temperatures by yourself for at least a week? If you are planning to kayak across a major body of water for weeks, have you tried a few weekends sleeping out on the water? You would be amazed how many set out without ever testing themselves on a smaller scale.

Terry navigating crevasses on Mt. Olympus.

PART FOUR

Financing

Adventure resumé

If you're a nobody in the expedition world and you don't have a rich uncle, you have some work to do. If you expect to raise sponsorship money, you will need an adventure resumé. Every explorer started under the tutelage of someone else. This means that you may have to start small.

Consider what skills and experience you have compared to what you want to achieve. Is the gap small or seemingly insurmountable? Having a grand vision is what takes you to incredible places. That same vision can excite sponsors, too.

Before striking out to raise funds, be ready to answer the question:

"What have you done before?"

Camping at the county campground a few feet from your vehicle isn't going to cut it. Your sponsors will expect you to show that you have the skill and experience to complete your expedition. You need to have done at least one trip (if not more) that simulates the scale of what you plan to do. If your trip will take two months, plan to

Financing

take more than one trip that lasts two weeks. The tougher and more impressive you can make it, the better. Sponsors will not offer up cash to someone without real qualifications and a good sales pitch.

Even if you don't plan to raise money, you still need to build a resumé. People have paid to climb Everest and have never climbed other serious mountains. Guide services make it possible. However, you need to ask yourself honestly if what you plan makes sense based on your skill level.

The challenge of building the resumé can be significant. There are some people who have the financial resources to take on an Everest climb having done little before that. If you have that financial capacity, then all the better. If not, keep reading.

How do I get the money?

The two approaches to funding your expedition are to pool your team's money or to pursue sponsors. Sponsors can include donations from individuals, companies, or organizations. Your approach to reaching each of these groups varies.

Individual donors require the least effort after their donation is made. Depending on what you offer people, the work during and afterward can be minimal. Make sure to do the work you promised, though. If you promise a phone call from the summit of a mountain, make sure you follow through.

Companies and organizations will require significantly more for their investment in your effort. You may need to provide articles, photographs, videos, and be present at one or more events. Stipulations and guarantees will often be attached to these funds. The reward of having your five-figure expedition fully funded will not come without a cost.

Self-funding

Funding an expedition yourself is arguably the easiest way to raise cash. Although raising the money can feel daunting, it requires the least sales effort compared to any other technique. All you need to do is convince yourself that the expedition is worth the effort.

ADVENTURE EXPEDITION ONE

Alastair Humphreys, a British polar explorer, is a big proponent of self-funding and enjoying small trips. He discusses the value of starting small in his book *Microadventures*. Does that mean you should trade your big dream in for sleeping under the stars in a local park? Not at all.

The concept of starting small will help you build up to something bigger. Just because your dream expedition is big doesn't mean it has to cost a lot. Humphreys wrote that it's possible to cycle from Britain to Japan on £1,000 ($1,300USD in 2018). Although that amount seems extremely low, he cycled around the world in four years. It's possible.

Clair and André from www.puncturesandpanniers.com reported a budget of £12,000 ($16,000USD in 2018) for their eighteen-month trip from Britain to Japan. Their blog shows that they did travel inexpensively, but nothing like Humphreys. Even though the difference in cost is large, saving that amount isn't out of reach for most people. Their blog suggests that they did splurge on some things like alcohol while visiting tourist sites.

In either case, consider that you will be living in your tent for much of the time on a similar trip. There may be times you will be invited in by strangers. However, there may also be times when strangers will cause you problems. But also consider that with a tight budget it will cost only $25 a week to save money for a major expedition. Skip the expensive latte drinks at your local coffee shop. When you feel like spending that money, transfer the $5 into a special expedition savings account. Every time. You'll be amazed how quickly you can build up the funds for an expedition.

It is possible to convince family members to financially support your expedition as well. For some, this may be a viable alternative. For others, there may be no support at all. Selling people on the viability, the chances of success, and what you will bring back will have an impact on how much funding you can raise.

Time

Depending on your earning power, thrift, and resourcefulness, it may not take long at all to save for an expedition. Depending on the

Financing

trek, you may only need to raise a few thousand dollars. The biggest challenge is your ability to save the money and dedicate it to your expedition.

Effort

Are you willing to take on a second job? What can you do without or sell to seed your fund? One key to this is to open a separate savings account that's dedicated to your expedition. Should you take the money out for something unrelated, you'll be much more conscious of the spending.

In tourist towns like Jackson, Wyoming, locals may work two or three jobs during the busy tourist season to save money, then travel for two months in a far-off location. You must balance what you believe are real necessities versus niceties. It can be instructive to seriously consider what is really necessary beyond basic bills. According to the Acorns Money Matters report, the average American spends $1,100 a year on coffee. If you diverted expenditures from the "nice to have" category into your expedition fund, you may discover the ability to fund your expedition quickly.

Risk

You reduce some of your responsibilities by using your own cash to fund an expedition. Because you are spending your own money, you are not beholden to anyone else. There are no external pressures to achieve your goal, only your internal pressure to succeed and justify the expense.

After expedition

Once you complete your expedition, your goal is to be in a position to return to your regular life with few if any obligations. Hopefully, you will not be carrying debt from the expedition. If debt looks unavoidable, consider delaying your expedition. Unsecured debts such as credit card debts tend to be a persistent strain on your financial future. Also, remember that you likely will have a period of time when you will not have any income while on your expedition.

The major advantage of self-financing a trip is avoiding obligations to other people, organizations, or companies. There is no one to keep

ADVENTURE EXPEDITION ONE

happy, do appearances for, or who may make you feel guilty should you fail to succeed. Do not underestimate the amount of pressure a sponsor can put on you and your team.

Non-profit funding

There are entire communities of non-profit organizations that raise money for causes or benefits. How will your expedition tie into these? Consider that you will want your beneficiary to be the primary reason for your trek. People have abused charities by using them as fronts to fund their trip while having little to do with the actual charity. How will you avoid this mistake and make it clear that your goal is to support your non-profit partner?

Another option to support your expedition is to create your own non-profit organization (referred to as a non-profit in the rest of the text) to pay for your expedition. There are many entities dedicated to as many causes, from saving feral cats to combating global warming. Whatever non-profit cause you choose, be aware that the effort level can be significant. This can provide a way to use your expedition for more than just the experience, but also to advance a cause you care about. How you balance this effort will take serious planning.

Time

The time required to connect with or establish a non-profit is significant. In addition to training and planning for your expedition, you will need to grow and nurture your non-profit. You have to establish the viability of your effort, connect with your community, and build a following. This may take months but more likely years to build into a viable project. For those who are skilled at sales and fundraising, this may be a difficult but achievable undertaking. For those who are not, you need to be willing to enlist skilled help or to reconsider your approach.

Effort

Making and maintaining your connection with a non-profit will turn into a part-time job. If you are creating your own non-profit,

Financing

look at it as a second job. You will not be able to work just eight hours a day. Legitimate non-profits are a major undertaking and will rapidly consume your time. An effort like this can take years to become financially viable.

If you are connecting with an existing non-profit, much of the basic groundwork will already be done for you. However, the non-profit will expect a moderate to major amount of time and energy directed at their efforts, along with the major challenge of preparing for your expedition.

Risk

The risk of connecting with an existing organization is relatively low and enables you to get off to a quick start. However, there is a real risk of your expedition never coming to fruition. What will happen when your opinion and the sponsor's diverge? Will you be able to sustain your relationship and continue with your expedition?

Creating your own non-profit to support an expedition is a higher-risk activity. If you are not familiar with the process and are not fully dedicated to the effort, there's a chance of failure. You must ask yourself if you are genuinely dedicated to the non-profit that sponsors your expedition. If you are not, your reputation is at risk.

After expedition

A non-profit will expect a significant amount of effort before, during, and after your expedition. You must plan to be at events, speak for them, and do continuous work. Make sure that whatever you plan, the commitment has a defined time frame. You want to have a clear contract of what expectations you must meet, when they need to be completed, and how you will sign off.

If you have created your own non-profit, presumably this organization will live long after your expedition has been completed. Are you confident that you will continue to dedicate a portion of your life to this effort? If so, then the satisfaction of running your own non-profit will be its own payoff. If not, reconsider this option.

ADVENTURE EXPEDITION ONE

Crowdfunding

Crowdfunding websites have become the go-to method for people trying to raise funds for projects and causes. These resources have expanded people's ability to connect with an entire world of potential sponsors.

Time

For individuals, you need to expect that you will need a large group of donors. There are books and websites dedicated to raising cash via crowdfunding sites. You will need to devote a significant amount of time to preparing and pre-advertising your campaign.

Once your project goes live, you will only have a limited amount of time to raise all of your funds. This is highly motivating but also restricting. Are you prepared to dedicate nearly all of your time to this effort? Consider that you still need to be training for your expedition, too. With a multi-person team, consider who are your best sales and media people. The team member who spearheads this crucial part of your expedition is essential and will be under a lot of pressure.

Effort

The common amount people contribute to a project on crowd-funding sites is $5–$10. If your expedition costs $20,000 and your average donor contributes $7, will you be able to convince nearly 2,900 donors to support your expedition? People are successful all the time with these sites, while other projects are never adequately funded.

Consider how good you are at sales and advertising. Promoting your idea and making people excited about it will be a challenge. With so many people posting their adventures on social media, you will need to spend significant time advertising and building excitement for your trip.

Risk

All crowdfunding sites will charge a significant amount of your fundraising cash, from 10 percent up to 25 percent. Make sure you account for this.

60

Financing

Some crowdfunding sites are an all-or-nothing deal, while others allow partial funding for a project.

You might notice the proliferation of crowdfunding sites. Have you ever wondered why that is? The effort from the website, financial, and legal managers is arguably low for their return on investment. In trade for providing a place to promote your project, brokering the money, and providing a community, these services reap an incredible income.

A distinct benefit of a crowdfunding site is that it can give you access to a community that would normally be beyond your reach. However, this means that your pitch may be completely lost amongst the thousands of other teams trying to raise funds for their projects.

Something you can learn from a crowdfunding site is what works and what doesn't. Whether you use this crowdfunding or some other funding method, you can quickly learn what attracts donors. These sites can require a significant time commitment to maintain near-constant communication with sponsors.

Often there is a deadline associated with a crowdfunding project. What if you choose an all-or-nothing site and miss your six-figure budget by a few hundred dollars? You risk losing all the money from your sponsors.

After expedition

The return on your investment of time can be potentially huge. There are countless stories of those who used their crowdfunding project to raise incredible sums of money. It's possible to raise far beyond what you're trying to achieve. Remember that you'll need to budget a non-trivial percentage of the funds raised to go to the website service fee.

As crowdfunding sites adapt and change over time, there will be more iterations and rule changes. These services have been an incredible boon to people trying to raise funds. Be aware that a funding site may develop a poor reputation that you are unaware of. As they are relatively new to the fundraising world, the future is uncertain. As long as you're able to raise funds and satisfy obligations to individual donors, you have done a successful job of fundraising.

ADVENTURE EXPEDITION ONE

Traditional sponsors

The classic way to pay for a significant expedition is to find sponsors willing to provide funding. From the time of Christopher Columbus to today, explorers are constantly searching for someone to pay for their adventures. The sales and value pitch to potential sponsors will make all the difference in your potential success. It will be a significant advantage if you have some connection inside the organization you're selling your idea to.

Consider the people you know in your immediate and extended circle of acquaintances. Do you know someone who works for a law firm, tech company, or alcohol distillery? Through your research, you will discover that people have used all of these and more to support their efforts. The options for potential financial support are endless.

Outdoor equipment companies receive requests for sponsorship nearly every day. Their response to you will be, "Why would we pay for your trip when we can fund our own?" Be ready with a response that shows the uniqueness of your expedition.

The book *You Want to Go Where?* by Jeff Blumenfeld is an excellent resource for an in-depth examination of what it takes to secure significant corporate sponsors. He discusses the process of successful and failing efforts to contact companies.

The value proposition is everything for a sponsored expedition. What do you have to offer a company besides having them pay for your grueling vacation? Often, the advertising value is the most significant value you can offer a company. If you have the ability to attract media attention, sponsors may be willing to take a look at you. Consider how much a half-page ad costs in a major US newspaper. If you can be featured in an article that covers that space, you can sell your advertising value based on that rate.

Often companies will offer in-kind support. That is, they will give you socks, outwear, tents, and the like. These can be major savings to your expedition and they are well worth pursuing. However, if you require flight support to a remote location, only cash will make it happen. You cannot pay for a flight with hand-warmers or other donated gear.

62

Financing

You or someone on your team must be media savvy. The ability to write, take compelling photographs, and generate video footage is an essential requirement for a modern supported expedition. Your sponsor company will want to use your media in their advertising. If you don't have multi-media skills, start developing them now.

Make a film about a weekend camping trip. Have your friends honestly evaluate it. If they aren't impressed, a company who can afford a television crew certainly won't be. Thanks to social media and video-sharing websites, today's standards are high. How many followers do you have on your video channel? If it's ten, be prepared for rejection. If you have 100,000 followers, someone will be interested. All of these people are potential customers of your sponsor. It really does make a difference.

Sponsors will also require you to carry insurance. They will need backup and contingency plans should things go awry. Have all of these planned for, in written form, and ready to send out. If a contact is interested and they ask for these materials, you need to be able to send them promptly. If you prepare like a professional, people will take you seriously.

Time

If you are someone with excellent connections, you may discover that it's relatively easy to fully fund your expedition. For a newcomer, you may find the fundraising process very difficult. Your track record is everything. Do you have an experience that demonstrates your grit such as a unique first or a major guided climb (like Denali or Everest)? If not, start with planning that preliminary expedition.

You will experience all of the challenges of a salesperson and more. The time required to cultivate a relationship with a sponsor can be more than you are willing to commit to. Famous expeditions have nearly come to an end simply because adequate funding could not be raised.

Effort

The effort needed to secure a sponsor for a major expedition can be daunting. Thirty years ago, you were required to deliver photographs

ADVENTURE EXPEDITION ONE

and a tiny bit of video. Now, you are expected to produce media that matches the quality of a major media production company. With the advent of the smartphone, you have the ability to photograph, video, and write about your experience on a device that fits into your pocket. Anything less simply isn't acceptable anymore.

Teenagers with a phone or a GoPro are producing stunning videos. If you can't match or beat them, you are in trouble. The ability to produce quality media comes on top of proving your ability and resourcefulness in completing an expedition. The larger your funding requirement, the bigger the challenge will be.

Also, note that many companies will refuse to sponsor you if your expedition is based on a charity. If you are raising funds for cancer, you may find rejection at every turn. Companies often want semi- or exclusive control of the media relating to your adventure.

Risk

The major advantage of securing financial sponsors is the reduction of your financial risk. It's much easier to use someone else's money on a risky activity. However, there's the risk that you will simply never secure enough sponsorship to make your expedition happen.

You need to weigh how much effort it will take you to attract sponsors. If you are not a natural salesperson or don't have a compelling personality, this will be a difficult approach. Do you have the ability to network with people naturally? Can you keep someone enraptured at a cocktail party? If not, finding a sponsor can be a major challenge.

After expedition

All sponsors will require something after you return. Some may require that you be present at their next three upcoming trade shows. All will require photographs, writing, and video footage. Be careful with what you offer sponsors. While you are fulfilling your obligation to them, you won't be working and making money to move on with your life. Every person's experience will be different.

Should you decide to write a book, create a film, or go on a speaking tour, what level of commitment will you make with your sponsors? Will they retain rights to the expedition and media? How will you manage this? Never assume you own the rights when someone else is paying for your trip. Make sure everything is perfectly clear at the outset of your trip. Otherwise, you may be in for unpleasant surprises afterward.

Another advantage of securing a major sponsor will be the company's willingness to work with you in the future. If you succeed and deliver the goods, you'll have a salable track record that can translate to future funding. Even if your current sponsor declines to support your next trip, there is a good chance that their employees know someone who will.

Training by dragging a tire up a mountain.

Porters hauling heavy loads up Kilimanjaro in Tanzania.

PART FIVE

Physical Training

Physical preparation

Nothing will detract from a successful start to your expedition as much as being physically and mentally unprepared. Sure, you will become "trail-hardened" after a week of backpacking, but those first days would have been so much more enjoyable if you had been physically ready for the long days of activity you are taking on. The sources for fitness and training information are endless. What should you really do to get in shape for your expedition? The answer to that question will depend on your baseline fitness level and what you are about to attempt. Make sure you start early enough!

Many people who have less than a stellar baseline fitness level will need a minimum of three months of physical training to get ready for a new, challenging physical test. Budget more preparation time if your baseline fitness is poor, if you are getting older, or if you are taking on a completely new challenge (for example, long-distance swimming or rowing for a novice).

ADVENTURE EXPEDITION ONE

> If you are leading a group on an expedition, make sure that everyone knows what will be expected of them in terms of fitness. If the trip will involve four to twelve hours of uphill hiking carrying a pack each day, all of the group members need to show up ready to perform. The group can only travel as quickly as the slowest member. Members of an expedition group will be understanding and patient with a group member who becomes sick or injured and needs to slow down or take a rest day. But there will be significant angst if someone shows up who is simply not ready to walk four hours a day. That unprepared person has just jeopardized the trip of a lifetime for the rest of the group.
>
> If you are joining a group on an expedition, you don't want to be that person. For example, on only Day Two of a group trek in the Solo Khumbu region, one of our party announced that she could not go on walking because of knee pain. She apparently hadn't "tested out" the knee adequately during her pre-trip conditioning.
>
> She went on to let the group know that she would need to hire a pony in order to continue, and she expected the group to pitch in to pay for the cost of her pony. You could hear the murmur rise from the group, "I'm not paying for your pony!" —*TW*

Depending on the difficulty and support for your expedition, there are two schools of thought on how hard you need to train. For fully supported expeditions like a Kilimanjaro climb, a base training program should suffice. However, for unsupported expeditions like a team climb of Denali or rowing across an ocean, every moment you can pour into training will pay off and even save your life.

Supported expedition training

The basic training suggestion is this: plan for resistance work (weights or body weight) three days a week to build strength and muscle mass. Devote alternate three days a week to cardio work, and

PHYSICAL TRAINING

make this as specific to your trip as you can. For example, if you will be backpacking across a mountain range, then spend time hiking with a weighted backpack (full water bottles work well) and ankle weights. If you will be pulling a heavy sled on skis but are training in the summer, harness yourself to a heavy tire and drag it uphill. It is important to not over-train. Vary your activities. Make sure you build one rest day a week into your schedule. Use an occasional cardio day to do something different: hike, swim, or play soccer with friends. Write your training schedule on the calendar. Stay motivated. There is nothing like your anticipated expedition to keep you motivated to train. When I have a climb to look forward to, I am much less likely to "blow off" a workout session.

Once you are in good baseline shape, try doing interval training once weekly. Interval training will help improve your cardiovascular fitness more quickly and you will notice the rapid gains. For example, after being well warmed up on a bike ride, pedal at almost maximum intensity for 90 seconds, then pedal at a slower pace that allows you to recover for two and a half minutes. Repeat this sequence four or five times in the first weeks of training and build your intervals from there. You can work out something similar if you are running or swimming.

Once we get to a certain age (around 50), we lose about two percent of our muscle mass annually *unless* we do something about it. Regular resistance work combats and even reverses this trend. This is why we all tend to become flabbier as we age. Having more muscle increases our basal metabolic rate, thereby increasing the calories we burn even when not exercising. So a regular program of resistance work will help all of us stay more strong, lean, and fit as we age, a worthy goal even if you are not planning an extreme expedition.

Don't neglect good nutrition as you train. Carrying an extra twenty pounds up that peak as fatty tissue is the same as putting a

ADVENTURE EXPEDITION ONE

twenty-pound rock in your pack. Your pack will be heavy enough already! If you melt off some of that extra fat with a good diet and exercise program in the months leading up to your expedition, you gain a lot of satisfaction from seeing your body perform by moving up that mountain or across those snowfields more efficiently.

Extreme or long-range unsupported expedition training

The exact training you'll need for an intense or dangerous expedition includes all the above and more. You'll need to discover where your limit is early on in your training. High up on Denali or on Everest is not the place you want to discover that your training wasn't up to par. It's not uncommon for climbers to train 25 hours a week for a Denali expedition. Only training ten hours will leave you slow and sluggish on these extreme peaks.

Speed is safety in the mountains and most anywhere else. That is not to say you should rush. Instead, you need to have the ability to pick up the pace should the need arise. Poor weather has overwhelmed many an explorer who couldn't find shelter in time.

There is the danger of overtraining, too. You must listen to your body. There is pushing through fatigue and then there's developing a permanent injury from pushing through the pain. Each person's body is different. You must take this all into consideration when preparing for a tough expedition.

If at all possible, train harder than what the physical demands of the expedition will be. When you're weeks into your journey, your body and mind will already know what being at maximum output is like.

For marathons and the like, conventional wisdom suggests not running more than 80 percent of the race distance. I found out the hard way that wisdom was wrong for me. Once I hit mile twenty-one, my body came to a total stop. Other people at the same pace had the same thing happen. After crossing

PHYSICAL TRAINING

a bridge in the San Diego Rock 'n' Roll Marathon, everyone around me stopped running. We became the slow walking mass.

I thought my legs had failed me, like everyone else. In retrospect, that was not the case. My training plan and my dedication to it was what failed. I was not injured or dehydrated. This distance was new to my body. It responded by shutting down.

Do not find yourself in this situation in the field. Teach your mind and body what the real deal will be like. Create the best simulation you can. Train in the worst weather, while respecting your safety. If possible, train at least at a level that you expect to encounter. There are fewer surprises for your body when you have undergone the toughest training.

Reading John Vonhoff's book *Fixing Your Feet* is highly recommended. There are few activities or expeditions where you do not need to pay thorough attention to your feet.

Great nutrition overview

There are literally thousands of nutrition and diet books and blogs out there. So what really works? After a lifetime of his own study and review of research findings, and his own efforts to stay fit as he ages, Terry will distill great nutrition for a lifetime down into a page for you.

Remember the discussion above that people tend to lose muscle as we age, and how this leads to a lower basal metabolic rate? What that means in practice leads to the first nutritional principle: portion control is critically important. Remember that great high school athlete who shows up at his 20-year reunion and is unrecognizable because he has gained so much weight? That's because he kept eating like a high school athlete when he was no longer exercising so hard and, more importantly, when he has a lower basal metabolic rate because he has less muscle. So here's my first strategy: the small plate diet. Serve your meals on a small plate (e.g. 7½ to 8½" diameter). Lunch or dinner

ADVENTURE EXPEDITION ONE

will fit on it without looking lonely, and if you don't refill, you have successfully limited your caloric intake to no more than it should be.

Next, what should you put on your plate? Here are a few simple guidelines that will keep you lean and healthy. First, the plate needs to be full of color. If it is all a different shade of brown, you have some improvements to make. Divide your plate into quarters. Half will be vegetables and/or fruit, a quarter grains (whole grain bread, brown, red or wild rice, quinoa, etc.) and the last quarter "protein" (for the healthiest choices, go for vegetable sources—beans come in all varieties and have many health benefits over animal sources of protein).

Drink plenty of liquids and mainly water. Watch the fruit juices, they are loaded with natural (and some with added) sugars. Most nutritionists will advise you to eat the piece of fruit instead of drinking the tall glass of juice. It comes down to portion control again. That glass of orange juice may be the equivalent of eating six oranges! Also, avoid other high-sugar drinks like sodas.

Snacks? Go for it! You are exercising regularly and it's normal to be hungry between meals. Just make healthy choices. Here's how: avoid the pre-packaged highly processed and high-sugar choices that line the store shelves. Limit your snack to something that will easily fit in your hand, and it should be from the plant kingdom. Examples: nuts, whole grain pita with hummus, vegetable sticks with hummus, avocado spread on whole grain bread… you get the idea. If you make choices like this, you can snack every three hours until your next mealtime and you haven't done any damage to that lean machine you are cultivating.

The best foods to choose are whole foods that are not highly processed. Shop for most of your groceries at the periphery of the grocery store, where all those fresh, colorful plants are. If it comes in a package with a long list of chemical-sounding ingredients, avoid it. Grains should be whole and unprocessed. Rice should be eaten brown, not highly processed into white rice. Avoid packaged foods with lots of added sugar.

And finally—use spices! There is no reason why your diet should taste bland or be boring. How about a wonderful vegetable curry over forbidden rice for dinner, with some slices of kiwi for dessert? There are lots of wonderful cookbooks available. Be creative.

Physical Training

Adventure-specific training

Each expedition has specific requirements for training. The universal requirements are building cardiovascular capacity and using weights or resistance to build muscular strength. If you are biking across South America, you may not want to bulk up. However, polar expeditions require that you start out with some extra body weight—enough weight to lose.

Speak with your physician and a certified trainer experienced in your expedition area prior to beginning a serious workout program. It's important to discover physical problems early on so you can safely deal with them.

There is no practical way to convey all the training necessary for every type of expedition. Seek out qualified sources for what you are doing and plan from there. Many types of expeditions will have common suggestions for workout programs. However, their philosophy, approach, and intensity may vary considerably. Remember that if you're not sweating and struggling during your workout, you're not pushing yourself to become stronger. Balance this against avoiding injuries. Even professional athletes struggle with pushing themselves without risking injury.

As it has been said, "No one ever drowned in their sweat."

Maintaining your body is a full-time job.

Climbing toward Camp 2 (11,200 ft / 3,414 m) on Denali.

PART SIX

Skills

Overview

To cover all the training, knowledge, and experience you'll need for your specific expedition is impossible. There are just too many variations and possibilities in the world for a single book. So why does this chapter even exist? There are commonalities throughout all expeditions that we can share. The mechanics of logistics, equipment, first aid, and the like are similar across all trips. Understanding what you might need for your specific trip is up to you, but this section will guide you in your planning.

The universality of knowledge needed to succeed is vast, and yet it is small. Speaking with other explorers, you'll discover that what you need to succeed in the overall trip is not unlike anyone else's expedition. That's what makes this material fascinating. You can actually take what you learn here and apply it to any expedition. Once you take your first small and mid-scale trips, you'll begin to discover the specifics of what you need. But the concepts of ingenuity, perseverance, and having a strong spirit are universal throughout the adventure world.

ADVENTURE EXPEDITION ONE

For example, it's important to understand how to take care of your body regardless of the conditions. Whether you are rowing across the middle of the Atlantic by yourself or on a distant peak in Russia, the concept of dealing with blisters is exactly the same. The sun can burn you whether you are in Antarctica or the Sahara. The need for taking care of your body is no different. Sure, in the Sahara you need loose, flowing clothes, whereas in Antarctica you need a parka—but the concept of protecting yourself from environmental conditions is exactly the same.

This chapter also provides you with research material. As an example, this book does not attempt to cover all the material in the United States Air Force Survival Manual. But what this book does give you is an overview of what you'll need. It will then direct you to various sources to round out your knowledge.

The gap between a solo and team adventure is immense. As a soloist, you are responsible for everything. But if you are part of a team, you might think that you will only be responsible for yourself. You might consider yourself a climber on a team and nothing else. Food, logistics, first aid, and weather can be the purview of someone else. So why would you care to have the knowledge that a soloist has? In a mishap, you might find yourself an unintentional soloist.

The American Alpine Club publishes a journal of mountaineering accidents every year. Frequently, a team made up of a pair of climbers ends up turning into a soloist trying to rescue their partner. Once one person is injured or disabled, the other climber finds himself or herself in the unenviable position of being a solo rescuer. And, on top of that, they have also become the initial search and rescue team.

This is not to say that every adventure will result in disaster. Far from it. If every expedition ended with rescue, humans would never likely venture out. The risk would be too great. The hope is that everything goes according to plan and everyone has a good time. It's when things don't go according to plan that the adventurer needs to have the wherewithal to get themselves and their team out of trouble.

What about the soloist? They have the advantage of not relying on anyone. How is this an advantage? Everything is up to that single person. There is no worry that someone else might create tension or cause the trek to fail. The whole of the mission is embodied in the

SKILLS

soloist. Yet, on the other hand, the soloist is responsible for everything that happens. There is no one there to offer support, to help figure challenges out. Or to provide the physical company that can keep one going when things get really tough.

The gap between a solo and team expedition is large. The requirements demanded of the single person are not only the sum of the individuals that would make up a team. Instead, these factors are multiplied because the strain on the individual traveler is multiplied. Fatigue, emotional challenges, and problems requiring more than one person make going solo many more times difficult than going with a team. For certain expeditions, these factors can make the challenge an order of magnitude more difficult. That's also what makes going solo so much more interesting.

> Guided climber job: climb, help out when requested
>
> Solo climber jobs: leader, motivator, logistics, first aid, navigator, meteorologist, cook, communication, transportation, mechanic, etc.

There is no comparison between a guided and a solo trip. This book assumes you are either leading a trip or traveling solo. Depending on the position you take in your adventure, the jobs listed above can be delegated or taken on. It all depends on what level you are running your adventure at. There is every advantage to having skills in all of those jobs. You may not be the actual person assigned to any of them, but your ability to lend a hand can make the difference between success and failure. Even if you purchase a guided trip, you may discover that you have to take on more roles than you anticipated.

Skills for success

You and your team must have skills for success. There are multiple disciplines that must be covered on a long expedition. In order to

ADVENTURE EXPEDITION ONE

build success, one or more team members must provide each of these skills. If you are a soloist, you must possess most if not all of these. Yet, all of these traits by themselves will not add up to success. They must be combined in a synergistic approach, where each person understands their role and what it means to the team. Below is a list of the fundamental skills a team (or soloist) must possess to have a chance at succeeding on their adventure:

- Leadership
- Expedition manager
- Ability to motivate
- Confidence
- Adaptability
- Versatility
- Ability to comfort others
- Problem-solving
- Medical expertise
- Mechanical expertise
- Navigational expertise
- Ability to mediate
- Communication skills

Only a few of the above are hard, quantifiable skills. For example, hard skills are carpentry, programming, accounting, or landscaping. Most of the listed skills are commonly referred to as "soft skills." Without these, the chances of long-term success during an adventure are lowered. And the longer the trip is, with more people, the less likely you are to succeed without them.

From an analogous perspective, any company requires some or all of these skills. Without them, the organization becomes disillusioned and rapidly loses morale and direction. All of these soft skills are also people skills. Even with a solo expedition, successful adventurers must have the ability to choose a path, motivate themselves, and be adaptable to countless situations.

Below is a discussion of the value, cost, and relative importance of some of these skills:

Skills

Expedition manager

The person responsible for maintaining and updating the expedition at home is called the expedition manager. This person will act as a liaison between the expedition team and the outside world. He or she will make decisions about direction or problems and keep the team informed about any pertinent developments.

The expedition manager carries a great deal of power, often including recommending recalling the expedition. It's important to have someone fully vested with the team and in constant communication with it. In the event of an emergency, the expedition manager will be responsible for coordinating rescue efforts, too.

Even when an expedition is a solo venture, having an expedition manager is important. If nothing else, the manager can direct rescue efforts for the soloist. It's common for long-distance Antarctic expeditions to have someone responsible at home make the call to perform a rescue. The expedition manager should have the final say on what to do in the event of problems. This person should be experienced, levelheaded, and highly responsible.

Leadership

Virtually nothing gets done without some type of leadership. Humans need decision-makers. They may also have to act as decision-maker to themselves. Such a person has to decide the direction, the value of a task, the value of team-level gear, to evaluate relative risk, and to provide guidance for the team.

Leaders must also fulfill the role of time manager and clock-watcher. This task can be delegated to someone else. However, time is everything on an adventure, regardless of the scale, distance, and finances. Time is the absolute limiting resource for any expedition. Poor time management causes expeditions to fall behind, miss goals and deadlines, and possibly to fail.

Often, a person is either assigned the leadership role or assumes the position over the course of an expedition. If assigned, team members delegate the final authority of decisions to the leader. If assumed, team members defer to the leader for important decisions. In either

ADVENTURE EXPEDITION ONE

case, the leader takes input from various team members, depending on the situation. Then, using that input, he or she makes a decision that's best for the team.

For a solo expedition, the same person acts as both leader and counsel. This is one of the main reasons solo expeditions are more challenging than team expeditions. The soloist must make not only the final decision but must also provide input from different perspectives. This person has to consider factors that may not have occurred to them before. There is a risk in this, as it's challenging for a single person to maintain the perspective of multiple individuals. Without such input, it's easier to make a mistake based on incomplete or incorrect reasoning. The soloist is best advised to be highly skilled, confident, and adaptable because of the additional burden placed on them.

Ability to motivate

The motivator is the cheerleader for the team and the person most focused on the expedition goal. This person may also be the leader of the team but can also be another team member. The motivator tends to be the person who has the most positive disposition. He or she tends to be the least negative, looking for the best in all situations, and someone who gets along well with everyone in the team.

The soloist must be the ultimate motivator. This person needs to have an internal drive. The single adventurer must be the person who gets up despite poor weather, fatigue, and hunger. Only with dedicated emotional and physical training will a soloist be successful. Ability to train regardless of conditions is a hallmark of the motivator, the person who sees a job to do and completes it.

Confidence

Team members and soloists alike must possess some level of confidence. Whether it is in their leader, the mission, or their skills, everyone must have confidence. Confidence is also heavily related to trust. These two emotions are crucial to achieving the goals of any adventure. If one loses trust, one loses confidence. The opposite is also true.

Skills

Training builds confidence in an individual and a team. It is the quality of understanding that a person has the ability to achieve a given task. People complete tasks but that does not mean they have confidence in themselves. Often, it is instilled by the affirmation of other people. Artists struggle with confidence in their abilities and talents. When others validate a particular skill, a person becomes more confident that what they're doing is valuable and appreciated.

Confidence in leadership and the possibility that the adventure's goal is attainable is paramount. Only with confidence can a team or individual make it through challenging conditions. Lack of confidence can lead to indecision, poor choices, and even the failure of an adventure.

<u>Adaptability</u>

Humans are one of the most adaptable creatures on the planet. We have the ability to live in virtually any environment, though sometimes the only way we can survive is with specialized shelter and clothing. With permanent bases, humans can even live in Antarctica through the dark winter. However, people must pass a psychological qualification test before they're allowed to overwinter at McMurdo or at the South Pole. As there is no practical possibility of rescue, it's important to know a person can handle the isolation and perpetual darkness outside.

The one place on land where people cannot spend more than a day or two is above 26,000 feet (8,000 meters) on the world's highest mountains. The human body begins dying above that altitude due to the lack of oxygen. Above 20,000 feet, the body has difficulty repairing itself in order to stay healthy. Minor injuries or illnesses can turn into major problems because of this.

Adaptability is a mental and physical characteristic of humans. One can become more tolerant of cold, heat, wind, or waves. Being adaptable to an environment means not only having the proper equipment but the correct mentality. If a person decides that they're unable to handle a place, their attitude and energy deteriorate, making the adventure a task at best and torture at worst.

ADVENTURE EXPEDITION ONE

<u>Versatility</u>

The adventurer not only needs to be willing to adapt to a different environment and lifestyle during an expedition; he or she also needs to be versatile. In order to succeed in varying conditions, you have to be able to perform many unfamiliar tasks that are rarely necessary while living at home. You might find yourself repairing a broken piece of equipment one moment and caring for a stricken team member the next.

Versatility is a function of willingness to lend a hand throughout the adventure. The more you put in extra effort, the more valuable you become to the team.

As a solo adventurer, you must be everything all the time. Whether it's navigator, medic, or motivator, you are the specialist and the generalist. This is not a function of attitude alone, but training as well. To be truly successful in a solo venture, you will need to put more time into training and preparation.

<u>Ability to comfort others</u>

When the team or you yourself are struggling, someone must take on the role of comforter. Although humans like to think that they're invincible, that is far from the case. The person you are at home, how you feel and comport yourself, will be different out in the field. Your natural personality will be exposed and raw under difficult circumstances. If you are naturally a drill sergeant, that will come out. On the other hand, if you naturally fall into the role of comforter, that will come out, too.

For team adventures, it's important to figure out what everyone's tolerance and personal needs for emotional comfort are well before striking out. Discovering that one person is a hard driver while the others need a softer touch a few weeks into an expedition is far too late. It behooves you to ensure everyone's personalities mesh. If not, you need to know how to manage people with conflicting personalities before a situation becomes unmanageable.

As a soloist, you must learn how to keep yourself going when you're having a difficult time. One of the best ways to figure this out about you is to take small and mid-scale adventures prior to embarking on the full expedition. Knowing what keeps you going or burns you out

SKILLS

is important to your success. As a soloist, the author prefers the drill sergeant approach, as much for the motivation as the humor. You will also discover that when you are by yourself for an extended period of time, you'll often talk out loud to yourself. Although people joke about this trait, hearing your thoughts can be productive and help you work through issues.

Problem-solving

The person who can solve problems on an adventure is invaluable. They are typically a mechanic or engineer. This person will have a knack for figuring out technical problems and identifying a pathway to repair whatever is amiss. Although it's good if every team member has the ability to repair their own equipment, some people are more naturally inclined to make quick and efficient repairs.

Again, as a solo adventurer, you must have the ability to repair every piece of equipment given what you have available. As this book focuses on long-range, large-scale adventures, it is rare to be in proximity to a store where you can purchase supplies. Instead, you must be able to take what you have and make the repair. Often, the fix may not be optimal or visually appealing. It only needs to serve the purpose of keeping the team safe and moving forward.

Medical expertise

There is no adventure in the world where first-aid skills may not be required. A simple slip of a screwdriver can turn into a life-threatening injury if not handled properly. A large team might even have the luxury of having a professionally trained medic. Next to the navigator, your medic is the most indispensable. For multi-week or months-long trips, having someone with substantial medical knowledge can keep the team safe and healthy. They might even save someone's life in an emergency.

If a particular team member is the designated medic, it may be necessary for the team leader to defer leadership temporarily during a medical crisis. Often, nurses, paramedics, and doctors train to be calm in otherwise calamitous situations. Having someone with a calm demeanor can help assuage the discomfort of the injured as well as the other teammates.

ADVENTURE EXPEDITION ONE

As a soloist, you are also the medic. It behooves you to take, at the minimum, a basic first-aid course through a recognized organization. If possible, take a longer, more intensive training course. One can never have too much emergency medical knowledge in the wilderness.

Navigational expertise

In ocean, polar, or desert landscapes, the navigator may literally have the team's life in their hands. Becoming lost in the featureless ocean or the ice fields of the Arctic or Antarctic can spell almost certain death for all involved. Although modern communication technology helps mitigate this risk, equipment still fails. Competent navigation will keep the team on schedule, heading in the correct direction.

Ability to mediate

The role of a mediator is often taken care of by the expedition leader. This person's job is to resolve conflicts between team members, sponsors, or local authorities. It's not uncommon for an adventure to run into issues with local authorities. Again, it's best to establish who is most qualified to handle conflicts prior to departing. In a difficult situation, knowing who is the best go-to person is invaluable.

Communication skills

Keeping in contact with the outside world has become increasingly important with sponsored expeditions. With satellite communications, it's possible to be in contact across the entire globe. An expedition's communicator needs to be a person who is adept at speaking with the media and sponsors. Their job is to update progress, provide status reports, and report the adventure story. This person may or may not be the team leader, though typically that's their role. The media contact person may often be someone who remains at home.

Transmitting video and pictures to home can be cost-prohibitive. The team in the field might transmit an image or small video to the communication manager for further distribution. This person will, in turn, transmit the communication (writing, photos, video) in a more polished form to the media and sponsors.

Skills

Rescue mentality

Every expedition, whether it is a team or an individual, must consider the possibility of something going wrong, requiring a rescue effort. Everything looks fine from a comfortable seat at home while studying maps. But when people are in the field, a minor stumble on a rock can turn an otherwise uneventful trip into a struggle for survival. Making a turn at the wrong canyon has been the fodder for the *I Shouldn't Be Alive* television show for many years. A common theme running through virtually all of these television shows is either an injury or becoming lost.

Usually, the people portrayed in the show have made little or no provision for rescue. One of the stories adapted into a feature-length film was the story of Aron Ralston. He ventured out into the remote canyons of Utah by himself. He was familiar with the territory, knew his skills, and was comfortable traveling alone. Then, the unimaginable happened. He fell down a canyon and his hand was pinned by a large boulder. After several days of being trapped, he made the unimaginable decision to amputate his trapped hand with his pocket knife. He escaped from the canyon and was soon rescued.

The critical mistake he made was not informing someone about his plans, particularly his intended route and when to expect his return. If he had prepared for the possibility of an accident requiring rescue his story may not have become the larger-than-life drama it is today.

An adventure to a remote location always entails some risk. Without this risk, the activity just doesn't have that element of excitement that we seek. In polar regions, expeditions are required to carry hundreds of thousands of dollars in rescue and repatriation insurance. Due to the remoteness of these locations, the cost of rescue is immense.

Below are some of the questions you need to have solid answers for prior to embarking on your adventure:

- How do you plan for rescue?
- What will your risk mitigation plan be, given different sets of circumstances?
- How much will it cost to recover your team from the remotest location you are traveling to?

ADVENTURE EXPEDITION ONE

- Where are the rescuers coming from?
- How will rescue be initiated?
- How will medical needs be taken care of?
- Do you have enough insurance to return you to your home country?
- What's the longest you'll need to be self-contained before rescue can be initiated? (This is a major consideration in polar regions and major mountains, where weather can forestall a rescue for a week or more)

To summarize, here are your options for rescue:

- Communicate with the outside world and call for help
- Hug a tree and wait for rescue
- Attempt self-rescue

Each approach has advantages, drawbacks, and complications. There are human factors, cost, and time considerations. If a rescue is truly needed, rarely is time on your side. Frequently once an expedition needs rescue, there is a pressing need for it. That means that, in some way, a clock is counting down until someone or the entire team perishes.

Whatever you decide, do not rely solely on your cell phone for rescue. This book assumes you will be far afield. As such, you will likely be far from a service area. This point cannot be emphasized enough. It is easy to forget that most of the globe does not have cell phone service.

The great difficulty in becoming lost is that your mental map of where you've been does not mesh with the planned route. Once this confusion sets in, it causes a series of mental missteps. You'll attempt to reconnect with your perception of where you should be. This can be a frustrating experience, as becoming lost creates a feeling of helplessness. Human adults pride themselves on knowing where they are. When this knowledge fails, a fear response is common.

What was once familiar and enjoyable suddenly becomes unfamiliar and threatening. When you stop to evaluate your position, your

Skills

physical position will not change. As the feeling of unfamiliarity settles in, staring at the map, GPS, or surroundings creates a change in your psychological position. Your confidence may erode. And, in the worst case, panic may set in. This causes people to make irrational decisions.

This is where the idea of "hug a tree" originates. You choose a tree, rock, or whatever is comforting to become your new base camp. Once you have a base, you can begin recreating your mental map of the surroundings. Your nerves will calm and decisions will be easier to make, reducing the chance of making the situation worse.

As an adventurer, you may find yourself far away from where you began your trek. This may make the concept of staying put to wait for rescue seems absurd. It only takes one wrong turn on a trail or choosing the wrong canyon to become lost. Consider the options below:

Stop and attempt communication for directions

This approach assumes you have two things: a communication method and the ability to determine or share your position. Presumably, if you know your rough position, you can save rescuers significant effort. This strategy is effective for teams coordinating with each other or a base station.

Perhaps your expedition needs to connect two separate parties. Perhaps you encounter unexpected geographic, weather, or political conditions. Information your expedition management shares with you may dictate much of what you do. Labor- and cost-intensive, this style of expedition requires a large coordinated effort.

Retrace the route

If you have the ability to retrace your route to your last known point, you may discover your original route. This is ideal, as you do not risk anyone else in a rescue. Once you become confident of your position, you can strike out again. You'll also have the added knowledge of the wrong path.

However, this approach can create a worse situation. If you cannot confidently return whence you came, you'll become more disoriented. This is common for people who become lost.

87

ADVENTURE EXPEDITION ONE

One trick to traveling through unfamiliar areas is to glance over your shoulder at regular intervals. This helps create a mental map of the world behind you. Even though you've traveled through an area, it will look completely different when you turn around. Glancing backward creates a mental map of both directions. If you ever need to retrace your steps, you'll have a better chance of returning to the correct path.

<u>Adjust and reconnect with the desired path</u>

Can you figure out where you are accurately? If so, you can bypass retracing your route and move toward your destination. This will help you recover lost time that route retracing costs. This approach is risky, too. If you become lost during your attempt to reconnect, the situation can become worse.

This approach should be used with care. Be confident about where you're going. You may also find impassable terrain such as cliffs, canyons, or rivers. If this occurs, you may lose more time recovering yourself than had you retraced your route.

I had just this experience after being caught in a sudden storm and whiteout conditions, with sustained winds over 100 mph and temperatures below zero near the summit of Mt. Shasta on a solo spring climb. I knew that it was critical that I start my down-climb in the right location, or I would risk being way off track as I moved further down the mountain. Visibility deteriorated so badly and suddenly that for much of the down-climb I couldn't see my feet, let alone any physical features that would help to orient me.

Once I had made my way down several hundred feet, I knew where I was by the hard blue ice underfoot. I was on a steep glacier to the south of where I needed to be. I decided to adjust course to get back into the proper descent route

SKILLS

more to the west by following a new compass bearing. I soon encountered a cliff that I couldn't safely down-climb. Retracing the safe route until I was below the cliffs, I re-adjusted course again, holding the compass up under my chin to stay on course in the zero visibility.

This strategy worked up to a point. I eventually rejoined the proper descent route but was not able to recognize it in the whiteout and continued on the adjusted compass heading until I was again lost and could not find the parking lot or my car. By now, darkness had set in and the storm was abating, so I decided to continue down until I found a road at the base of the mountain, where I was finally able to get help finding my car after twenty-eight hours of continuous climbing. —*TW*

Hunker down and wait until help arrives

Another solution to being lost is to establish a camp where you are and wait for help. This assumes you have no way to communicate with the outside world. You will be at the mercy of time and your backup organization. You need to have told someone where you were going and when you plan to return. Until your team believes you're in trouble, you'll need to be self-contained.

If you have not left a plan or return time with someone, you may be in for a long wait. Since you are planning a major adventure, you and your team's lives depend on someone knowing your plans and whereabouts. Do not depart without leaving your emergency contacts, team list, trip plan, itinerary, and equipment list with your manager or a highly responsible person.

Should you choose to use the stay-put method to handle being lost, you must consider how long you can wait. The more remote the location, the lower the probability of being found. Some countries have no reliable search and rescue. Discuss this scenario with your team well before departure. Stress and fear will affect team cohesion. If you have an established procedure, you'll be less likely to make rash decisions.

ADVENTURE EXPEDITION ONE

One peculiar behavior that has been observed with lost travelers is the propensity to hide from rescuers. Although it seems contradictory, it happens. The embarrassment of being lost makes people act in unpredictable ways. If you suspect people are searching for you, do everything you can to be found.

Fingernail rescue

If there is a pressing need to evacuate the team, there may be no other choice than to attempt a self-rescue. You may need to drag yourself or your team out by your fingernails. Search and rescue (SAR) teams put their lives at risk when they execute a rescue. If conditions are too dangerous, SAR will not deploy until conditions are less risky. The rescuer's (and medic's) motto is "Don't become part of the problem."

If you're in a remote region of Earth, you may need to be able to rescue yourself. If the weather is poor in Antarctica, no flights will come looking for you until conditions are safe. The same is true for most places in the world. SAR teams have a threshold for the risk they are willing to accept. That means you're on your own to extract yourself. If conditions are too dangerous for SAR teams, consider what risk you are in.

The challenge of self-rescue is more difficult than can be imagined from the comfort of home. Hunger, cold, and heat take more of a toll than the uninitiated realize. Being away from family, friends, and home can be overwhelming. Whatever happens, never give up.

Avoiding being lost in the first place

The advent of modern satellite and cellular phone communication has enabled people to put themselves into situations beyond their skill level.

More than one ranger in the Grand Canyon National Park will tell stories of people calling in for helicopter rescue because they are simply cold, tired, and hungry. The park may or may not deploy an expensive helicopter rescue.

Another cause for rescue in the Grand Canyon is people being overconfident. Nearly every table in the cafeteria at the South Rim

SKILLS

visitor's center has a flyer depicting a rugged-looking man in his early twenties appearing strong and confident. This person is made out to be the archetypal tough man who should be able to handle any circumstance. Yet the flyer indicates that this person most often fits the profile of the typical rescue victim. He walks too deep into the canyon at the wrong time of day or year, with inadequate training or supplies. He soon finds himself in a life-threatening situation. Underestimating the difficulty causes many rescues every year on mountains and in parks around the world.

Modern communication is no substitute for planning, training, and proper management of self and conditions. Yet every year, more and more people rely on these devices to get them out of situations beyond their training. One of the goals of this book is to help you understand what you need to know about your adventure.

Deciding when to call in a rescue is a significant decision. All team members should be in agreement that a rescue is necessary. If there is a chance that the team can extract itself from a situation without unreasonably risking someone's life, it is well worth considering.

As a soloist, there may be no other choice than to sit and wait. There are countless stories of injured people dragging themselves out of danger. Deciding how to manage an evacuation is tough. A clear-headed evaluation of conditions must be made. Are you simply frightened, uncomfortable, and unsure of yourself? Or is there a real risk of injury or worse if you continue?

Sponsorship will weigh significantly on your decisions. There will be internal and external pressure to succeed that can cloud your judgment. A trusted expedition manager can help make these decisions easier. They will not be hungry, tired, or worn down so are more likely to evaluate circumstances with a clear mind.

Testing yourself and your team with small and mid-scale expeditions will help refine your approach. Placing yourself in uncomfortable but low-risk circumstances will train you for tougher times. Some cold, dark, and hunger will reveal if you are ready for the main event.

ADVENTURE EXPEDITION ONE

> I spent weeks at night skiing across Yellowstone alone, in complete darkness, in the dead of winter, during storms. These treks were excellent training for my mind. I learned to deal with solitude, blindness, fatigue, and fear of the unknown. These trips were excellent preparation for skiing across Antarctica alone. Even though the challenge was many times greater, I was familiar with how I handled pain and fear. —AL

Teamwork

The longer the expedition, the more important it is for everyone to be able to help with all tasks. Unless the expedition team is large enough to justify specialized personnel, being able to do any task reduces strain on everyone. Assigning individuals regular duties, such as cooking, camp creation, or gear repair is a common approach. Discover who has the best skills before leaving.

This is especially important when conditions or weather deteriorate. It's easy to assign duties and stick to them in comfortable times. But when a raging ice storm appears out of nowhere and destroys your camp, being able to do anything required can make the difference between an entertaining story and having a trip-ending crisis.

Certified outdoor education

There may be specific certification organizations like the Boy Scouts, NOLS, PADI, and the like to prepare you. Any time you need training and you are unsure of whom to go with, seek professional guidance. Contact people in the industry and ask them what they recommend. It's important to ask more than one person if you don't know them personally. It may take significant time to find the correct resource.

Skills

Self-sufficiency

The importance of being self-sufficient in the event of separation from your party cannot be overstated. It is not uncommon for teams to spread out during the day. Some people are naturally faster than others. For some treks, this may never happen. Often, however, the fastest people may arrive hours before slower team members.

Consider the what-if scenario. What if you become separated from your party and are unable to rejoin them? This may be for any number of reasons: weather, nightfall, injury, snowfall, becoming lost, etc. If your party tends to separate, are you self-sufficient so that you can survive on your own until you are reunited with the others? If not, you are putting yourself, your teammates, and your entire adventure at risk.

Decide if the party can safely separate during the day before setting out. Having a significant speed difference in team members can induce significant stress into an already tough trip. These are serious questions to consider when traveling in remote locations. They need to be answered well before the actual separation takes place.

Discipline

If there were one measure to determine if a team (or soloist) is going to succeed on an expedition, that essential trait would be discipline. Lack of discipline is the primary thing that can break down progress, damage morale, and hinder success.

One of the reasons polar expeditions fail is because the members are not disciplined about sticking to their schedule. Occasionally sleeping in an extra half hour or stopping fifteen minutes before the scheduled break will not impact the overall expedition. But repeating this habit daily will rapidly eat into travel time. Over the course of weeks, a half hour here and a quarter hour there translates to days of lost travel. The window for travel in polar regions is strictly limited due to weather and ice conditions. Small increments add up to a significant loss over time.

Adventure Expedition One

The value of keeping to a regular schedule cannot be overstated. If you are unable to wake up at three a.m., you are likely not an alpine climber. If you cannot rise at six a.m., you are not likely a long-distance trekker. If you cannot make yourself ski for a full nine hours, you are not going to make it as a long-distance polar explorer.

Maintaining a regular schedule for endeavors spaced over long periods of time is paramount. By being strict about your schedule and regimen, you will find comfort in knowing you can handle the workload. Once you allow yourself to slip one day, it becomes easier on the following day. Soon you will find yourself impossibly behind schedule.

This is not to say there is no room for fun and enjoyment. Far from it, in fact. If you or the team are not having a good time, problems will arise and threaten the expedition. The team needs to continually manage the balance between covering the distance and maintaining a positive attitude.

Deteriorating discipline brings health problems, too. Not eating, drinking, cleaning, or brushing teeth one day may be no big deal. But before you know it, an entire week has passed. What was a manageable issue can turn into a major problem.

> As a younger trekker and climber, I often made the mistake of wanting to prove my toughness by pushing on for hours without a break for water or food. I learned a valuable lesson about group leadership on the first guided climb I joined on Aconcagua. While we were moving up the mountain, the lead guides enforced a five-minute stop approximately every hour so that team members could stop to drink and eat a few bites.
>
> At first, it seemed like these between-meal stops were too frequent and would slow us down, but the leaders were disciplined about limiting the stop to just five minutes every sixty to ninety minutes. Doing this kept the group moving smoothly and efficiently. This pace allowed for the weakest team members to keep up and have a successful climb. The guides demonstrated great team leadership and discipline. —*TW*

Skills

The same principle of discipline applies to daily gear inspection. People can push through fatigue and hunger but gear generally cannot. If equipment requires regular maintenance, stick with the schedule. If it's worth bringing, it's worth maintaining. Experienced long-distance travelers are careful about weight. A broken item in your kit can feel like carrying a stone, and worse, can end a trip.

Begin training yourself early on if you're not already a disciplined person. Discipline takes a long time to develop into a habit. The commonly held belief is that if you do something regularly for at least twenty-one days, it will develop into a habit. This is an excellent benchmark for either developing a new skill or breaking a poor habit. You'll need to be committed to doing something for twenty-one days.

Discipline does not develop overnight. This is a personality characteristic that requires effort and energy. At first, you will struggle and fail. By degrees, the effort will become easier. Eventually, you will stop noticing the difference. If you can do this, you can discipline yourself to be consistent enough to achieve incredible feats.

Social courtesy

One of the overlooked items on a team expedition is maintaining common social courtesies. People might become lax in their "pleases" and "thank-yous" for simple actions. The deterioration of personal relationships is slow. Once festering irritation sets in, it can be difficult or impossible to repair.

Ernest Shackleton was famous for enforcing a high level of courtesy and decorum on his *Endurance* expedition. He ensured his crew observed courtesies each time, every time. This kept the level of interpersonal respect high and this maintained morale through the disaster of losing their ship.

An individual may be an incredible contributor to a team. Maybe he or she is the best climber, rower, or skier. Yet, if they're abrasive to the rest of the team, they may become a detriment rather than an asset. Determine this well before committing to the final roster of your expedition team.

95

ADVENTURE EXPEDITION ONE

Discovering everyone's personality quirks is important. If someone is awesome in other aspects but cannot get along with another team member, question whether this person should really be on the team. You want everyone to have the best time possible. Having someone who is incessantly negative can do irreparable damage to your team. People like this are often not worth the benefit they bring.

Patience

Depending on the circumstances, bold action can lead to success. At other times, patience makes the difference between returning safely and dying. There is no practical way to dictate what each situation requires. Experience is thought to be the best teacher. However, what may have worked once may have only been a matter of luck.

Know that summit fever is contagious and it can lead to a disaster. When you and your team's instinct says to remain in camp, think hard before venturing forth. Other teams may move up a mountain but that doesn't mean your team should. They believe they can make it. Consider the risk factors: supplies, fatigue, timing, weather conditions, your team's condition, etc. If you believe conditions are too dangerous to move out, then do not move out.

Climbers are frostbitten, injured, and killed on Denali (Mt. McKinley) every year from a lack of patience. Continuing up the mountain when you are up against a departure deadline or supplies are running low is not a good reason to risk permanent injury. Be willing to sacrifice months of training and effort and the large expense of the expedition to come home. The mountain, continent, or ocean will be there next year. It's important that you and your team are, too.

Survival Skills

What happens when everything goes wrong?

The farther afield you are, the higher the consequences can be. Without basic survival skills, you may be putting your very life at

SKILLS

risk on your adventure. Knowing what might keep you alive in any particular circumstance will also boost your confidence. You'll be able to help others through problems.

There are many survival experts throughout the world. No matter where you turn, there seems to be a new survival expert with a television show, knife set, or a new kit to sell you. Adopt their information with care. Just because they look like they're roughing it on television does not mean they're actually "surviving." Many of these shows have camera crews, production support, and safety experts along for the ride.

Internet resources are always suspect. Can you verify the information beyond marketing hype? Learning survival skills involves more than reading a screen or being in a classroom in a calm, safe setting. Learning to survive requires experience in the field to see how you adapt.

There are countless survival books on the market. Start with these resources:

USAF Survival Manual
Boy Scout Handbook
Boy Scout Field Book

Each of these books has been tested by a vast array of experts in their field. They are excellent starting places for your expedition.

The *USAF Survival Manual* has been used for decades. This voluminous text is used as a resource for training pilots who may be downed far in the field, in unknown territory, during combat. It is one of the most comprehensive manuals available today. The book covers everything from meteorology to food to staying alive in hostile territory.

The *Boy Scout Handbook* and *Boy Scout Field Book* have been tested by millions. Britain's Lord Baden-Powell originally developed the Scouting program. He was dismayed at how many young men perished in the field from lack of basic knowledge. Though the program has changed over the years, the fundamental information in the book is as useful today as it was a century ago.

97

ADVENTURE EXPEDITION ONE

Survival Essentials

What are the real survival essentials? This list might surprise you. When a survival situation arises, the first priority is keeping yourself and your team alive. As such, the list of priorities is based on the hierarchy of their importance. The first item is required. Without it, the second item will be of no use. And the third item is less important than the second for the same reason.

Note the list does not contain any tools. The most important tool you have is your mind. If your adventure goes awry, your mind is your most important resource. The theory is based on how long you can live without this particular essential. Many lists focus on outside resources and disregard more important internal forces. Below is an adventurer's survival list based on the priority of importance, followed by a discussion of each.

1. The will to survive
2. Oxygen
3. Core temperature
4. Positive outlook and hope
5. Ingenuity
6. Protection from injury and toxins
7. Shelter
8. Water
9. Food
10. Fire

The will to survive

This item rates above everything else. The moment you lose your will to live, you won't last long in a survival situation. You can be dead in seconds without the desire to live. Take, for instance, falling through ice and becoming trapped. If you decide at that moment to give up, you'll be dead in moments. But if you want to keep fighting to live, you move on to the next most critical survival item.

Skills

<u>Oxygen</u>

Without it, you'll be dead in four minutes. If you don't have the will to survive, you will not last even that long. Humans are oxygen breathing and have a voracious need for it. Above 26,000 feet (8,000 meters), there is not enough oxygen to survive for long. If you find yourself trapped above that altitude, you may last a day or two. But it's likely you'll die from hypothermia, bringing you to the next survival priority.

<u>Core temperature</u>

Human beings are warm-blooded. Although the body is tough and versatile, it malfunctions without heat. Warmth is what keeps blood circulating, the brain functioning, and metabolic processes working. If you allow your core temperature to drop below 91.4 degrees Fahrenheit (33 degrees centigrade), you become confused and have poor muscle coordination. At 89.6°F (32°C), shivering stops and an important mechanism to maintain body heat is lost. Once your core temperature falls to 84°F (29°C), you can experience cardiac arrest, and this becomes increasingly more likely as your core temperature drops further.

How quickly your temperature drops is dependent on environmental conditions. Cold water immersion is much worse than exposure to cold air. If you are feeling cold and are experiencing poor muscle coordination, you must act quickly to reverse the process. If a teammate is cold and confused, and especially if you notice that they've stopped shivering, you have an emergency on your hands and you must act decisively. Review the section on hypothermia for more information.

<u>Positive outlook and hope</u>

You have to believe that you will make it through this situation. If you think that you are doomed to die, you will slide into despair. A positive attitude is the key to your continued fight for survival, regardless of the conditions. As long as you believe you have a chance, you can keep going. Think up all the reasons you need to stay alive. This will help muster the mental and physical strength you need.

ADVENTURE EXPEDITION ONE

Ingenuity

The next priority is figuring out what to do. In a survival situation, something has gone wrong. Do you have the ability to figure your way out of it? With a positive attitude and a belief that you will make it, you have a good chance. But if you can't figure out what to do with what you have, you're still in danger. Figuring out ingenious methods for utilizing what you have is key to making it through. A piece of gear that seems useless can end up making all the difference.

Protection from injury and toxins

This is an all-encompassing survival requirement. If you are in danger from immediate injury or toxins your survival is at risk. This survival element is variable around the world. Examples include dangerous animals, spoiled food, and poisonous plants or water. Regardless of which element is threatening you, it's important that you figure out a way to neutralize the risk.

Shelter

In order to protect yourself from the elements and other dangers, you will need some sort of shelter. Only in perfect weather can humans sleep without some type of shelter. You may survive for a day or two without it, but you will soon be overwhelmed. Even the boughs of a tree can provide shelter from wind, rain, or snow and raise the temperature around you a few degrees. Shelter also provides important psychological support.

Water

Typically water is listed high on the items required for survival. But as you can see in the above list, water is not nearly as important as the above items. You will be overwhelmed without the higher priority items. But soon, you will not survive without water. This is heavily dependent on environmental conditions. People have survived without water for a little more than a week. In a hot desert or cold polar regions, you may not last three days. Assuming higher priority needs are managed, water will quickly become a pressing need.

Skills

Food

If you have made it through the first few days of your ordeal and you have water, food will be foremost on your mind. When you are dehydrated, you cannot digest food well. Conventional wisdom suggests you can survive thirty days without food, but this depends on conditions. You may live a month without food, but you will not be functional after two weeks; you will be incredibly weak. After three weeks, you'll be lucky to be moving.

Fire

To round out the list, fire is helpful to long-term survival. Assuming you've managed all other items, a fire will do the following for you: keep you warm, bolster your spirit, purify water, cook food to make it more digestible, and keep animals at bay. It can be used as a rescue signal. Though fire isn't absolutely necessary for survival, it makes the experience more comfortable. Fire can be used to improve attitude, a much higher priority.

First aid

For the safety and health of a team expedition, every team member should be trained in basic first aid. Unless your expedition has a specially trained medic, first-aid knowledge will help the team keep going. If only one or two members are first-aid trained, the group may be more vulnerable.

Having everyone knowledgeable and with similar training can also cut down on conflicts over how to handle an injury situation. The military and coast guard rely on this premise. If all team members are equivalently trained, people can be interchanged. Everyone will have confidence, knowing that basic problems will be handled correctly and efficiently.

For solo expeditions, professional first-aid training is essential. When you are in the field by yourself, you are the only person who can take care of minor problems. As long as your life is not in immediate danger, knowing how to patch yourself up will keep your expedition moving forward. You will always be more confident

ADVENTURE EXPEDITION ONE

knowing as much first aid as you can acquire. Once an injury exceeds your skills and equipment, you will be forced to evacuate. However, you must be able to stabilize yourself prior to rescue. If you are unable to handle a significant emergency until help can arrive, your life is at risk.

Refer to the medical chapter of this book for further details.

Field diagnosis tricks

Self-diagnosis in medicine is rarely recommended. But when you are a thousand miles away from a basic clinic, you have no alternative. Treks through the far reaches of the globe will expose you and your team to risks outside daily experience.

As a soloist, one of the first problems you will discover is looking where you normally cannot. Suppose you need to take a look at your lower back. How are you going to accomplish this? There are two practical options. The first is to use a mirror. In order for this method to be effective, you'll need a glass mirror. Metal survival signaling mirrors are not optically clear enough to achieve this end. This means you'll need to pack a specialized and fragile piece of equipment just for this purpose.

An inexpensive lady's compact is the best option if you choose to carry a mirror. The plastic protects the glass. In a pressing situation, the plastic cover may also come in handy. Still, a single mirror is useless if you need to look anywhere from your buttocks up to much of your head. You will need a second mirror to accomplish this. Examine your setup at home. How many mirrors and handheld items do you need to look at the back of your head or neck?

Almost all expeditions carry some type of digital documentation equipment. Usually, this is in the form of a camera. It might even be your smartphone. When off, the screen is a serviceable mirror in adequate light conditions. But consider the camera itself.

If you have practiced taking a selfie (i.e. taking a picture of one's self with one's own camera), you have the basis for an excellent field inspection tool. You may discover detail you never thought possible. It may take several attempts, but you can take a high-resolution shot

SKILLS

anywhere on your body and use the camera's review mode for instant inspection. It may take some experimenting, but even the middle of your back is easily inspected using this method.

If for some reason using your hands is difficult, use the camera's self-timer. Place the camera wherever you need and set the self-timer. In seconds you will have more detail than an entire series of mirrors could ever provide.

Consider the problem of a wood splinter in the middle of your back. If you are traveling through a wooded location or are on a solo boat voyage, all you have to do is lean up against a piece of wood or a tree to have this happen.

Instead of considering how you might extract that splinter, consider the best alternative—avoid the injury altogether. As a soloist, you must be vigilant at all times to avoid any injury. What can normally be taken care of in minutes at home can turn into festering misery in the field. It may make sleep impossible. Should your injury become severely infected, you may need to be evacuated as a result of a minor initial injury.

When you are in the field, whether by yourself or as a team, minor problems can become major disasters. The farther afield you are, the greater the risk is. You must change your mentality when traveling afar. Take a little extra time. Be more conscious of what you are doing with your body in order to avoid even minor mishaps.

Cold climates and solar radiation

As quickly as hot climates can injure or kill you, cold climates can become dangerous even more quickly. If you lose your tent during a storm, you can perish from exposure in a short time. This happened to a Greenland trekker. Your only enemies in Antarctica are the cold, sun, and crevasses. In the Arctic, add open water (at 28.5°F) and polar bears to the mix of dangers.

Paradoxically, one of the challenges of traveling in cold climates is keeping cool and protected from the sun. With exertion, you can quickly become wet from perspiration, and the wet clothing under your shells will then make it more difficult to regulate your body temperature. As you exert yourself, pay attention to what is happening and adjust or vent your clothing before you become wet.

Frequently trekkers hiking across Greenland's tundra will develop sunburn and parched lips. It is easy to forget the power of the sun when traveling to sub-polar or polar climates. In these locations, the sun is relentless and may never set. You must have a plan to deal with the scorching sun in high-latitude locations. Whether it is through chemical or clothing protection, have a plan for dealing with the sun.

This is especially true on snow or the water. In these environments, it is as if there are two suns. The snow and water reflect a significant portion of the ultraviolet radiation. We are all familiar with snow blindness, but you can also develop the same condition, called river blindness, on water. A sunburn under your chin, on the roof of your mouth or inside your nostrils is painful.

In Antarctica, the sun is your best friend and your worst enemy. It will keep you warm. But without wind, it will broil you. Without eye protection, your eyes will sunburn. This happens in minutes, not hours. The severity of burns received from the sun in Antarctica cannot be understated. The snow surface reflects up to 98 percent of all solar radiation. This means you are under a glaring sun coming from all around you. In polar regions, you will rely on clothing rather than sunscreen as protection from solar radiation: sunscreen freezes, soils your protective clothing, and is heavy.

Personal hygiene

In order to keep yourself and your team comfortable and happy, special attention needs to be paid to personal hygiene. The military has emphasized this for centuries. They know all too well the dangers of failing to maintain a standard of cleanliness. Disease can spread quickly. It can render challenging conditions unbearable or, in the worst case, kill. The goal of maintaining personal hygiene is to prevent something from becoming a first-aid problem. The human body is adaptable and tough. But without regular maintenance, it can become a cesspool of disease and misery.

Skills

A daily shower

When at home, you regularly shower. In the field, this may be impossible, especially in polar climes. On many adventures, water is one of your scarcest resources. Yet, it is one of the most important. You cannot afford to squander water on a comfortable shower. Or, in sub-zero temperatures, it may be altogether impossible. And washing clothes is another matter entirely.

What is the consequence of not taking a shower for months at a time (that is, beyond the odor)? Consider how a small rash can become a major annoyance. Rashes can come from anything. Unwashed clothes build up bacteria and oils from your skin and hair. This is unavoidable.

Personal hygiene is paramount to keeping yourself and your team in good health. A rash or outbreak of acne can lead to real misery. Should these annoyances develop into more serious infections, they can become major problems.

One common solution is to take a sponge bath. This technique is used in field hospitals and is a simple way to clean your body. However, sponges only last so long. After repeated use, the sponge itself can be full of bacteria and needs to be swapped out. This means knowing how many sponges to carry. Sponges are light but can take up significant space in your pack. Pre-compressed sponges can help the volume problem. But on a long journey, you will wonder if those sponges are worth space they consume and weight they add to your pack.

What are you to do with the sponge once it is exhausted? You don't want to just cast it aside, littering the landscape you came to explore. You'll want to squeeze the water out and pack it with the rest of your trash. Extract as much water as possible. Otherwise, you will be carrying unnecessary weight.

Also, will you bring soap or hair care products? Both of these items pollute waterways. Non-biodegradable soaps kill marine life. These products are heavy. Their containers cannot (generally) be used for anything else. Spilled soaps and shampoos will make rations and water inedible and undrinkable.

At home, all of these problems are literally washed down the drain. The municipal water system is designed to properly manage these

ADVENTURE EXPEDITION ONE

waste products. But when you are in the wild, you must manage your waste.

These are all significant considerations for team expeditions, too. With a large group of people, cleaning and human waste disposal must be considered. See the section on camp maintenance for a further discussion.

Another problem regular showers keep at bay is bacterial and fungal infections. As you will be wearing the same clothes for weeks if not months, it is easy to develop infections. Look up ringworm and fungal infections (toe, groin) for the proper way to manage these.

If you have foot fungus, commonly referred to as athlete's foot, you must prevent its spread. To keep the problem contained, label your socks L and R with a permanent laundry marker. This way, if you develop a problem, it will be restricted to a single foot. Little is more frustrating on a long trip than spreading a controllable problem all over your body.

Self-cleaning trick

If you are drinking tea on your expedition, you already have cleaning sponges with you. Once you have made your drink and have exhausted the teabags, here is a good secondary use for them. If you squeeze the water out, you have a handy sponge with which to clean yourself. In cold environments, put the used teabag on your head, under your hat. This will dry out the bag and eliminate extra water weight.

One advantage to the teabag method is odor control. Instead of smelling like body odor, you will smell of lemon ginseng or chamomile.

Caveat: try this method at home prior to embarking. You may discover that you have an allergic sensitivity and may develop a skin reaction to some tea ingredients. This is best discovered at home before your trip.

Teeth

Remember the scene from the movie *Castaway*, where Tom Hank's character has to knock out his aching tooth with an ice skate? This example is extreme but is a good illustration of what a toothache will

SKILLS

drive someone to do. A month or more prior to embarking on an expedition, visit your dentist and have a thorough examination and cleaning performed. If a tooth is bothering you now, imagine your disappointment when you are turned back from summiting Everest because of crippling tooth pain.

Maintaining teeth on a long expedition is important to your comfort and health. Forgetting a toothbrush and toothpaste on an overnight camping trip is a minor inconvenience. Forgetting this on a three-month expedition can lead to problems. Speak with your dentist about tooth maintenance on a long trip. She or he can recommend the best tools.

One thing to note is toothpaste usage. Toothpaste commercials show a large, attractive glob of paste on the brush. On an expedition, this is wasteful and unnecessary. You only need a pea-sized dollop. Speak to your dental professional about this. Carrying more toothpaste than you will need for a long Arctic expedition only adds unnecessary weight, and managing the weight of your load is critical for success. The author was able to stretch one travel-size tube of toothpaste to sixty days of use.

On a long trip, flossing is also important. Bacteria can build up at the base of your teeth, causing decay and damage. Also, if a piece of food becomes lodged between teeth, floss will enable you to extract it. Food jammed between teeth is distracting and painful, especially in the field. Being distracted by a toothache can cause you to miss other details, possibly leading to another problem or an accident. Measure your average length of floss while home to establish a baseline of how much you will need during your adventure, and then add ten percent extra. You may find yourself in the field longer than planned. Floss is handy for repairs, too. Use non-shredding classic thread floss. Other types will shred or break, making them useless.

Halitosis can result from oral neglect, too. Sharing a tent with someone with wretched breath is something no one wants to experience. As the expedition leader, reminding team members to maintain oral health may feel awkward, but it can prevent future problems.

Adventure Expedition One

Hair

Hair and scalp maintenance is a topic with as many opinions as there are people. It's a good idea to experiment on short- and medium-range expeditions prior to your main adventure. What may be tolerable for a weekend may become intolerable after a week. Take care to keep your scalp clean to prevent skin infections that can become a more serious problem.

Depending on conditions, men will find shaving facial hair helpful. If a mask is required for an expedition, such as in polar regions, eventually your face mask will freeze to a beard. This requires painful and discouraging removal every time you need to eat or drink and can be prevented if you take the time to clip or shave. Also, clean your face mask regularly, as bacteria can build up inside at an alarming rate.

Nails

On long expeditions, it is easy to forget about fingernail and toenail maintenance. Over a period of several months, nails will grow significantly. Bring a tool to not only cut but file nails. This may be your multitool, as many come with files. During a multi-month expedition, spend a few minutes every week inspecting and filing your nails. You will catch problems early before they become more serious.

Skin

Your skin serves critical functions in maintaining hydration, controlling your body temperature and acting as a defense against certain infections. But human skin is susceptible to sunburn, dehydration, cuts, abrasions, rashes, acne, chilblains, frostbite, etc. It is your first and best line of defense against the ravages of the world. When properly maintained, it will keep you protected and comfortable.

An in-depth discussion of skin maintenance is beyond the scope of this book. Discuss this with your healthcare professional and experiment well before embarking on your trek.

One common problem explorers encounter in polar climates is chilblains. These lesions are not frostbite. Rather, they are the skin's reaction to chronic exposure to cold. Chilblains of the thigh and stomach are common in cold, windy locations. Chilblains cause

SKILLS

patches of the skin to die and sluff off. This leaves painful, open sores, which can be prone to secondary bacterial infection. Avoid these at all costs. Once they develop, they are difficult to cure until you return to warmer weather. More details can be found in the medical chapter of this book.

<u>Feet</u>

Your feet are everything on any expedition. If they are painful or injured, you can be debilitated and miserable. Proper maintenance of feet is critical to your enjoyment of your adventure. The moment you detect a hot spot or sore, stop. Pushing through foot pain for a day can result in lost days of travel. This is important for all of your team members to understand.

People will often push through foot problems because they are afraid to slow down the team. After the pain becomes unbearable, then they cannot walk at all. Ultimately, this costs the team even more than a ten-minute stop to take care of a hot spot. See the medical section for more details on the care of hot spots and blisters. Read the book *Fixing Your Feet* by John Vonhof. It is a comprehensive text on maintaining your feet.

<u>Eyes</u>

Eyes are fundamental to everything you will do on an expedition. Bring eye protection in the form of sunglasses or goggles. And bring a backup pair. If you are traveling for more than a month, bring an additional pair on top of that. A wind-driven, flailing tent pole can smash your goggles. If you have already lost one set, you will be down to no backups. It happens. This is an area where having a few backup options is never a bad idea.

Avoid eye sunburn at all costs. In snowy climates or on water, wear eye protection at all times. You will not notice the damage until it is too late—usually that night or the next day. Then, your eyes will feel like they have a handful of sand in them. Bright light will be unbearable and you may not be able to get your eyes open at all. At best, your vision will be blurred and you can be temporarily blinded.

ADVENTURE EXPEDITION ONE

If you require prescription eyeglasses, bring at least one spare pair. On long journeys, bring two spares. They can be damaged or lost. Although expensive, consider becoming blind in the field. Treat glasses with the utmost care. There are no opticians or labs in the middle of nowhere.

If you use contact lenses, bring extras. They are generally not recommended on long expeditions. Maintenance is simply too difficult and it's easy to develop an eye infection. Talk with your eye care professional about your specific needs.

Note: If you are traveling to polar latitudes, bring an eye mask. It is nearly impossible to sleep without an eye cover in 24-hour sunlight. These are well worth their weight.

Ears

You may not give much thought to your ears until they hurt. Then, that is all you can think about. In cool or cold climates, bring ear protection. This will help prevent an earache. Also, keep your ears clean, being careful not to damage your sensitive ear canals, which are lined by thin, sensitive skin that can be damaged even by a soft cotton swab. Be gentle! When not showering for weeks or months, the grime buildup can lead to ear infections.

Speak with your doctor about any specific ear issues you may have. This must be taken care of prior to departure. If you need special medicines, bring extra. Do not count on purchasing these wherever you are traveling to.

Note: If you are going to be sleeping in a tent in windy conditions, bring a pack of earplugs you have tried out overnight. You will be surprised at the level of noise and sleep will be all but impossible.

Before embarking on a long adventure, figure out what works best on test trips. Here are some important considerations. Figure out how much toilet paper you use per day. Consider your exertion level and changed diet. You may need more than you expect. However, it's nearly impossible to carry enough in snowy climates when you're eating a high-fat diet.

SKILLS

> Hard-packed snow is adsorbent and an effective toilet paper substitute. However, use it too slowly and it will freeze your skin. Wiping too quickly will shred your skin. Experiment with your technique in similar conditions prior to leaving. I budgeted two squares of toilet paper per bowel movement during my solo Antarctic expedition. —*AL*

Hot climates

Special care must be taken in hot climates. There are many ways you can be injured in hot locations. The list is too exhaustive for this text. And, depending on where you are traveling, specific techniques are required to stay safe. The danger is not only from the heat but also from animals and plants you may encounter in the region. Often, creatures and plants in hot climates are tough and toxic. There is a unique knowledge required for each desert and jungle around the planet. You will need to do your research. Consult an experienced source for where you are traveling.

Here's another thing to note about hot locations, particularly deserts. Without the steadying influence of the ocean, temperatures can swing wildly from day to night. Even though temperatures may be above 100°F during the day, at night the air can drop below freezing. Cold climates are arguably easier to manage: they are only cold and colder. Only if they warm up above freezing will you face additional challenges. Trekkers in desert climates must be prepared for large daily temperature swings.

Hydration

Keeping properly hydrated during an adventure is one of your biggest challenges. Not only do you need to find or produce clean water, but you also need enough of it. And, on top of that, you need to ensure the rest of your team is drinking enough water. When at rest, hydration is not a major problem. But when hiking through the middle of a desert, it becomes a matter of survival.

Adventure Expedition One

One of the difficulties people run into is the fear of drinking too much and needing to relieve themselves. Before departing, establish a system and timing for people to take care of this basic need. Often, inexperienced trekkers will suffer parched throats from "holding it", waiting for an opportune time. Sometimes this may not come for hours.

With mixed gender teams, the challenges escalate. Creating a toilet plan for people so they are comfortable and have their privacy is a responsibility of the expedition leader. Discuss what will work given conditions and travel, and make sure it works as you train together. Everyone will appreciate your efforts.

To keep your team healthy, you must make sure your water supply is as clean as possible and free from pathogens. The only guaranteed way to kill water-borne pathogens is to bring the water to a boil. Once the water is boiling, remove the heat and let the water cool.

Boiling water is a fuel-intensive activity. This is why chemical and mechanical treatment of water is so popular with trekkers. There are many water purification products on the market. Each has varying effectiveness in killing bacteria, protozoa, and viruses in water.

Something all chemical treatments and most filters cannot remove from water are chemicals and heavy metals. This may be a problem if you are near mines, agriculture, ranches, or manufacturing sites. Even though these facilities may be long gone, their contamination can persist for years if not decades. Arsenic, lead, mercury, and other chemical toxins will not be removed by common filtration systems. Boiling will not remove or neutralize these toxins either. Desalination systems can remove salt ions from water. But you still can't be sure, especially in a wilderness situation, if a desalination system will adequately purify your water. If there is even a remote likelihood of chemical or metal toxins in your water, find another source.

One advantage of cold-climate travel is the availability of ice and snow. Make sure the frozen water is free from contaminants and is fresh. The snow that fell weeks or months ago can be laden with bacteria and air-borne contaminants. Again, boiling, filtering or otherwise treating the melted snow is highly recommended.

Skills

Nutrition

In order to be successful on any long adventure, you must have proper nutrition. On short trips, it's possible to eat low-quality food. However, the longer you are in the field, the more apparent nutritional deficits become. Not only do nutrients affect your energy level, but they also support positive emotions and a strong immune system. Without all systems in your body working at full capacity, you will not do as well as you could. The only way to keep yourself strong, happy, and healthy is by eating a diet matched to your activity.

Carolyn Gunn, the author of the *Expedition Cookbook*, suggests planning for 4,000 calories per person per day for a high-altitude mountain trip, in the ratio of 60-65 percent carbs, 20-25 percent fat and 10-15 percent protein. That amounts to about two pounds of food per person, per day, not counting packaging.

Calories

The number one thing you need while participating in any activity is calories. Without these, you will quickly tire and come to a grinding halt. Although you are able to live for weeks without food, that does not mean you will function well. In fact, if you are rowing a boat, climbing a mountain, or dragging a sled, you will need to eat frequently. On polar journeys, this will mean eating as often as every seventy-five minutes.

Except on adventures with a base camp, you will find hunger to be a constant companion. It is difficult to eat more than 6,000 calories per day while engaged in strenuous travel. Any more than that and you will feel overly full. However, you may be burning upwards of 9,000 calories per day. What you often experience in these high-exertion activities is that you are constantly hungry, you will then eat, and feel temporarily satisfied. Before your next rest break, you will find yourself famished again.

Your success is dependent on properly managing your eating schedule. If you decide to skip a meal or two in the interest of making more distance, you will suffer for it, maybe not immediately, but the next day. When you are pushing at your maximum the whole time,

ADVENTURE EXPEDITION ONE

any reduction in fuel (food) to your body will become apparent. Arctic expeditions have failed because the team chose to eat less in order to conserve resources for later.

Eating less than you planned for the day will have definite consequences. Your energy will drop. The distance you cover will decrease. Your attitude will deteriorate. Teamwork will falter. The reason to reduce rations is to ensure you have enough supplies to make it through your journey. This happens to many expeditions. It's not always a function of poor planning. Unanticipated weather or conditions may slow progress, necessitating reduced rations.

The opposite is true, too. If you bring too much food, you will be hauling unnecessary weight and will travel slower. This will translate to more time required in the field. Your body will be stressed under the load and may be injured.

Figuring out the proper amount and correct type of calories requires repeated experimentation well prior to departure. You do not want to discover two weeks into your journey that you cannot stomach a particular type of food. This is where the value of medium-distance training trips becomes apparent. Only by testing yourself for more than a week on your expected diet will you discover problems. You may learn certain foods don't agree with you while you're under mental and physical pressure.

Also, avoid being picky when choosing your daily ration. Implement a random whatever-you-grab-is-what-you-eat rule. This will prevent you from consuming preferred foods too early in the trip. If you make this mistake, you will be left with only less desirable foods at the end of your trip when you need the best in order to keep your energy and morale up.

Whatever you choose to eat, make sure it is something you can sustain yourself on for months. If you discover some food to be intolerable and you have no way to resupply yourself, you have a conundrum of needing the calories but despising the food. Learn what works for you early. Some people can eat anything. Others are sensitive and require specific foods. If you have a team, rigorous planning to establish a diet that everyone enjoys will go a long way to ensuring success. Nothing demoralizes a team quicker than food

SKILLS

problems. In a half-day, what was once a fun journey can turn dismal if people don't enjoy their food. Expedition food tends to be bland and uninspired. Unless you have the ability and resources to make fancier fare, make sure your team has a tolerance for boring, repetitive food. Your expedition truly depends on this.

Be aware that when under physical strain, strongly spiced foods may not agree with some people. These people may handle spicy foods without trouble at home. Yet, these same foods may cause stomach upset in the field. Figuring out what people can handle prior to departure is important. Dealing with digestive issues is unpleasant enough at home. Doing so high on a cliff is another matter entirely.

If someone has a particular food allergy, you must be doubly careful. It is best not to bring any food that a teammate is allergic to. Eliminating the source eliminates the chance of a serious or fatal reaction. Determine what food allergies exist prior to departure. Ensure this person has an unexpired epinephrine autoinjector (EpiPen®) with them at all times, regardless. Some foods may contain trace amounts of allergens that can cause an unexpected reaction.

Some authorities may not allow an expired epinephrine autoinjector through customs. Ensure the autoinjector expiration date is beyond the last possible date of your return to home. Also, bring the prescription or doctor's note. This may help you with issues with authorities while traveling.

> Whole or crushed peanuts do not digest well. This has been the experience of other explorers, too. Every bowel movement reminded me that the peanuts in my food bars made it all the way through my system without breaking down. —*AL*

Salt intake

One of the particular challenges with traveling far afield is the problem of too little salt intake. This problem is more common in hot environments. In its extreme form, it can lead to a condition called

ADVENTURE EXPEDITION ONE

hyponatremia, where the level of the sodium electrolyte in our body fluids drops. This condition occurs when humans drink too much water and do not have enough salt in their body.

Hyponatremia feels similar to dehydration. You feel like you need to drink more water, which only exacerbates the problem. Eventually, the person's muscles will cramp up. This again will make you feel like you need more water. In fact, drinking more water at this point can cause more problems. If the sodium level drops far enough, seizures and incapacitation can occur.

Signs around the major hiking trailheads in Grand Canyon National Park warn of this problem. In most circumstances, as long as we are eating regularly, we get plenty of sodium from our food. However, when exerting yourself strenuously in a hot environment, hyponatremia can happen, particularly if meeting your fluid needs requires a large volume of water. Salty foods and salt supplements are both options to avoid this problem. These can be found in running and some sporting goods stores.

Consult your doctor prior to dramatically increasing your salt intake. There are adverse health problems that can arise from too much salt intake. This is where learning how your body handles expedition-similar conditions is important. Only by knowing how you respond to strenuous conditions will you be able to plan for what you need.

Trace mineral intake

Another challenge that can crop up in the field is the lack of trace minerals in your diet. Calcium, sodium, magnesium, and zinc are all essential for proper muscle function. Often, expedition food combined with physical strain will deplete your body of these trace minerals. Runners or other long-distance athletes, including expedition members, may experience cramps that simple salt pills might not alleviate.

This text mentions trace mineral intake for your information only. Consult a licensed medical or dietary professional prior to making any change in your diet. This is especially important with trace minerals and salts, as over-consuming these can adversely affect your health.

SKILLS

Logistics

In order to put together a large-scale expedition, you will need to become a master of logistics. Some adventures require only a few hours to put together and you can be in the field for months. However, most require significant planning. Some may even take a decade to come to fruition.

> Logistics: the things that must be done to plan and organize a complicated activity or event that involves many people.

The farther afield you are, the more important logistics become. Organizing support staff, participants, transportation, spare equipment, safety, and the like are major tasks and can become full-time jobs for the people involved. Often, major treks like Antarctica, the Arctic, ocean crossings, and major mountain climbs require months of full-time preparation by participants. You will discover during planning that physical training, gear acquisition, and organization will preclude a full-time job.

The more you prepare, the more smoothly you can anticipate that your adventure will unfold. Is it possible to over-prepare? Possibly. But is it easy to under-prepare? Absolutely. Sometimes, your life may depend on particular equipment. If this is the case, you must be confident that your gear is sound and that you have a backup plan. If your life is dependent on one or more pieces of gear, treating them as a life-support system is the best way to look at them. You do not want to be paralyzed by over-analyzing problems. But you must also consider backups and redundancy to those backups for anything your life truly depends on.

Logistics planning techniques

In today's world, most communication is digital. Managing equipment and planning requires skill in organizing lists, people, and transportation. There are many ways to keep track of

ADVENTURE EXPEDITION ONE

all the factors you need to consider. For as many technologies as there are available today, sometimes simple methods are more efficient.

Some adventurers draw things out on a whiteboard or large piece of paper. With everyone in the room, this is the fastest way to put all your team's thoughts together. You will be able to visualize items, connections, and paths to what you need. Writing down everything allows your brain to treat ideas as real. When ideas are discussed but not written down, they are difficult to manage and understand, especially when planning as a group.

Once written down, people can more easily identify problems or conflicts that were not apparent before. It is common to have a room full of people talking about an idea and all seem to agree. Once they leave the room and begin discussing items individually, differences appear. Soon, what was originally agreed upon is disputed. This problem is just as common with two-person teams as it is with multi-thousand person organizations.

Write everything down

To eliminate miscommunication, write everything down. It may seem like it takes too much effort. But when your adventure is strained because of misunderstandings, you will learn the hard lesson of the weakness of purely oral communication too late.

Once you have everything written down on a board or large paper, you'll need to transcribe this material to a digital document. There are various options for how to do this. Whatever method you choose, it needs to be easy to share between all participants.

Your chosen method should not rely on people having specialized smartphones or expensive or difficult-to-use software. The moment planning becomes too difficult for people to do, they will fail to do it. Again, this happens with teams of any size.

Should your adventure require major planning and dependence on a sequential series of events, consider planning software. Some people make a career out of using this type of software. Do not undertake using planning software unless you are proficient and dedicated to the process.

Skills

For anything but the most audacious adventures, most expeditions only require simple text documents and spreadsheets. Whichever computer platform you are using, make sure all involved parties are able to easily share the documents. Incompatible files bog down sharing and frustrate everyone.

The KISS (Keep It Simple Stupid) principle is valuable for your entire expedition. Given a choice, choose the simpler alternative unless there's a compelling reason otherwise. Simpler means less to go wrong. You will already encounter many challenges. Avoid compounding an already complex operation.

Consider online and cloud-based sharing with caution. Although these services have gained popularity in recent years, they carry a significant risk. If a hacker acquires your username and password, all of your data may be compromised, contaminated, or destroyed. For, as secure as computers can be, even the biggest companies with multi-million dollar computer security have been hacked. Do not believe hacking and theft will not happen.

Back up everything off-line

Losing all of your expedition information only needs to happen once to ruin your plans. This may cause you to lose sponsors if they believe you cannot manage your digital assets properly. If you're unable to keep your files safe, they will ask how you will manage yourself or your team in the field. Avoid a data loss disaster with off-line backup. An inexpensive USB thumb drive is an excellent backup. For a few dollars, you will sleep better at night knowing your adventure documents are safe.

Although cloud data services are extremely popular, consider what happens if someone hacks into your account or computer and deletes everything. Ransomware attacks are prevalent. Also, what happens if someone on your team accidentally corrupts or deletes a critical file? Do you have a backup? What happens if someone doesn't have an Internet connection?

Also, choose a calendar system everyone can use. Make it easy for team members to look up critical calendar items at any time without your intervention. Peculiar things happen when planning for an

Adventure Expedition One

expedition. The goal is to make it easy for everyone to see when critical events and deadlines are.

Navigation

Keeping on course is everything to reaching your destination. Navigation is essential to any expedition, whether climbing a mountain or crossing an ocean. Becoming misdirected or lost can:

- Put the team behind schedule
- Exhaust your supplies prematurely
- Damage morale
- Put you in a dangerous situation or location

If you fall behind schedule, you may miss achieving your goal. You may have to eat less each day to stretch your food out. People become disheartened when lost. It saps energy, erodes leadership confidence, and morale plummets. In the worst case, you may wander into risky areas and put the lives of your team or yourself at risk. Becoming lost is a major problem!

On some adventures, you may be on an expedition of discovery. Your plan may be to explore an unmapped area. This may be to open up a previously unexplored area to the world or it may be to discover a new species. Perhaps your adventure may be to find a long-lost city. The key task in these expeditions is returning to civilization. Discovering a lost Incan city in the jungles of Guatemala is of no use if you can't find it again or return to civilization to share your discovery. Local guides may be required.

Even on short weekend trips, navigation is a critical skill. Stories of lost hikers routinely fill the news. Often, these people are only a few miles from help. Even with modern technology, people frequently become lost. It has been argued that over-reliance on cellular phones leads people to take risks beyond their skill level.

The longer the expedition, the more important navigation becomes. If you are traveling hundreds of miles, a few degrees error can add up to missing your destination by miles. You can end up

SKILLS

in the wrong drainage or on the wrong mountain or miss your campsite.

Whoever manages navigation is under a great deal of pressure. If a single individual is responsible for determining travel direction, ensure they are competent. The entire team's life depends on their decisions.

As a soloist, you are the navigator. This makes going solo many times more difficult than traveling as a team. When tired or stressed, humans can make poor decisions. Teams have the ability to reason out an error that a single person may make. A soloist has no such luxury. This is one of the reasons that soloing is both dangerous and alluring.

Accurate time-keeping is key to navigating unmapped areas or the open ocean. Latitude can be determined with charts, sextants, and a few calculations. However, there is no simple way to manually determine longitude without accurate time-keeping. This is why so many expeditions rely on GPS technology.

One of the dangers of team navigation is "group think." This occurs when a dissenter's voice is squelched, even though they may be correct. Some people are not comfortable with conflict about travel direction and risk. People may assume someone else knows the best route. Teams get lost together. Peer pressure is a significant factor in becoming lost.

Major travel decisions must be made with care. If there is constant discord about the correct course, team morale may disintegrate. Establishing leadership is important prior to departure. The team must have confidence in the leader's competence.

During the great age of long-distance Polynesian ocean travel, the most important person on the boat was the navigator. They were more important than the chief, the fishermen, or the religious leader. If the navigator fell ill or died, there was a good chance that no one would survive. Becoming lost in the vast Pacific Ocean nearly guarantees a tortured death from starvation and exposure.

ADVENTURE EXPEDITION ONE

Orienteering is using a map and compass together to determine position and travel direction. Although the concept of using a map and compass together appears simple, their use can confuse even the seasoned adventurer. It's important to practice and understand:

How the compass works
How the map and compass can be used together
Magnetic declination
Common errors

Study an authoritative book and take a class on orienteering to learn this essential skill. Taking a course offered by a local professional is valuable. Beginning a wilderness trip without this essential skill invites disaster.

The night sky can also be used for navigation. Understanding the constellations and their positions in the sky can help you stay on course. Polaris, the north star, can be used in the northern hemisphere. Star navigation in the southern hemisphere can be more problematic. However, don't rely exclusively on celestial navigation. The weather may render the stars invisible, making direction-finding impossible.

Some places on Earth have inaccurate maps. In other places, maps are essentially useless. The Antarctic plateau and the Arctic Ocean are two examples of places where accurate maps do not exist. There are no landmarks on the vast Arctic Ocean. In Antarctica, there are few high-resolution maps available. The countless square miles of ice can all look the same from the ground.

For ocean navigation, sea charts are available. Many, but not all, coastal regions are accurately charted. Marine maps and charts identify underwater dangers. Charts of remote islands and rarely visited places may have errors and omissions. Shoals, reefs, and wrecks may be poorly marked or omitted. Consult an authoritative source for the most accurate available ocean navigation.

Modern technology has made navigation easier. The primary tool for this is the GPS (Global Positioning System) unit. Small handheld units can, in clear sky, accurately locate someone within a few yards

SKILLS

of their exact position. For travel in unfamiliar territory, these devices are incredibly useful.

However, GPS devices can fail. They do not work well (or at all) in steep canyons, near large obstructions, or in a heavy canopy. If the GPS is essential for the travel and safety of the expedition, bring at least two with redundant spare batteries.

Even with available modern technology, bring a compass and map. If the team's GPS fails, how will you navigate? Without a map (built-in, electronic, or paper), a GPS unit can only provide waypoints and travel direction. If there is a mountain or body of water in the way, the GPS may provide little help. A GPS cannot think for you.

For the purpose of historical re-creation, an expedition may choose to use only a sextant, compass, and map for travel. Although modern technology has made travel easier, it has also reduced some challenges in the process. Using historic techniques may be the goal of your expedition.

In polar latitudes, the difference between what a GPS shows and the reality on the ground can be extreme. A GPS is designed for orthogonal grid travel. However, the convergence of longitudinal lines in polar locations causes confusion. If a GPS has the ability to compensate for the difference between the position near the poles and magnetic declination, learn how to use this feature prior to departure.

I encountered this problem during my solo expedition in Antarctica. Near the South Pole, a GPS will continue to indicate travel direction should be toward 180° south. Over 720 miles of travel, it's easy to be off by a few miles. GPSs have the ability to correct for magnetic error near the pole, but either I didn't understand how to use it or my GPS unit didn't support this feature. Even though I was three miles from the South Pole station, I couldn't see it. —*AL*

[See *Antarctic Tears* for more details.]

ADVENTURE EXPEDITION ONE

Weather and the Elements

Weather is a major variable to consider on any expedition. You can have the best team, but when dangerous weather moves in you will all be sitting it out. Humans have been to every climate on Earth but we can only handle so much. Even with the correct clothing and shelter, people die. Wind and precipitation can destroy the best equipment.

Whatever the weather could be like, based on your study, be prepared for it and more. You want to be able to handle the worst mountain, ocean, jungle, or ice cap weather. There is a delicate balance between having enough gear and too much. Too little gear invites danger yet too much gear slows you down.

If you are headed to an extreme environment like high mountains or polar areas, be wary of equipment you have not extensively tested. Will Steger wrote in his book *North to the Pole* that even though his gear worked well in freezing Minnesota weather, it wasn't up to the task on the Arctic Ocean. He had to purchase tougher and warmer equipment.

If you are on a long Antarctic expedition, the sun will scorch any exposed skin. Sunscreen is of no use here, though. It is heavy so you can't carry enough for three months, it will freeze solid, and it will soil adjacent clothing thereby reducing its insulating properties. The only option is to stay completely covered up. Research and speak with others who have been there before.

Rescue and medical insurance

If you are traveling to a distant and extreme location, rescue and recovery insurance is advised. Some transport companies and countries will require you to carry an appropriate amount of insurance. It is not uncommon to be required to have a $300,000 policy for Antarctic and Arctic expeditions. Some mountaineering companies strongly suggest a policy, too.

Relative to the cost of a rescue, insurance is inexpensive. Although it seems like a needless expense, an evacuation for a significant injury can easily cost tens of thousands of dollars. Make sure to budget for this.

Skills

Many major companies do not cover the polar regions. Few insurance companies cover travel north or south of 80° latitude. Make sure to ask about details of the policy before purchasing. Speak with your insurance agent about your specific activity so that you obtain a policy that actually provides the coverage you need.

It can take an immense crew to lead twelve climbers to the summit of Kilimanjaro.

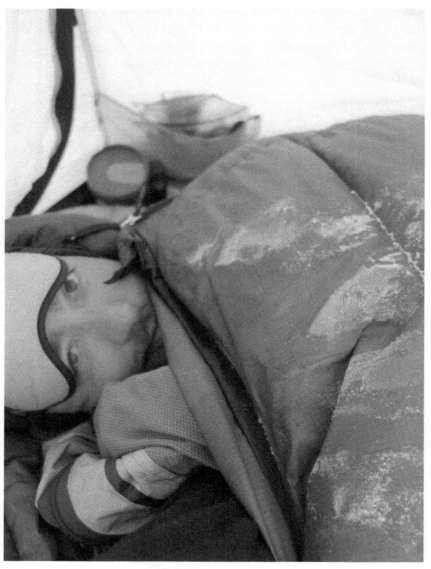

The proper sleeping bag and headware can make all the difference between joy and misery on an expedition.

PART SEVEN

Equipment

What do you actually need?
For any significant adventure, you need the following fundamentals:

Clothing
Sleep system
Shelter
Cookware
Navigation
First aid
Communication

You can pursue any human-powered adventure with the above. If your expedition requires a kayak, bicycle, aircraft, vehicle, or some other mode of transport, you can still use these lists as a good starting point.

Ten essentials

You've considered the fundamental priorities for survival. What are the most important tools to bring along on an expedition? There are many lists of what is essential. Depending on your adventure, this list

ADVENTURE EXPEDITION ONE

may grow but it won't likely shrink. Carrying these items will take you nearly anywhere in the world.

Also, these items are chosen because they're difficult if not impossible to replicate in the outdoors. There are natural substitutes for some of these items. However, it may be beyond your resources or skill to acquire them.

1. Pocket-knife or multitool
2. First-aid kit
3. Extra clothing
4. Rain gear
5. Water bottle
6. Flashlight or headlamp
7. Trail food
8. Matches/fire starter
9. Sun protection
10. Map and compass

Recommended items beyond the Ten:
Whistle and mirror
Water purification
Insect repellent
Toilet paper (small roll)

Pocket-knife or multitool

Depending on what your adventure is, more than a pocket-knife may be necessary. And even a multitool might not be enough. You might need an entire chest of tools if you're using a vehicle (land, water, air) to transport yourself. But of all the tools you might need, a cutting tool will be invaluable. It's impractical or impossible to replicate a sharp knife or a complex tool like pliers in the outdoors.

First-aid kit

Your life may literally depend on carrying an adequate first-aid kit. Even if you only carry a basic kit, this may make the difference

Equipment

between making it and not. After spending any time in the outdoors, you will likely need some type of first aid, even if it's just for a blister on your foot. Without this, you or your team can be miserable or in danger. Refer to the medical chapter for comprehensive recommendations.

Extra clothing

Even for a day hike, carrying a warm coat can make all the difference. If you find yourself stuck in the woods overnight, a jacket can be a life-saver. On a longer adventure, extra clothing is required. You will need to handle cold, hot, wet, and windy conditions. Adventures covering weeks if not months will encounter varied weather conditions and extra clothing is mandatory.

Rain gear

When it rains or snows, you, your team, and your equipment can be soaked in minutes. Without protection from water and wind, the onset of hypothermia can be life-threatening. What is easy to deal with at home by stepping inside is completely different in the outdoors. In winter or polar regions, you will substitute a parka or another heavier outer shell for rain gear.

Water bottle

In order to travel more than a few miles, a water bottle is essential. You cannot go far without water. Water containers are difficult or impossible to replicate in the wild without spending significant effort and time. Often, you will need multiple containers, depending on your adventure. Note that soft water containers and hoses can freeze in cold conditions. Test your water system in matching temperatures prior to embarking on your adventure.

Flashlight or headlamp

Except in polar regions in the middle of summer, you will need a light source. Modern flashlights or headlamps are versatile and can last a long time. However, they can also fail at the worst time. Always carry spare and backup batteries. If you are on a sub-freezing

Adventure Expedition One

adventure, use lithium batteries for your lamps. Lithium batteries are lighter but more expensive than other battery types. They function to −40°F/C and can deliver far more energy than alkaline and nickel metal hydride (Ni-MH) batteries.

Trail food

Food for your expedition is dependent on: the destination, mode of travel, and time in the field. When possible, select highly nutritious, calorie-dense foods. Freeze-dried or dehydrated food is commonly used. The water has been removed to save weight and is added prior to consumption. Though expensive, it may be the only option if you are traveling under human power.

Matches/fire starter

For more than a few days in the field, you will need something to light a fire. This may be for comfort, warmth, cooking, or water purification. Bring spares and backups. Once this resource is depleted, it is extremely difficult to start a fire using primitive methods. In addition to whichever fire-starting method you choose, the author suggests carrying flint and steel. It is unaffected by altitude, temperature, or moisture.

Sun protection

Unless you are traveling exclusively in the dark, some type of sun protection is important. Without clothing or chemical protection, the sun will deplete your energy, burn your skin, and damage your eyes. This is especially important on water or in snowy environments. For long expeditions in polar environments, sunscreen is impractical. You will rely on eyewear and clothing alone. Sunscreen makes clothing dirty, will freeze, and is heavy.

Map and compass

When modern technology fails, a map and compass can keep you on course. It takes study and practice to learn to use a map and compass well. Do not attempt to figure out how to use a map and compass for navigation when you need it most. Practice these skills

EQUIPMENT

in the field before leaving. Note that magnetic declination is severe in polar regions. See Navigation in the previous section for further discussion.

Bonus essentials

The following items are not in the classic ten essentials list. As you read through them, consider how they can benefit you in a survival situation.

Whistle and mirror

If you or your team become lost, signaling rescuers becomes important. Your voice does not carry any appreciable distance. Yelling will wear you out quickly. If your communication technology fails, you need an ultra-light backup. The sound of a whistle carries an incredibly long way. Flashes from a mirror can be seen miles away. (See the USAF or BSA *Handbook* for proper use.)

Water purification

In virtually all environments on Earth, water purification is recommended. Humans have a low tolerance for waterborne pathogens. Ingesting unclean water can rapidly incapacitate you. The only guaranteed method of purifying water is boiling for a couple of minutes—longer at altitude. All other methods provide varying degrees of purification.

Insect repellent

In most areas of the world, insects are a nuisance. In tundra climates, summer insects can be crippling. In some regions, insects carry disease and can make you very sick. Research these medical issues and consult your qualified medical professional beforehand.

Toilet paper

This simple product will keep you clean and comfortable. However, it must be kept dry and it takes up space. There are few substitutes in the wild that will fill the job of toilet paper.

131

Adventure Expedition One

Gear minimalism

Outdoor gear contributes billions of dollars to the economy. Magazines, manufacturers, and retailers keep busy creating, improving, marketing, distributing, and selling gear. Mountains of money are spent on equipment every year. For any adventure you are going to undertake, you will need some essential gear to help you make it through. One of the questions that will keep you up at night is:

What do I bring with me on this adventure?

As this text is dedicated to providing you an overview, it's impractical to provide a list of all the gear you might need. The needs of a trans-Pacific rower are different from an Everest climber, which are different from a Gobi Desert trekker. There are some fundamentals you will need regardless of your adventure. The key consideration of whatever you bring is:

Bring nothing more than you need.

The first inclination of a weekend backpacker is to carry gear to cover every eventuality. After a wild buying spree, their backpack is laden with the latest ultra-light gear. And, once you buy it all, it weighs fifty pounds! And this is for a one- or two-night trip in the summer when the weather is expected to be fine.

> Recommendation: The longer the expedition, the earlier all of the gear needs to be purchased. For other expeditions not at Antarctic scale, I was buying things the day before. This was a horrible mistake. Not only does the gear need to be tested, but also it needs to be tested early. Less than three weeks before the expedition is not the time to be ordering items by second-day air delivery. It wastes money and it puts the entire endeavor in jeopardy.

EQUIPMENT

> For all my major expeditions, my goal now is to have all equipment in hand two months prior to departure. This saves stress, time, and money. The last two months prior to an expedition are busy with peak training, media interviews, and completing travel arrangements. The last thing you want to be doing is running to the store or clicking online to buy last-minute items.
>
> Last-second gear acquisition caused me much lost sleep, both because of late-night chores and stress. Your expedition will be stressful enough. Don't add to it. —*AL*
>
> *"Bring no untested weapon into the field."*

Consider an example: an expedition backpacker named Terrell. He feels confident that there is no circumstance his team's mountain of technology cannot handle. After reading countless reviews online, he believes his trip through the Jedediah Wilderness in Wyoming will be easy and comfortable. Even though he's never backpacked at altitude and over a long distance, he's confident.

He purchased a tent with integrated LED lights to read by at night. All the comforts of home will be with him. With this sizeable load on their hips, he and his teammates should be as comfortable in camp as one could possibly be in the wilderness.

What is wrong with this scenario? The backpackers experience the pure drudgery of carrying this ponderous load for nine hours for several days.

Every time Terrell removes the pack, he feels his spine decompress. By the end of a rest, he dreads slinging the weight onto his back. Also, he grows worried. Terrell has been unable to cover anything like the mileage he originally planned. He hoped to cover forty miles in two days. By the end of his first full day, he's barely covered ten.

This scenario is not as absurd as it first appears. Modern-day backpackers routinely carry thirty or more pounds for one or two nights

133

ADVENTURE EXPEDITION ONE

in the wilderness. Food, shelter, backup supplies, and comfort items all add up quickly. What drives Terrell to carry such a load?

Fear

At first, fear doesn't seem to make sense. Isn't Terrell carrying only what he needs? This is where the complexity comes into play. What, exactly, do you "need" with you to travel along trails through the woods? Equipment is purchased based on the fear of the following:

Cold
Hunger
Dehydration
Injury
Lack of daylight
Lack of company
Becoming lost
Discomfort
Dangerous animals

Each of these fears, and other unlisted ones, will drive you to make decisions about what you bring. Should you be a professional survivalist, the most you might bring is a knife on many trips. As your trips extend into farther-away places, you may need to supplement your gear with backups. But, again, carrying backups is based on fear of something. This fear may be fully justified, though. In Antarctica, if your stove fails and you have no backup, you may perish before help can reach you. In the middle of the ocean, if your desalinator fails, you will suffer the same fate. Your fears will determine every gram of equipment that you carry with you.

Enter the concept of *base weight*. The term base weight is what you are carrying that will not or cannot be reduced during the trip. Base weight is everything minus food, fuel, water, and any other consumables. This weight remains the same throughout the adventure. If you travel to the point that you are completely out of food, fuel, and water, you have reached the base weight of your pack.

Equipment

Terrell started out with a base weight of thirty pounds. On top of that, he planned a luxurious two pounds of food per day. He is also carrying extra water, as he is unsure of where the next water is along the trail. He plans to have at least two liters (quarts) on him at all times.

Plus, he's brought several fuel canisters. They are all half-full and he wants to use them up on this trip. Terrell planned for three days of travel. His final pack weight, at the start, is:

Base weight: 30 pounds
Food (three days): 6 pounds
Water (start with one gallon): 8 pounds
Fuel canisters (three half-full): 3 pounds

Total backpack weight: 47 pounds

Terrell is carrying the equivalent of six gallons of water on his back. Once he consumes his food, his pack will still weigh thirty-three pounds (base weight plus two liters water plus empty fuel canisters). As our theoretical backpacker has only traveled ten of his forty miles in the first day, he is stressed. How will he cover the necessary mileage in what is left of his weekend?

If Terrell came across a trash dumpster, he could jettison some weight and still make it. Otherwise, he is in for a difficult haul. What he once envisioned as a pleasant stroll through the woods has now become a struggle to reach his destination. He begins thinking that he might have to turn back.

He is also carrying the psychological burden of attempting a trip beyond his skill and ability. Perhaps a friend dropped him off, so returning to the starting point isn't an option. Terrell is now in a precarious situation. He told his friends he was going to bomb this trail out with time to spare. There was nothing that was going to stop him.

Meanwhile, in Georgia, Sheila has begun her thru-hike of the Appalachian Trail. She has taken many short and mid-scale backpacks prior to departing on the 2,190-mile trail. She knows her body, its limits, and what she needs to bring. Her needs are few.

ADVENTURE EXPEDITION ONE

Her backpack base weight is ten pounds.

Sheila will be hiking through fourteen states. She plans to be on the trail for three months. Though traveling in summer, she's prepared for any weather she might encounter. Her plan is to cover fifteen to twenty miles per day, depending on elevation gain.

As Sheila's father drops her off, she is confident and buoyed. Though she's excited, she's also scared. She has fear, but it's only fear of being away from her family for so long. Her fear has nothing to do with her gear. It's tested and trusted. She's been in precarious situations before and knows how to handle herself.

When Sheila arrives at the first post office along the trail, she sees fellow-backpackers who are weary and beat. They are mailing much of their pack contents back home. Their feet are bleeding from torn blisters. Their backs are sore. They are disheartened. Sheila chats for a few moments with a few people. She hikes on, confident and smiling.

Although Sheila will cover many times the distance that Terrell will, her pack base weight is one-third of his. How is that possible?

The longer the trip, the less you need

In order to cover significant distances, you must be critical of every gram of gear. Even if you are traveling by kayak, vehicle, or plane any excess weight will soon be felt. Extra weight will result in fewer miles covered or more fuel consumed. If you are carrying your pack, you will soon be sensitive to even the slightest change in pack weight.

> I dragged the equivalent of a twenty-six cubic foot refrigerator-freezer across Antarctica. Every time I stopped, I brushed snow off the sleds to lessen the weight I had to drag. While traveling, I even began thinking of ways to grind off the edges of my sleds.

136

EQUIPMENT

> I made a serious effort to remove every unnecessary item from my Antarctic expedition gear, including clothing tags. After removing every jacket, glove, and pant tag, I saved a quarter pound. I even cut the strings off my tea bags. Small items add up.
>
> This was all in an attempt to reduce weight any way possible. The desire to cut weight will occupy your mind as much as hunger.
>
> *En largo camino una paja pesa.* (On a long journey, even a straw weighs heavy). *—AL*

Although reducing weight is important, do not render useful items useless. Cutting the handle off a toothbrush to reduce a few grams is beneficial from a weight standpoint but is detrimental to the utility of the tool. Consider that you will be using this twice a day for the duration of your expedition. If the handle is too short and you need to brush wearing gloves, you may add more irritation to the experience. This, in turn, reduces enthusiasm and drains energy. Your toothbrush is one of your essential tools, so don't ruin it.

When modifying gear, ensure the basic utility remains unimpaired. If you drill holes in a piece of metal to save weight, will the piece still hold up after three months of use? Consider how long your tools and equipment will need to last to bring you home. They will receive more battering in the field than at home. Extremes in temperature, humidity, vibration, and dirt wear everything down quickly. Unless you are completely confident, don't remove or reduce something beyond how it was originally designed.

When you return from your trip, open your gear list spreadsheet. Create an additional column. As you remove each item from your pack, note how much you used it. You will gain knowledge that will inform your planning for your next adventure.

What would have happened if this item fell out of my pack?

Since you didn't use it, and presumably the item isn't for rescue or first aid, what purpose did it serve? Often, you will discover items you've carried for years have only been rocks in your pack. It takes time to be comfortable with less. So, often, people are conditioned to bring more.

Bringing too much can reduce comfort and risk safety. If you are carrying too much weight, your footing will not be as solid. Your joints will be strained. You can recover from a stumble with a light pack. Stumbling with a heavy pack can result in serious injury.

When you have discovered what you have been carrying for no apparent reason, leave it at home. Then take a shorter trip. See what happens. On returning home, what did you discover about that missing item?

On any adventure, safety is paramount. Do not eliminate items that place you at risk. Figuring out what these items are can be a painstaking process. Depending on the strength of your fear, you may have difficulty leaving behind items that you believe you need. Only through experience can you work through this process.

One of the tricks to cutting equipment weight is using items for more than one purpose. Every expedition has different possibilities for multipurpose utilization. Consider all of the items on your gear list. If possible, lay everything out in a room. Place similar materials together. Look at each item. Think about how you would replace it if you lost a particular piece of gear. If there is no need to replace the item, do you even need it?

Clothing

Your body requires basic protection from the elements as you travel. Your basic garments will keep you warm, cool, and protected from the elements and from insects. There are endless choices of styles and options. Start with designs that have been proven by other expeditions and then branch out from there.

The key to traveling comfortably in any condition is to use a layer system. Using layers will allow you to adapt to nearly any weather

EQUIPMENT

conditions you will encounter. This system is superior to wearing a shirt and then a single heavy coat. If you find that you are too cold with only the shirt but are too hot with the coat, you have few options. You will struggle with this kind of system, unable to adequately vent heat with the single jacket.

Overheating is both unpleasant and dangerous. The discomfort of being too warm is one problem. You may find yourself feeling nauseous and sapped of energy. But sweating in your clothing can lead to hypothermia in cold environments. Once your clothing is sweat-soaked, it will chill you the moment you stop exerting yourself. Sweaty clothing is also unpleasant to wear. Salts and oils in your sweat will soil everything and cause rashes or pimples. Both lead to problems in the field. See the medical section for further discussion.

One fundamental question to decide on is if you are going to use synthetic or natural fibers or a mix of both. It is important to test how your body reacts to different fibers under various conditions. What may feel comfortable at home may be unpleasant in the field. The key factor in your undergarments and base layers is that they wick sweat away from your body. The only fabric that does not readily perform this action is cotton.

There is a saying in the outdoor community that "cotton kills." This is because cotton retains moisture (sweat), dries slowly, and soils quickly. These factors cause you to become cold because the cotton garment stays wet. As a test to see this for yourself, take a cotton t-shirt and a light synthetic shell jacket and drench both. Then hang both and see how long each takes to dry. Depending on conditions, the cotton t-shirt may still be moist three days later. If you found yourself in a downpour of rain with only a cotton shirt, you would stay wet far longer than is comfortable. Also, cotton tends to stretch out when wet. What was once a cool, comfortable shirt will now be a heavy, sodden dishtowel.

The one place where cotton may be advantageous is in hot and humid conditions. This is the one environment where synthetic clothing may be uncomfortable. One of the design advantages of technical adventure clothing is the advent of venting systems. Shirts

ADVENTURE EXPEDITION ONE

with slats in the back or the underarms have made synthetics livable in humid environments.

The natural fabric that remains popular is wool. Newer weaves and blends have eliminated the scratchiness of the fiber. Higher quality, more expensive products tend to have the best feel and wear characteristics. Thin wool shirts feel comfortable in warm conditions and keep you warm in colder climates. Thus far, it is the most enduring and versatile fabric. It does a great job of wicking water away from your skin and dries quickly. Wool also does well at retaining heat and will continue to keep you warm when wet.

Another major advantage of wool over synthetic fibers is the ability to combat odor. Synthetic fabrics have a propensity to retain and encourage bacterial growth. This, in turn, builds odor and can cause skin afflictions. After wearing the same shirt for weeks on end, this is not a minor consideration. Polypropylene is arguably the worst at odor retention.

I used the same polypro shirt over my ten-day, one-hundred-mile trek across the Greenland tundra. After five days, the shirt was unpleasant. By the tenth day, it had the odor of an organic garbage dump on a hot August afternoon. As the weather was always at or below freezing, washing the shirt in a lake or river was impossible. Doing so would have prevented travel until the shirt was nearly dry.

In situations where I cannot wash out my clothing regularly, wool ends up being a better option than any synthetic. I've worn wool shirts in the backcountry for several consecutive days without developing the stench that occurs with a synthetic fiber shirt. *—AL*

Shell layers

Breathability is also a major factor in mid-layer and outer shell clothing selection. Even if you select a breathable, wicking undergarment, a shell (outer jacket for wind, sun, and snow protection) that doesn't allow for sweat to evaporate will both overheat and soak you.

EQUIPMENT

For virtually any adventure, you will need some type of shell jacket. This will protect you from wind and precipitation. Which choice you make will be dependent on the expedition you are undertaking.

There are two types of outer shell materials, referred to as hard and soft shells. This terminology refers to the pliability of the fabric.

Classic rain jackets are hard shells. This means the fabric is relatively stiff and can make a crinkling sound when folded. Hard shells also create a "zif zif zif" sound when you move. These jackets can be light to extremely heavy, depending on the fabric and features such as pockets, hoods, pouches, and added insulation.

Soft shells are a relatively new category in outerwear. Their goal is to retain the waterproof quality of hard shells without the stiff feeling and noise. These jackets tend to be made of thicker material than their hard-shell counterparts. Because of this, they can be heavier while fulfilling the same purpose. They also may not keep water out in a downpour. As soft shells are thicker, they can provide an additional level of insulation that hard shells do not.

The one challenge with all waterproof outer shell jackets and pants is their breathability, the garment's ability to allow moisture to escape while keeping rain and wind out. If a jacket has zippers under the arms, be aware the jacket may not ventilate well. There are two major competing fabrics in the outdoor shell pants market: Gortex® and eVent®. Basic coated nylon is an option but allows for little to no ventilation. Search the Internet for the latest updated information about the relative advantages of these and other modern fabrics.

If you are traveling to polar climes, you will also need a fur ruff around the face part of your parka hood. Fur placed in this manner creates a microclimate around your face. It will cut nearly all the wind and moderate the noise. The warmer microclimate around your face helps reduce the chance of frostbite.

Perhaps the most surprising value of the fur ruff is the extent to which it cuts down the roar of the wind blowing around you. After exposure to wind sound for a long time, you can develop anemomania, where you become uncontrollably anxious about the direction of the wind. As there are incessant headwinds in Antarctica, you need something to protect yourself. A fur ruff is the solution.

Shelter

On most any adventure, you will need shelter to sleep in at night. Whether to keep moisture, cold, insects, or animals at bay, a shelter provides the protection needed to enjoy a good night's sleep after a strenuous day of travel. The most common type of shelter used for adventures worldwide is a tent.

Variations of the modern nylon tent can be found from children's versions to ones tough enough for polar travel. As with sleeping bags, the variety of tents available on the commercial market is mind-boggling. Different tents are designed for various objectives: weight reduction, weather resistance, insect control, wet conditions, mountaineering, etc. A tent that is designed to shave every gram of weight off will likely be incapable of handling gale force winds.

Tents also come in single- and double-wall variety. A single-wall tent will have a rudimentary fly that does not come to the ground. Rather, it only covers a portion of the tent top. Double-walled tents are designed for tougher weather conditions. The outer fly covers the entire tent and extends all the way to the ground.

In cold weather locations, you may experience the tent door zipper freezing shut. This can be caused by several factors: condensation, respiration, or meltwater from rain or snow freezing as the temperature drops. You may find that the zipper has completely frozen shut.

Whatever you do, avoid using the flame of your stove to free up the frozen zipper. That's a recipe for disaster. Applying open flame to melt the ice without setting fire to the nylon is difficult. If you only melt but don't drain off the water on the zipper, it will refreeze as you move the heat. This drives water further into the zipper.

Also, avoid using your hands or another body part to heat the zipper. You may end up with frostbite before you thaw the

Equipment

zipper. In extreme cold, your skin will freeze before the zipper heats up.

Instead, use a water bottle filled with hot to boiling water. Open what vents you can in your tent and heat up water. Once it is as hot as you can get it, pour it into your water bottle. Using gloves to hold the bottle, place it against the zipper pull. As the ice melts, gently unzip the tent. Be gentle, as you do not want to damage the plastic teeth. Once the zipper is thawed, flex the teeth back and forth and brush them out with a small brush. This will remove the ice.

It is important to figure out what caused the zipper to freeze in the first place. Make changes to your system to prevent this in the future if possible. This problem may be unavoidable in polar climates.

In most environments, keeping the door or windows slightly open will help reduce condensation. If you completely close your tent, you'll find yourself moist or even soaked in the morning. Your exhaled breath contains a surprising amount of moisture and it will condense and accumulate on the inside surfaces of your tent. This remains true in sub-zero temperatures.

To avoid being showered with condensation inside your tent, keep the windows open. If you have windows on both ends, open them both a small amount. Maybe more if the humidity is high or you have more than one person in the tent.

With open windows or slightly open doors, it will be colder but you'll stay drier. If everything is wet in the tent, you'll be miserable. And if frost builds up inside the tent, it can soak your sleeping bag, endangering your life. Keep the tent interior as dry as possible.

Vestibules are useful tent features for cold or wet travel. A vestibule is an extension to the fly creating a covered porch. You can store food, gear, and even cook in a vestibule. Note that this is dangerous and should only be done in extreme weather locations.

ADVENTURE EXPEDITION ONE

Do not be lulled into believing nylon only a fraction of an inch thick can stop animals from entering. Scents from your food and toiletries can attract animals. Discovering a hole chewed in your expensive tent is disheartening. Larger predators like bears can tear through wooden walls, roofs, and doors, so they can penetrate a tent in moments. Follow local regulations and recommendations regarding food storage where animals are an issue.

Tarp tents are also a viable shelter for long-distance backpacking. These shelters have several unique advantages over tents. They keep condensation at bay, are lighter, and can be roomier than tents. They are common on the American Pacific Crest and Appalachian Trails. As you begin backpacking longer distances, you'll find that, for a while, tents provide initial psychological comfort. But over weeks of carrying the weight, you'll begin fantasizing of a way to cut weight any way you can.

The authors have used tarp tents in the Sierra and Rocky mountains in downpours and snowstorms. With a little adjustment and work, they slept as comfortably as they would with a tent. Pitching a tarp tent can require more effort than a free-standing dome tent. A well-pitched tarp can withstand a significant storm. If positioned correctly, it can provide a more comfortable night than a tent in stormy conditions. Use a net to keep insects at bay in buggy areas.

Sleep system

For any adventure, you will need some type of sleep system. The universal tool for this is the sleeping bag. The varieties, manufacturers, and warmth levels of sleeping bags are innumerable. Some long-distance backpackers even sew their own sleeping quilts. You may opt for a sleeping quilt, too. This can be treated as a bedroll. There are advantages and disadvantages to each. As with other gear, price does not always equate to quality.

The main considerations for sleeping bags are:

Equipment

Styles

There are two fundamental designs for sleeping bags. The first is rectangular and the second is a mummy. Rectangular bags are more spacious, do not retain heat well, and are heavier for their comfort rating. Mummy bags are designed to more closely fit a person's shape. The name comes from the sarcophagus shape of the outer material. They are more weight- and warmth-efficient than rectangular bags. Specialized features like drawstrings and baffles are often incorporated into mummy bags as well. If you are planning on a cold climate adventure, mummy bags are the best alternative.

Insulation material

There are two main insulation materials used in sleeping bags today: down and synthetic fibers. Natural down, the insulating feathers from geese and ducks, is still the warmest insulation per weight available. Down also compresses better than synthetics. Do not place blankets or heavy objects on a down bag, as that will compress the insulation and make the bag colder. However, a down jacket thrown over your bag can add to your warmth if needed. The one major failing of down is that if it becomes soaked, it loses its insulating value. Down also takes a long time to dry. It is critical to protect a down sleeping bag from moisture. Use a waterproof stuff sack while traveling and protect it from moisture in the evening. If you are going to be in a perpetually wet environment or there's a high chance of soaking your bag, a synthetic bag may be a better choice.

Arctic explorers may use a combination of synthetic and down sleeping bags. As humidity is high in the Arctic, a person's warmth will drive moisture into a down bag, reducing its insulating value. The trick is to put the synthetic bag inside the down bag. The idea is to keep the down farther away from the water vapor given off by your body as you sleep.

Another technique used by some explorers to reduce this problem is to line their sleeping bag with a waterproof sleeve called a vapor barrier. This keeps perspiration and water vapor from permeating the sleeping bag. Though this solves the problem, vapor barriers are not comfortable to sleep in.

145

ADVENTURE EXPEDITION ONE

Warmth rating

How comfortable you are in a sleeping bag is dependent on two factors: the amount of insulation in the bag and how warm you sleep. The temperature rating on a bag may be rated to comfort or survival. If the temperature drops to the rating of your sleeping bag, this difference is important.

These numbers are highly dependent on the sleeping warmth of a person. If you tend to sleep hot, you may do fine with a lighter bag. But if you sleep cold, you may need a bag rated ten degrees below the coldest temperatures you expect to encounter.

Bag length

If you are six feet tall, purchase the six-foot-six sleeping bag. If you compress the insulation with your feet or head, you reduce the warmth of your bag and you will be cold. Typically, this happens in the foot area, which is much more vulnerable to cold. Make sure to test proper length in the store before purchasing.

Left or right-handed zipper

Manufacturers can place zippers on either the right- or left-hand side of a bag. This is a personal preference. If you are a soloist and tend to sleep on one side of your tent, this will determine which side zipper you choose. Some bags can be zipped together, mating a right and left zipper bag.

Baffles

Tubes or baffles are found on high-end expedition bags. They are often found on bags rated at −29°C (−20°F) and below. There are neck and zipper baffles. A zipper baffle is a small tube of insulation that is sewn in along the zipper to reduce the cold spot. As zippers provide no insulation, this is an excellent design feature. It will keep you much warmer.

Neck baffles are large insulation tubes sewn around the neck area of a sleeping bag. This allows you to separate the body and head area, preventing cold drafts from coming down the length of the bag. Independent drawstrings are found on the entrance and the neck

Equipment

baffle, allowing individual control of each. Some will find this a bit too claustrophobic, but often the warmth the neck baffle provides is well worth it.

Seam tape

Seam tape is a specially sewn stiff material that is sewn along the zipper of higher-end sleeping bags. The idea is that the seam tape prevents the zipper from snagging the bag fabric. Cheaper bags suffer from this problem constantly. There is nothing more frustrating than snagging a zipper in the middle of the night when you are in a hurry to relieve yourself.

Cooking

While on a long expedition, you will find that you'll need one hot meal per day. It is possible to eat cold food over a period of weeks or even months. However, your morale will begin to fail. You'll find activities unappealing. You may even lose heart. You'll start to think of reasons why you shouldn't be on your adventure. Your mind will slowly begin to rebel against you. Even the hardiest long-distance travelers find they need to consume one hot meal a day, preferably for the evening meal.

Some explorers have completed tough expeditions and climbs without hot food. Take Nanomi Uemura, for instance. He's one of the most celebrated adventurers in all of Japan. Uemura was the first man to trek to the North Pole alone. He then climbed Denali solo, the first person to do so. He forsook hot food in order to save pack weight. Although he reached the peak of Denali and left a Japanese flag to prove it, he perished while climbing down.

Stoves

Assuming you plan to eat hot food during your expedition, you'll need a stove for the job. There are many variations available on the market and new ones are introduced every year. There are even stoves which generate electricity with integrated USB ports for charging electronics.

147

Adventure Expedition One

All stoves require some type of fuel. Depending on where you are in the world, one or more of these fuels may be the most common.

Well prior to departure, make several tests of water boil time in your cooking system. Test different setups for the best efficiency. For a short weekend trip, there is little consequence to improving boil time by thirty seconds. On a trip of several weeks or months, this savings adds up. The better your stove system, the less fuel you will have to carry. The lower your weight, the faster you can go.

Stove types

White gas
White gas is arguably the most popular fuel today. It is used on 26,000 feet (8,000m) peaks and in polar regions. It is one of the most efficient fuels, is clean and is easy to ignite. The fuel requires preheating to burn properly. These stoves are also prone to flare-ups if too much fuel or pressure is applied at the burner. The fuel is carried as a liquid and pressurized by hand, making them adaptable to virtually any altitude and environment. The disadvantage is that this makes them more complex and prone to problems than other designs.

When these stoves are first ignited and then extinguished, the incomplete burn of the fuel causes carbon build-up, fouling the fuel jet. This clogging can prevent the stove from working safely or at all. Consequently, manufacturers have designed features to help users eliminate carbon build-up. If your expedition will be far from help and for an extended period of time, a repair kit is essential. For Arctic and Antarctic travel, a complete backup stove and spare pumps are necessary.

Propane and butane canister
These stoves are popular among trekkers and backpackers. The fuel is already pressurized, so it burns properly and almost instantly. This is advantageous compared to white gas. They are also not prone to flare-ups either during start-up or use. However, canister stoves are sensitive to altitude and do not burn well above 10,000 feet (3,000 meters). Some stoves are designed with an integral pot for maximum efficiency.

Equipment

Determining the remaining fuel in a canister is difficult in the field. It's common for trekkers to bring extra canisters, increasing their load. Canister stoves require no significant cleaning with normal use. Their simple design reduces the chance of problems in the field.

To achieve the best efficiency out of these stoves, improvise a windscreen and heat exchanger. On a long trip, the fuel savings from the screen will be worth it.

Alcohol

Denatured alcohol is commonly available at sporting goods and hardware stores in the United States. It is available at marine stores around the world, as this is a common fuel for sailing. It is a popular fuel with long-distance backpackers on the PCT, AT, and CDT trails. The reason for this is two-fold. Many use self-constructed stoves out of easily obtained materials—most notably aluminum cans. These primitive stoves have nothing intrinsic to go wrong. They do require a windscreen. The only real problem you might encounter is spilling the fuel or tipping the stove over. For longer trips, they are not as efficient as white gas stoves.

Kerosene

What was once the most common adventure fuel is now rare in the western world. It can still be found in some countries. Certain stoves are designed to burn multiple types of liquid fuel, kerosene among them. Some countries may only have kerosene available.

Kerosene has a high heat to weight ratio. The one major disadvantage is that it requires a strong heat source to vaporize and ignite the fuel. Kerosene requires you to light an alcohol paste (or other accelerants) to pre-heat and vaporize the fuel prior to cooking with it. This requirement for kerosene to have a starter heat source makes white gas a better option.

Wood/charcoal fire

Using locally available cooking fuels is rare for most adventures. Without a stove to retain the heat, these fires are inefficient. Also, collecting natural fuels can be hard on the local environment. Avoid

ADVENTURE EXPEDITION ONE

removing live wood from trees in all but the most extenuating circumstances. Should you choose this method, collect dead fallen wood.

Open fires also tend to give off sparks, which damage synthetic fabrics. If you are in a fire-prone or drought area, open fires must be handled with the greatest care. Charcoal or dung may also be available where you are trekking. These fuels are smoky and heavy. Modern fuels provide significant advantages in heat delivered per ounce carried.

All the disadvantages aside, natural fires are psychologically comforting. Not only can you cook with them but they also give off enough heat to warm you. If you are chilled and need warmth, starting a fire can be critical to staying alive. If your team's morale is flagging and needs a boost, start a campfire if possible. It may be exactly what you and your team need.

<u>Stove safety</u>

If you plan to use your stove in the tent, be *exceedingly careful*. It is easy to burn your tent down. It's recommended to use a stove in your tent only when you must—on high mountains or on polar expeditions.

Also, there is the risk of fume build-up inside a tent. When igniting a white gas stove, the initial combustion generates carbon monoxide. This is especially problematic at high elevation or in extremely cold climates. White gas stoves require a warm-up time before they begin burning properly with a blue flame. Until the fuel is hot, it does not vaporize and burn correctly and cleanly. Be extremely mindful of this.

<u>Stove efficiency</u>

On long trips, you want to do everything you can to reduce fuel use. Whichever stove you choose, bring a windscreen and heat exchanger. Many commercially available liquid fuel stoves come with a flexible aluminum windscreen. This prevents air motion from stealing heat away from your pot.

Equipment

On cold polar or high-mountain expeditions, a heat exchanger will also increase your fuel efficiency. It works by drawing hot air from the stove along the sides of the pot, improving heat transfer. This device is a bit heavy, but on long trips is worth its weight.

Food Storage

Food storage while sleeping in your shelter is a major consideration. In areas where bears or other significant predators are prevalent, proper food storage outside your shelter is sensible and may be required by law. Bears are highly intelligent and endlessly persistent. They're powerful and highly motivated. Follow the local regulations and customs of the area you are trekking through.

Five days into a long trip is a miserable place to have your food rations stolen by a bear. Do not underestimate an animal that is capable of driving a motorcycle or tearing apart a locked car.

Communication

Staying connected with the outside world for long, sponsored expeditions has become a requirement today. No longer will a team depart on the high seas not to be heard from for months or years at a time. Modern communication technology makes it possible to stay connected everywhere on the globe. Satellite communication even makes phone calls from the middle of polar regions possible.

There are multiple reasons for the need for stable communications:

Emergency and rescue communication
Progress tracking
Updates to sponsors, supporters, and followers

The fundamental communication medium for expeditions today is wireless. Radio technology has been used since the turn of the 20th century. Ships were early adopters of the technology, as they needed a method to share their position and status throughout the world.

ADVENTURE EXPEDITION ONE

Certain communication services only cover part of the globe, where others are truly global. Fully investigate to confirm that what you plan to use works where you will be exploring.

Below is a list of communication technologies currently available.

Cellular phones

Modern cellular communication is ubiquitous around populated areas. Even in sparsely populated areas, it can be possible to call. Should the signal be weak, it may only be possible to send or receive text messages. It's best to research what phone service works in your area of travel. You may need to rent a phone or purchase a SIM card locally.

Do not rely on cellular phones in remote locations as your only means of communication. Too often, adventurers expect their phones to work in canyons, mountains, oceans, or other remote areas. People have become so habituated to continual coverage that they do not realize there are areas without cellular service. In rural towns, cell phone service can be spotty to non-existent.

Software on today's smartphones may rely heavily on a digital data connection to function properly. If this is the case with yours, be doubly careful. Remote locations may only have voice or text service.

The great advantage of smartphones is their ability to enable mobile access to the Internet. This can reduce your costs for updating your sponsors and supporters. Smartphones can be coupled with satellite phones. Paired together, you can have a functioning, if slow, Internet connection. Sending pictures and videos using this pairing is possible from even the North and South Poles.

Satellite phones

Once relegated exclusively to government and military use, satellite phones are now available to consumers. Expeditions use them all around the world. The base camps at Everest and on Antarctica are packed with elaborate satellite systems.

Only certain services cover Antarctica and the Arctic. It's important to verify your service coverage before purchasing. This information may be difficult to find in the mass of marketing materials.

EQUIPMENT

Often, it can take some time to purchase and test a capable satellite device prior to departure. Make your purchase months before departing. They take time to ship and set up.

These phones are delicate and fickle. They must be handled with care. Their batteries and digital display are sensitive to the cold and heat. If you are traveling to a far-off location, purchase a second unit and backup batteries for each.

Satellite phones can be connected to computers, digital pads, and smartphones. You can send long text, pictures, and even video. The data speeds are slow compared to cellular service. Do not expect to send large video files with a basic satellite phone.

These services are also expensive. You may need to budget several thousand dollars for satellite phone time. It is common for prices to exceed three dollars a minute of airtime. Plan your calls carefully to eliminate missed connections. Set a fixed time to call your home team.

Satellite phone signals are weak. Thick cloud cover, trees, canyons, roofs, metal, and other obstructions thwart them. You need a clear sky to have any hope of making a call. Charging satellite phone batteries is an important consideration, too.

Transponders

Another viable communication option is satellite transponders. There are many options available today. Some are consumer grade and are not highly reliable. Others are integrated with GPS units. Depending on the unit, they may offer either one-way or two-way communication.

Virtually all satellite transponders require a subscription service to function, similar to cellular and satellite phones. You'll either need to call the vendor or establish an account.

Make sure it is not easy to accidentally activate the emergency beacon mode (SOS). More than one news story has shown a rescue initiated from someone in no trouble at all. The reason it happened is the transponder's SOS switch was inadvertently activated. You don't want expensive helicopters scrambled due to your toothbrush clicking the SOS button.

ADVENTURE EXPEDITION ONE

Reading user reviews and understanding your device's limitations is important. If you are using this device as your last hope of communication throughout the world, make sure it's something that will keep functioning after some abuse.

Personal locator beacons

Popular with sailors, personal locator beacons (PLBs) are an emergency communication option as well. You may need to register your particular device with a service. There are different PLB services around the world, so you will need to research them for your use.

Short-distance radios (VHF, UHF, marine)

Handheld, vehicle, or boat-mounted radios are handy for short-range communication in the field. They are useful for communicating with nearby teams or a climbing base camp. The proliferation of inexpensive radios available at mass retailers means that nearly any team of people can have a good communication system.

CB (citizen's band) hand-held radios are also still available. They've lost their popularity compared to smaller and less expensive units. The one advantage to CBs is that the communication channels are not as crowded as with consumer radios.

One of the primary difficulties with these types of radios is their inability to communicate over significant distances. They can only communicate when there is a line of sight between the transmitter and receiver.

The same is true for marine VHF radios as well. They typically have far more power than handheld units, meaning they can transmit far greater distances. Add the increased power to the significant advantage of a mast-mounted antenna, and a boat can communicate twenty-five miles or farther.

A major failing of consumer radios is channel clogging. If multiple teams attempt to communicate on the same channel it may be impossible to understand each other due to interference. There is no privacy on basic radios. Anyone can listen in to the conversation. If important or sensitive information is to be relayed,

Equipment

consider more complicated units. Since anyone can purchase a consumer radio, the communication can be jammed inadvertently or intentionally.

Long-distance radios (HF, shortwave, longwave)

More powerful long-distance shortwave radios make communication possible over distances of a thousand miles or more. Often, these radios require a ground station and power in order to transmit long distances. Vehicle-based HF (high frequency) units make communicating far away possible, too. The Amundsen-Scott station at the South Pole has an over-the-horizon HF antenna capable of transmitting nearly anywhere on Earth.

All of these types of radios require a license. The license requirements are primarily dependent on operation frequency and power. Anyone can listen in, but only a licensed operator is allowed to transmit. The laws determining operator permits vary significantly between countries.

Power

The major challenges with remote communication are:

Power and battery life
Equipment fragility
Cost

In order to use any modern communication device, some sort of power source is necessary. Each phone, transponder, and radio will have its own type of battery. Few devices rely solely on AA or 9V batteries. There may be a secondary power pack to recharge the device.

The various battery chemistries dramatically impact performance. All batteries suffer from the effects of cold. Even the most advanced lithium and lithium-polymer batteries do not deliver as much power when cold, though they will operate down to $-40°$ F. Nickel metal-hydride (NiMH) will operate with reduced power delivery in sub-zero temperatures. Alkaline batteries will fail quickly in extremely cold environments. Be aware of flying restrictions with these batteries.

Adventure Expedition One

If you have the convenience of a base camp, a gasoline generator or large solar panel installation may be worth considering. Both have their advantages and drawbacks. Consult the manufacturer for more information.

Online and social media communication

There are many ways to share your expedition with followers, supporters, and sponsors. If it fits your purposes, the most common method is to create a dedicated website to the expedition. Here you can keep calendars, updates, and any important public information.

Creating an effective, engaging website is as much an art as it is a science. The philosophy of creating good websites changes from year to year. What works this year may be outmoded in three years. Expect that you'll need to make changes as you go.

You may need to invest a significant amount of resources to create and maintain a website. Unless you are proficient with web design, consider hiring the effort out. Given your high-priority responsibilities of training and connecting with sponsors, website management may overwhelm the number of hours you have available in a day.

Social networking sites are an excellent way to communicate with the people involved in your expedition. That said, be wary about relying on them for all of your communications. Should the site change its policies or make communication difficult, you will be in a pinch to redirect your efforts. Manage your online reputation ruthlessly. It takes little to ruin your reputation in the eyes of sponsors.

Remote Messaging

In the modern world of constant communication, many expeditions rely on an Internet blog or social media website in order to broadcast their news. It is arguably the easiest way to stay in contact and provide regular progress reports. The blog can be read by thousands (millions ideally!) and those people can comment, support, and provide valuable information to expeditions in the field.

One major challenge to staying connected to the Internet in the field is a stable data link. In far-off locations, there is no easily accessed Internet connectivity. As a consequence, radio and satellite

Equipment

communication must be relied on. Today's portable satellite hardware connects at low speeds, making transmission of media slow, unreliable, and expensive. Sending a lengthy, quality video from the field via satellite is exceedingly difficult.

Low-resolution pictures can be sent via satellite with relative ease. However, this requires a compatible phone, tablet, or laptop. Carrying this additional technology has several downsides. The team must carry additional weight in delicate equipment and batteries. Typing messages can consume needed sleep time. Typing on a touchscreen in the extreme cold is laborious and puts fingers at risk of frostbite.

One trick to reduce the burden of communication is to have a person transcribe audio communications back home. This reduces the burden on the expedition team. Send a voice message to a recording service and have the home team do the rest. Speaking the message eliminates worries about typing, grammar, etc. Lying in one's sleeping bag while talking on a satellite phone requires little effort. The audio recordings can be useful for future films and media activities.

Writing coherent, well-edited material from the field is difficult. A raging storm will hamper anyone from writing well. Typos may give the mistaken impression that your team is incompetent or careless. Have someone at home edit the text so you make your sponsors and yourself look good.

Recording the experience of the expedition

Along with the advantages of digital recording of an expedition, there are some significant downsides. Although the modern world expects instant communication, permanency and integrity are major problems. Digital recording devices can be easily erased.

Consider a hand-written journal. It does not corrupt or break, nor can it be hacked. Using a combination of waterproof paper and a waterproof pen, you can reliably record the experience. You can then hire someone to transcribe the journal when you return if your handwriting is legible.

I made a terrible mistake and lost my climbing journal on a flight home from Alaska. This was the first and, up to that point, the only time I had pulled it out of my bag during the flight. While in Seattle, I had to unexpectedly exit the plane. In the rush, I left the journal in the seat back pocket. By the time I realized it in the terminal, the cleaning crew had come through and it was gone.

Journals have been the best way for me to document an expedition. Waterproof paper with waterproof ink is completely reliable. With a waterproof pen, I've written in the Sahara, in the Arctic, and in Antarctica. Unlike an electronic device, I can squash the journal and it won't break. There are no batteries to worry about, and it works to −40°F. If it's colder, I warm up the pen in my shirt for a minute. This works even at −70°F. The only way this recording method can fail is if I lose it. When I return to Internet connectivity, I use my smartphone to photograph each page of the journal. I email the images to myself and back it up with a cloud service. That way if something happens to the journal, I still have the content. —*AL*

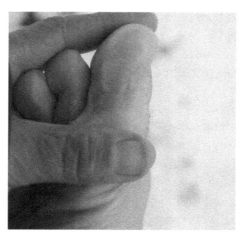

Proper foot maintenance will make or break your expedition.

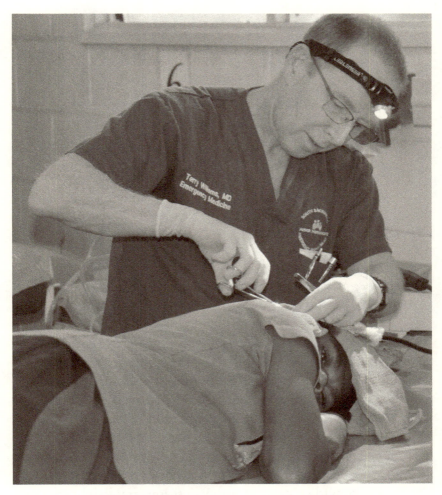
Terry performing surgery in the field.

PART EIGHT

Medical

Expedition medical issues

Terry M. Williams, MD
Emergency Medicine Specialist and Expedition Medical Doctor
American Board of Emergency Medicine (ABEM) Certified

Modern medical treatment is a constantly evolving field—recommended treatments and drug therapies are always being updated. All medical treatments discussed in this book must be evaluated using the most current information available in order to verify the recommended dose, the proper administration, warnings and, contraindications. It is always the responsibility of the licensed practitioner, relying on their training and knowledge of the patient, to determine the best treatment and proper dosages for each individual. Neither the publisher nor the authors assume any liability for any injury or illness related to the medical discussions in this publication.

Introduction

Being self-sufficient on a long expedition far away from medical help can be challenging. Your team's confidence will be greatly

MEDICAL

bolstered by the way that all of you plan, train, study, and research important issues together during the preparatory phase of your expedition. Neglecting medical training and planning will put yourself and your teammates at unnecessary risk. Enlist professional help if you need to.

The following sections will cover some of the medical issues that can arise on an expedition. You need to consider each as you plan and gather your equipment. Answer the questions below to improve your confidence that you're prepared for a major expedition.

- What medical problems can you expect to encounter in your expedition environment?
- What are the team members' pre-existing medical conditions?
- How do you prepare for predictable illness or injury that your team may face?
- How will you handle the special needs of elderly or child team members?
- Are you ready to handle the unique issues that female team members face?
- What level of first aid and wilderness medicine knowledge and expertise will you and your team be able to bring with you?

Planning for medical issues

A reliable and comprehensive resource for area-specific travel medicine recommendations is the Centers for Disease Control website, http://wwwnc.cdc.gov/Travel

Many health plans now offer consultation with a travel medicine clinic. Often done over the phone with a nurse who can review current recommendations, they can tailor recommendations to your specific health and medication history. They can order recommended vaccines, preventative treatments, and other medications for you to pick up at the pharmacy and/or receive at an injection clinic. If this service is available to you, take advantage of it.

ADVENTURE EXPEDITION ONE

Make sure you are up-to-date on routine vaccines before every trip. These vaccines include measles-mumps-rubella (MMR) vaccine, diphtheria-tetanus-pertussis vaccine, varicella (chickenpox) vaccine, polio vaccine, and your yearly flu shot. Keeping these up to date not only prevents serious disease but also means you will not have to seek out a tetanus booster if you sustain a laceration or bite on your trip.

In some areas, your travel medicine consultant will recommend vaccines for regional-specific risks such as hepatitis A (can be contracted through contaminated water), typhoid, hepatitis B, encephalitis, meningitis, or yellow fever. Medication to prevent malaria will be recommended in at-risk areas, along with measures to avoid mosquito (and other insect vectors) bites.

If your expedition puts you at risk of rabies exposure (contact with high-risk animals, caving), pre-exposure rabies vaccine may be recommended. If rabies exposure occurs while you are on your expedition, you will still need two more doses post-exposure. The pre-exposure vaccine reduces your risk and simplifies the process. Many of these vaccines and medications need to be given before your trip, so start working on this at least three months before your departure date.

Rabies

Avoid the common desire to pet or handle "house pets" such as dogs, cats, or other animals while traveling. Americans have become used to considering the risk of rabies as almost non-existent in pets. However, rabies may be very common in dogs encountered in rural villages. In northern India for example, 20 percent to 70 percent of dogs tested in recent years were positive for rabies. More than one-third of the world's rabies deaths occur in India each year, most of those when children come into contact with infected dogs.

Any exposure to a dog's saliva in an area like northern India, even being licked by a dog, will necessitate treatment for rabies exposure with wound care and a series of injections that will likely impact your trip plans. If you are planning

MEDICAL

extended travel to an area with high rabies risk (mostly Asia and Africa), your travel consultant most likely will recommend pre-exposure rabies prophylaxis. This series of shots does not complete your treatment in case of exposure. You will still need additional injections after you are exposed, so avoiding contact with potentially rabid animals remains very important.

Pre-existing chronic illness

Team members may have chronic illnesses such as diabetes or high blood pressure and may not be sure about how to handle problems when they arise. If anyone does have a chronic illness, they need to plan ahead with their doctor to discuss trip plans and answer questions.

Some illnesses may make your planned trip too risky. Discuss these risk factors with your doctor. For example, your mother with mild heart failure does well at sea level, having only minimal symptoms with exercise. She wants to join your two-hundred-mile trek through the High Sierra. Her doctor will be able to discuss the unique risks she would experience by exerting herself at altitude and let her know that particular trip is not appropriate for her.

The luggage that never arrived
While serving as ship's physician on a cruise, I saw several irate passengers on the first day of my clinic that needed their medications (and more!) replaced. It turned out that while one of the palates of luggage was being loaded aboard some of the suitcases toppled into the water and sank! So it isn't only the airlines that lose track of luggage. —*TW*

Make sure every team member brings all of their personal prescription medications and has enough for the entire trip. Never put

ADVENTURE EXPEDITION ONE

personal prescription medications in checked luggage—it may never arrive. If you need personal medical equipment (e.g. a glucometer), make sure it is in good working order and carry spare batteries (if traveling to a cold environment, buy lithium batteries). It is easy to make mistakes with medications and devices, as people are used to having access to help.

Four days into the approach hike to one of the Seven Summits, an older member of our expedition approached me in camp to let me know that he had diabetes and his glucometer had stopped working. He was exercising far more than normal and sometimes felt lightheaded on the trail. He was concerned that his blood sugar was getting too low. He reasoned that he should stop taking all of his diabetes medication, thinking that it was less dangerous for him to let his sugar run too high rather than too low.

His thinking was sound up to a point. I was very glad that he checked with me before he stopped his medication! On further questioning, it turned out that he was not having any clear symptoms that would indicate low blood sugar. More likely, his mild symptoms were from the altitude and exertion.

I had the chance to explain to him that stopping his medication could lead to a hyperglycemic (high blood sugar) diabetic emergency. In the remote environment we were in, that would be highly dangerous. We had no way to effectively deal with it in the field. It would require a trip-ending evacuation off the mountain. In the end, he was willing to settle on a dosage adjustment with some precautions and enjoyed the remainder of the climb. —*TW*

Traveler's diarrhea

Safe water and food is always a concern. Not much ruins a trip more quickly than the rapid onset of uncontrollable diarrhea and/or

MEDICAL

vomiting. A few precautions will go a long way toward keeping you fit for the expedition. Safe water and food is expected and taken for granted in low-risk countries, but you may be traveling to a higher-risk area.

Traveler's diarrhea risk worldwide:

- Low-risk countries include the United States, Canada, Australia, New Zealand, Japan, and countries in northern and western Europe.
- Intermediate-risk countries include those in eastern Europe, South Africa, and some of the Caribbean islands.
- High-risk areas include most of Asia, the Middle East, Africa, Mexico, and Central and South America.

In areas of the world where the water is not reliably safe food can be a danger, too. The recommendation in suspect areas is to only drink bottled or treated water and only eat food that is freshly cooked and steaming hot. The simple recommendation has been summarized as "boil it, cook it, peel it, or forget it." Eggs should be hard-cooked. Eat only fruits and vegetables you have washed in clean water (rinsed in a weak bleach solution) or peeled yourself. Only pasteurized dairy products are safe to eat if handled properly.

Don't eat food served at room temperature, food from street vendors, raw or soft-cooked (runny) eggs, raw or undercooked (rare) meat or fish, unwashed or unpeeled raw fruits and vegetables, unpasteurized dairy products, or "bushmeat" (monkeys, bats, or other wild game). It is okay to drink bottled water that is sealed, water that has been disinfected, ice made with bottled or disinfected water, carbonated drinks, steaming hot coffee or tea, or pasteurized milk. Don't drink tap or well water, ice made with tap or well water, drinks made with tap or well water (such as reconstituted juice), or unpasteurized milk. Carry a small container of alcohol-based hand sanitizer (containing 60 percent or more alcohol) and use it frequently.

Do you become "used to" or develop resistance to contaminated food or water? This is a common but mistaken belief. In short-term

ADVENTURE EXPEDITION ONE

travelers, bouts of traveler's diarrhea do not protect against future attacks. It is common for more than one episode of traveler's diarrhea to occur during a single trip.

A study of longer-term expatriates residing in Kathmandu, Nepal, showed that they experienced an average of more than three episodes of traveler's diarrhea per person in their first year. It makes no sense to try to "inoculate" yourself with the local water. Be as careful as you can with food and water, but be prepared. No matter how careful you are, you are likely to become sick at some point while overseas.

Traveler's diarrhea is the most predictable travel-related illness. From 30 to 70 percent of travelers will come down with it, depending on the destination and season of travel. Traditionally, it was thought that following the safe food and water rules above can prevent traveler's diarrhea. Studies have found that people who follow these rules may still become ill. So what do you do if you develop diarrhea? Preparation and having your medications with you is key, along with being meticulously careful about safe food and water.

Three different types of germs can cause traveler's diarrhea: bacteria, viruses, and protozoa. The most common culprit is bacteria, with current thinking that 80 to 90 percent of traveler's diarrhea is caused by bacteria. Both bacterial and viral traveler's diarrhea cause the sudden onset of bothersome symptoms that can range from mild cramps and urgent loose stools to severe abdominal pain, fever, vomiting, and bloody diarrhea. With norovirus (famous for recent outbreaks on cruise ships) vomiting may be more prominent. Protozoal diarrhea, such as that caused by *Giardia intestinalis* or *E. histolytica*, generally has a more gradual onset of less severe symptoms, with two to five loose stools per day.

The incubation period can be a clue to the cause of traveler's diarrhea:

- Bacterial and viral infections have an incubation period of 6–72 hours.
- Protozoal infections generally have an incubation period of 1–2 weeks and rarely cause symptoms in the first few weeks

MEDICAL

of travel. (There are exceptions such as *Cyclospora cayetanensis*, which can present quickly in areas of high risk.)

- Untreated bacterial diarrhea lasts 3–7 days. Viral diarrhea generally lasts 2–3 days. Protozoal diarrhea can persist for weeks to months without treatment.

What is commonly known as "food poisoning" involves the ingestion of preformed toxins in food. In this syndrome, vomiting and diarrhea may both be present, but symptoms usually resolve spontaneously within twelve hours. The main clue that it is food poisoning is that several people who ate at the same table become sick simultaneously. If you suspect food poisoning, the best strategy is to use an antiemetic (anti-vomiting medicine) such as ondansetron (Zofran), if needed, along with oral rehydration. The good news is that you should feel better within twelve hours or so.

I have contracted food poisoning several times over many years of travel. One of the most unexpected was from a breakfast buffet in Ireland. During the illness, I thought about how the food looked. In hindsight, the fruit containers had little fruit and a lot of juice while the meat and eggs didn't seem fresh.

After discussing it with my companion, we concluded that the buffet leftovers were put in a refrigerator and served the next day. The yogurt that I ate (my companion didn't have it) was likely the culprit. It didn't look right but tasted fine. I surmised it was shaken. It was probably allowed to warm up for hours and then placed back in the refrigerator at the end of the service. Humans will convince themselves of anything.

I failed to trust my instincts. It's easy to become complacent in western countries. This incident was similar to what happened to me in Egypt (train food) and Budapest, Hungary (unknown source). The food poisoning in Egypt took twenty minutes to develop. The Hungarian poisoning took a few hours

ADVENTURE EXPEDITION ONE

> but the results were all the same. I vomited violently every twenty minutes for eight straight hours.
>
> As a consequence, I no longer eat yogurt in hotels no matter where I am, even at five-star establishments. I'm never sure how well dairy products are handled. —*AL*

Antimotility agents are drugs that slow down the spastic contractions of your bowel and provide symptomatic relief of traveler's diarrhea. Synthetic opiates, such as Imodium (loperamide) and diphenoxylate (combined with a drug called atropine with the brand name Lomotil), can reduce the frequency of bowel movements and enable travelers to ride on an airplane or bus while waiting for antibiotics to clear the infection. Loperamide appears to also work by reducing your intestine's output of fluid.

The safety of loperamide, when used along with an antibiotic, has been well established. Loperamide can be used in children, and liquid formulations are available. In practice, however, these drugs are rarely given to small children (aged less than six years). If an adult comes down with diarrhea, the first thing to do is take an initial dose of Imodium (loperamide), two capsules of 2 mg each for a total of 4 mg. You repeat a dose of one capsule (2 mg) each time you have diarrhea as needed until it stops (maximum 16 mg/day, so you can repeat that 2 mg dose six times after the initial 4 mg dose). Most travelers with uncomplicated traveler's diarrhea will find that their symptoms are much improved or gone after just one or two doses of loperamide, along with prompt antibiotic treatment.

It turns out that 80 to 90 percent of traveler's diarrhea is caused by bacteria, and only 5 to 8 percent is caused by viruses. Protozoal infections are slower to manifest symptoms and collectively account for approximately 10 percent of diagnoses in longer-term travelers. No vaccines are available for most of the germs that cause traveler's diarrhea. There are vaccines that can prevent other foodborne or waterborne infections to which travelers are prone, such as hepatitis A, typhoid, and paratyphoid fever.

MEDICAL

Your travel consultant will also provide you with an antibiotic to use, if needed, for traveler's diarrhea. When do you take the antibiotic? The short answer is promptly. It is reasonable to try one or two doses of Imodium, but if diarrhea doesn't stop promptly, if it is severe or bloody, or if it is accompanied by fever, use the antibiotic right away.

Bacterial causes of traveler's diarrhea far outnumber other microbial causes, thus early treatment with an antibiotic for the common causes remains the best therapy for traveler's diarrhea. The benefit of treating traveler's diarrhea with antibiotics has been proven in numerous studies.

The usual first-line antibiotics include fluoroquinolones, such as Ciprofloxacin (Cipro) or levofloxacin. Increasing microbial resistance to fluoroquinolones has been noted in some regions. A potential alternative to the fluoroquinolones in these situations is azithromycin but resistance to this choice is also becoming a problem. The antibiotic that your travel consultant recommends will take into account the region you are traveling to, your age and medical history, and other medications that you are taking.

The antibiotic is not taken for long. A single-dose or one-day therapy for traveler's diarrhea with a fluoroquinolone has been shown to work well. The best schedule for taking azithromycin treatment is still being worked out. One study used a single dose of 1,000 mg, but side-effects (mainly nausea) may limit the acceptability of this large dose. Azithromycin, 500 mg taken once daily for one to three days, appears to be effective in most cases of traveler's diarrhea.

Your doctor might recommend a preventative treatment for traveler's diarrhea that does not use a prescription antibiotic. One recommended non-antibiotic prevention strategy is to use bismuth subsalicylate, which is the active ingredient in Pepto-Bismol. Studies from Mexico have shown that this agent (taken daily as either 2 oz. of liquid or two chewable tablets four times per day) reduces the incidence of traveler's diarrhea by approximately 50 percent. However, because of the number of tablets required and the inconvenient dosing, this is less commonly used as prophylaxis for traveler's diarrhea.

The use of probiotics has been studied in the prevention of traveler's diarrhea in small numbers of people. Results are inconclusive and this cannot yet be recommended. Active prevention is still the most effective option.

Is it possible to take antibiotics as a preventative strategy (prophylactic antibiotic therapy)? Prophylactic antibiotics are effective in the prevention of some traveler's diarrhea. On the positive side, medical studies have shown that diarrhea attack rates are reduced by about 90 percent by the prophylactic use of antibiotics. The prophylactic antibiotic of choice has changed over the past few decades as resistance patterns have evolved.

Agents such as Septra (trimethoprim-sulfamethoxazole) and doxycycline are no longer considered effective antimicrobial agents against the common intestinal germs. Cipro is the most commonly used drug and has been the most effective antibiotic for the prophylaxis and treatment of bacterial traveler's diarrhea, but increasing resistance may limit its effectiveness in the future. Cipro also has the potential side-effect of tendinitis and tendon ruptures. On strenuous trips, this can be a major concern.

At this time, prophylactic antibiotics are not recommended for most travelers because of the following factors:

- Prophylactic antibiotics afford no protection against nonbacterial pathogens and can remove normally protective microorganisms from the bowel, which could make a traveler more susceptible to infection with resistant bacterial pathogens.
- A traveler relying on prophylactic antibiotics still needs to carry an alternative antibiotic to use in case diarrhea develops despite prophylaxis.
- The use of antibiotics may be associated with allergic or adverse reactions in a certain percentage of travelers and may potentially contribute to drug resistance.

The use of prophylactic antibiotics should be weighed against the result of using prompt, early self-treatment with antibiotics when traveler's diarrhea occurs, which can limit the duration of illness to 6–24 hours in most cases. Notable exceptions: prophylactic antibiotics may be considered for short-term travelers who are high-risk (such

MEDICAL

as those who are immune-suppressed) or who are taking critical trips (such as engaging in a sporting event) during which even a short bout of diarrhea could affect the outcome.

Treatment of traveler's diarrhea caused by protozoa

The most common parasitic cause of traveler's diarrhea is *Giardia intestinalis*, and several treatment options are available, most commonly metronidazole (Flagyl). Cyclosporiasis is treated with trimethoprim-sulfamethoxazole (Septra). Treatment of amebiasis is with metronidazole or tinidazole, followed by treatment with a luminal agent such as iodoquinol or paromomycin. Luminal agents stay inside the bowel lumen (hence the name) and help to eradicate infection by eliminating immature parasites within the bowel.

If you have persistent traveler's diarrhea that has not cleared with the usual antibiotic therapy, you have to sort out which resistant organism or parasite you have with a laboratory test to accurately determine the cause and specific treatment. This is a situation where you will have to seek more advanced medical help.

Oral Rehydration Therapy

Fluids and electrolytes are lost in a bout of traveler's diarrhea, and replenishment is important, especially in young children or adults with chronic medical illness. In adult travelers who are otherwise healthy, fluid losses can successfully be replaced orally—severe dehydration resulting from traveler's diarrhea is unusual unless vomiting is prolonged and fluids cannot be replaced. Replacement of fluid losses helps you feel better more quickly. Remember to use only beverages that are sealed, treated with chlorine, adequately filtered, boiled, or are otherwise known to be purified.

For severe fluid loss, replacement is best accomplished with an oral rehydration solution, prepared from packaged oral rehydration salts, such as those provided by the World Health Organization. Oral rehydration solution is widely available at stores and pharmacies in most developing countries. It is prepared by adding one packet to the indicated volume of boiled or treated water—generally one liter. Travelers may find most oral rehydration solution formulations to be

171

ADVENTURE EXPEDITION ONE

relatively unpalatable, due to their saltiness. In mild cases, rehydration can be maintained with any palatable liquid (including sports drinks), although overly sugary drinks, such as sodas, can cause a worsening of diarrhea if consumed in large quantities.

If vomiting is interfering with rehydration, use an anti-vomiting (antiemetic) medicine such as ondansetron (Zofran). This is easy to take (you don't even have to swallow the pill—it is available as a dissolving tablet that melts on your tongue) and works well for most people. In severe cases where vomiting does not stop and dehydration cannot be corrected orally, intravenous therapy will be needed.

> If you don't have access to oral rehydration solution packets, here are a couple of easy recipes:
> Add 1 teaspoon of salt and 2 to 3 tablespoons of sugar to 1 liter of purified water.
> or:
> Mix 1 cup of orange juice (or other fruit juice) with 3 cups of water, and add 1 teaspoon of salt. Remember, the juice and water need to be safe!

Traveler's diarrhea in children

Children who accompany their parents on trips to high-risk destinations can contract traveler's diarrhea as well. There is no reason to withhold antibiotics from children who contract traveler's diarrhea unless they have drug allergies or are taking medications that may interact with the antibiotic. Consult your doctor before departing.

In older children and teenagers, treatment recommendations for traveler's diarrhea are the same as those for adults, but with appropriate adjustments in the dosage of medication. Among younger children, azithromycin is usually the first antibiotic choice, although some experts now use a short course of Cipro therapy (although this is not FDA-approved for this use in children) for travelers aged less than 18 years. Rifaximin is approved for use in children aged 12 and over. Again, consult your doctor for the best recommendation for your child.

MEDICAL

Infants and younger children with traveler's diarrhea are at higher risk for developing dehydration, so it is critical to start oral rehydration early—just wait a brief period for vomiting to calm down. Zofran can be used to treat vomiting in children and can help correct dehydration in the vomiting child so that you can avoid having to resort to intravenous therapy.

How much rehydration solution do you give? For children under two years, give 50–100 ml (¼ to ½ cup) after each episode of diarrhea; for children between two and nine years, give 100–200 ml (½ to 1 cup) after each episode of diarrhea; for children over ten years and adults; give as much as wanted, up to approximately 2 L (8½ cups) a day.

If you can't recall these amounts, don't worry. It's best to give fluids in a liberal amount that the child will tolerate. Breastfed infants should continue to nurse on demand, and bottle-fed infants can continue to drink formula. Older infants, children, and adults should be encouraged to eat and may consume a regular diet. This actually helps the gut to recover more quickly and the normal salt content in foods is helpful to replace losses. Children in diapers are at risk of developing diaper rash on their buttocks in response to the liquid stool. Barrier creams, such as zinc oxide or petrolatum, should be applied at the onset of diarrhea to help prevent and treat a rash.

Serious illness or injury in the field

If you are traveling in a group, you should have at minimum two members of the team with proper first-aid training. Obviously, if you are planning a solo trip, you are the sole resource. After all, part of the attraction of planning a solo adventure is the challenge of facing whatever happens on your own and rising to that challenge. But if you are in a group, what if the one trained person is the one who is injured or lost and they are no longer able to help? Having at least two trained members provides another margin of safety.

173

ADVENTURE EXPEDITION ONE

One of the great self-rescue stories in the annals of adventure is the story of Steven Callahan, who spent 76 days adrift in a small life raft after his sailboat suddenly sank in the eastern Atlantic. His epic story of the constant battle to keep his little raft afloat and survive on the most minimal rations of food and water makes riveting reading in his book *Adrift*.

He knew that he could expect no rescue and he would have to rely solely on himself in order to survive. He made fresh water with solar stills, but this critical piece of equipment kept malfunctioning and he had to limit his water intake to the minimum that would keep him alive. A small school of dorado fish (known as Mahi Mahi in Hawaii) followed in the shade of his raft and were his salvation. When he caught a fresh fish, he craved water so much that he found great pleasure in eating the fish's eyes and feeling the liquid from them soothe his parched mouth.

Self-rescue and first aid are the first steps in dealing with an illness or injury on your expedition. What if your group is in a remote area and someone is ill or injured beyond what you can care for in the field? It is time to put your evacuation plan into action. Develop your plan ahead of time, taking into account the details of your trip.

- How isolated or remote will you be?
- How will you call for help (satellite phone, cell phone, radio, sending a healthy member on foot)?
- What emergency transport options are available (strong porters with back slings, carried litters, rolling litters, helicopter, fixed wing, boat, ambulance)?
- Keep in mind that search and rescue organizations usually feel that a minimum of six rescuers is needed to transport one non-ambulatory victim by carried litter.

Once transported out of the wilderness, what are the capabilities of local healthcare facilities? You may be in an area where you want

MEDICAL

to insist on further evacuation to more capable medical facilities. Ask yourself if you want to risk a team member or myself by having surgery here? Or would it be safer to travel on to a more capable facility?

Research ahead of time and carry a list of local doctors and hospitals near your destination. Review your health insurance plan to determine what medical services it will cover during your trip. Consider purchasing travel health and medical evacuation insurance—a medical evacuation can end up costing tens of thousands of dollars. Carry a card that identifies, in the local language, each expedition member's blood type, chronic conditions or serious allergies, and the generic names of any medications they take.

Consider that some prescription drugs may be *illegal* in other countries. Contact the local embassy to verify that all of your prescription(s) are legal to bring with you. In some countries, medicine (prescription and over-the-counter) may be substandard or counterfeit (in suspect areas, you want to avoid having to buy medicines locally). Bring all medicines (including over-the-counter medicines) you think you might need during your trip, including extra in case of travel delays. Have your doctor help you get prescriptions filled early if you need to. Many foreign hospitals and clinics are accredited by the Joint Commission International and a list of accredited facilities is available at their website at https://www.jointcommissioninternational.org/about-jci/jci-accredited-organizations.

The National Outdoor Leadership School (NOLS) offers a wilderness first aid course, and more advanced courses designed to train wilderness first-responders. If you have no medical training, their first aid course is a great place to start. https://www.nols.edu/en/courses/wilderness-medicine/

Mental preparation

Knowing that you are well trained to meet the physical challenges you will face is your biggest factor in being mentally prepared. As

ADVENTURE EXPEDITION ONE

we just discussed, thinking through how you will handle medical emergencies is also critical. But there will be other mental and psychological factors to think about and begin working through as you plan your expedition.

Are you going solo? How will you deal with fatigue, fear, loneliness, stress, discouragement, and anxiety? How will you control your emotions if you are alone and become sick or injured? Hallucinations? Talking to yourself? All of these are common and foreseeable, so think it through ahead of time. It may help to discuss your thoughts with other experienced adventurers or write your thoughts down. Train for these situations mentally just as you have physically.

Go on a "shakedown" trip to test not only your equipment and physical preparation but also your mental readiness. Make the conditions mimic your expedition as closely as you can—similar altitude, weather, and physical challenges. If your solo trip will last a month, make the shakedown trip last at least a week—long enough to begin to experience some of these challenges.

Are you going with a group? Think through some of the group dynamics. Do expedition members know each other well before the trip? How well are they likely to get along? Are cliques forming and will that be a problem? Will romances develop that may be disruptive (or a pleasant surprise)? Will the top performers show patience toward slower or weaker members? Is there a group member who has scheduled travel so tightly that it might jeopardize the success of the entire group?

The trip leader will need to have a contingency plan in case the team needs to be split into faster and slower groups. How will the leader keep the team functioning well and communicating well? Given all the competing demands on our schedules, it is much more difficult to do a shakedown trip for a group expedition, but for a major trip, you may want to consider making it a requirement before your actual expedition.

Special considerations for women

You want to anticipate problems and plan for them rather than to address them for the first time in difficult conditions. There are few

MEDICAL

known gender-specific disadvantages when it comes to adaptation to extreme environments. For example, there is no difference in the incidence of acute mountain sickness between men and women. However, when it comes to adaptation to hot environments, females have a lower sweat rate than males and rely more on size differences and circulatory mechanisms for heat dissipation.

Due in part to these factors, females have been found to adapt to hot moist environments more easily than men, and men adapt more quickly to hot dry environments because of their higher sweat rate. However, with similar acclimatization and physical training, women are able to generate a similar sweat response to men and tolerate hot dry environments just as well. Because they need more time to mount this acclimatization response, it has been recommended that women planning an expedition to a hot dry environment allow a one- to two-week acclimatization period.

In somewhat cold environments, women tend to adapt better than men, partly because of thicker subcutaneous fat. In a more extreme cold, women may be at some disadvantage because of a lower muscle mass (on average), which serves to insulate and also generate heat during exercise. But overall adaptation to extreme cold seems to depend more on body size, physical fitness, and degree of acclimatization rather than gender.

However, there are some unique practical needs that should be planned for. For example, a menstruating woman's diet needs to be richer in iron, calcium, folate, and other vitamins than a man's in order to replace the regular blood loss and meet other nutritional needs. Vaginal infections and menstrual disorders, although not serious, are decidedly uncomfortable and may require treatment.

Women more commonly contract urinary tract infections and medication for treatment should be included in your kit. If sexually active on the expedition, contraception and prevention of sexually transmitted diseases should be planned for. And there is that practical gender-specific nuisance of needing some type of urinal guide if prolonged periods of bad weather are anticipated. A device called a Freshette, also known as a feminine urinary director, more commonly known as a pee funnel, is available. However, it is useless

ADVENTURE EXPEDITION ONE

in extremely cold environments such as polar regions because of rapid freezing.

In some regions of the world, special planning, precautions and security measures may be needed because of the increased danger to women from assault or sexual assault.

There are many special needs during pregnancy that are beyond the scope of this book. For example, pregnant women adjust to altitude more slowly and are more prone to severe altitude sickness. Pregnant women have more difficulty acclimatizing to hot humid environments and prolonged exposure to such an environment can be harmful to the fetus. Any pregnant woman should have a candid discussion with her obstetrician before planning to participate in an expedition—most likely they will ask you to wait until after your pregnancy.

Example of supplies for a woman's expedition hygiene and medical kit	Basic toiletries: soap, towel, toothbrush, toothpaste, dental floss, comb
Cotton underwear	Toilet paper in a plastic bag
Tampons and/or sanitary napkins in a plastic bag	Moisturizing lotion for chapped skin, lip balm, Vaseline (for severely chapped or cracked skin), skin adhesive or superglue
Freshette or pee funnel	Moist wipes (for cleaning up when water is limited)
Powder such as Gold Bond when facilities for personal hygiene are limited	Multivitamin with iron, calcium supplement
Acetaminophen for pain or a headache	Ibuprofen or similar non-steroidal anti-inflammatory medication for menstrual pain

MEDICAL

Zofran (Ondansetron) for nausea or vomiting (prescription item)	Cipro for urinary tract infection or traveler's diarrhea (prescription item)
Imodium for traveler's diarrhea	Miconazole cream or suppository or oral fluconazole (prescription item) for vaginal yeast infection
Metronidazole (tablets or vaginal gel) or clindamycin vaginal gel (prescription items) for bacterial vaginosis	Urine pregnancy test kit if needed
Conjugated estrogen (Premarin) or Medroxyprogesterone acetate for treatment of abnormal menstrual bleeding (prescription items)	

Special considerations for children

Wilderness travel with children places special demands on the child and parents, but also provides unique opportunities for a shared experience that will hold special significance for all. There are many obvious differences in the young expedition member. They are smaller and not able to carry heavy loads or travel as far or fast as their adult teammates. Their thermoregulation is not as robust and they will have a more difficult time in extremely hot or cold environments.

Children are more sensitive to sunburn and will need more carefully applied and re-applied sunscreen. Their requirements for rest, food, and drink are different and more frequent. Young children are more prone to becoming dehydrated if they become ill with diarrhea, vomiting, or high fever. They will require more supervision than adult teammates in order to ensure their safety (e.g. near cliffs, bodies of water, dangerous animals, etc.).

ADVENTURE EXPEDITION ONE

They are more prone to bite injuries and rabies exposure in high-risk areas because of their natural tendency to approach animals and risk being bitten on the head or neck. For these reasons, the CDC recommends pre-exposure rabies vaccines for children traveling to high-risk areas.

Preparing for travel with your child will involve much of the same preparation that you have already undertaken. You will want to meet with your pediatrician or travel consultant to make sure vaccines are up to date and to receive any region-specific recommended vaccines. You can also pick up prescription medications for traveler's diarrhea, malaria prevention (if appropriate), and other region-specific recommended treatments.

Talk with your pediatrician about the most appropriate oral rehydration strategy geared toward your child's age. Discuss any special medical needs or allergy problems your child has and make sure all of your questions are answered. Prepare your child emotionally for being away from home, and away from you if he or she is traveling with another family. Talk about how he or she will feel. Practice with short periods of separation before the big trip.

Families traveling with infants need to be particularly vigilant in monitoring their baby's health. Infants can become hypothermic (low body temperature), hyperthermic (abnormally high body temperature), become dehydrated, or develop serious infection more rapidly than older children or adults. Any fever over 100.4°F (38°C) in an infant younger than three months of age requires evacuation to a medical facility for evaluation.

Examples of supplies for a pediatric wilderness medical kit:

Basic supplies

- Identification and basic health information for the child, including health history and current medication use, allergies, blood type, weight

MEDICAL

- First-aid supplies—bandages, wound-cleaning supplies, antibiotic ointment, basic splinting materials, etc.
- Oral rehydration packets
- Sunscreen
- Insect repellent (less than 35 percent DEET)
- Age-appropriate emergency signaling device such as a whistle or air horn
- For infants—also include a bulb syringe, thermometer, diapers, and barrier cream (Desitin)

Medicines

Topical:

- Antibiotic ointment for wounds
- 1 percent hydrocortisone cream for itchy rashes or bites
- Antifungal cream (miconazole or clotrimazole) for yeast rash in the diaper area, groin, scalp, feet, ringworm
- Desitin cream for diaper area
- Permethrin (Elimite) for scabies or lice
- Antibiotic eye ointment for pink eye or eye (corneal) scratches (prescription item)

Oral:

- Oral medications should be brought as a liquid, chewable tablet, or tablets, depending on child's age. Discuss the appropriateness of use in your child and dosage with your pediatrician.
- Diphenhydramine for allergic symptoms, itching, motion sickness
- Dimenhydrinate (Dramamine) for motion sickness
- Acetaminophen for pain or fever
- Ibuprofen for pain or fever (avoid if vomiting)
- Claritin or Allegra for allergic symptoms
- Loperamide for diarrhea
- Oral rehydration salts

- Antibiotics appropriate for your child (discuss with your pediatrician). Might include amoxicillin, amoxicillin-clavulanate (Augmentin), azithromycin, ciprofloxacin. Make sure you understand when and how to use what your pediatrician prescribes.
- Ondansetron (Zofran) for vomiting
- Appropriate malaria prevention medication (discuss with your pediatrician)

Does your child need to carry an epinephrine autoinjector? (for severe allergic reactions)

High altitude prevention or treatment medications? (discuss with your pediatrician)

Special considerations for elderly expedition members

It is wonderful that so many people want to stay active and even adventurous as they age. The astronaut John Glenn was a heroic example, making a space flight aboard the space shuttle *Discovery* at age 77. The first American astronaut to orbit the earth became the oldest astronaut to fly in space. However, this wasn't undertaken without mental and physical preparation and meticulous planning.

Health risks associated with high-performance activities increase with age because physiological function declines, impairments can go unrecognized or under-appreciated, and chronic illness can take its toll. The degree of loss of physiologic function of our various organ systems can be approximated by the "one percent rule." Generally, we lose about one percent of our organ system functions yearly after about age thirty. However, this varies tremendously depending on genetics, the effects of chronic disease, and exercise and nutrition habits.

MEDICAL

We can each strive to have an impact on how gracefully we age and particularly how well we can perform on a strenuous expedition later in life. But it is important to temper our enthusiasm and be realistic about the risks we are willing to take given our limitations compared to when we were younger.

Elderly expedition members can have altered tolerance to hot environments because of multiple factors: chronic illness, medication affecting heat adaptation, altered thermoregulatory systems in the brain, vascular system and skin, metabolic disorders, heart disease, infrequent heat exposure, and more.

To prevent heat injury, elderly members of your team should first meet with their physician and discuss the planned activity to be sure it is appropriate given their health history. If cleared by their doctor, they should embark on a heat acclimatization program by exercising in a tolerably hot environment for about two weeks before the trip. Low-intensity exercise for 60 to 100 minutes daily at tolerable heat levels for seven to fourteen days before the trip can improve heat acclimatization. Other measures to reduce risk include maintaining adequate hydration and nutrition and avoiding the use of superfluous medication (good advice at any age). Estrogen replacement therapy for postmenopausal women (if indicated) can help with heat tolerance.

Cold exposure is more poorly tolerated and can be more risky among the elderly for several reasons. Heat conservation through the constriction of peripheral blood vessels is more sluggish; the metabolic rate is lower; and chronic diseases such as cardiovascular disease, diabetes, thyroid disease, and others can alter thermoregulation.

It has been known for a long time that cold exposure is one of the triggers of angina (heart pain) in patients with coronary disease. Cold exposure also worsens high blood pressure. Ultimately, prevention of cold injury is best achieved from learning through experience. Train by making shorter trips into the cold wilderness with a trusted partner so that you can acclimatize and test your clothing, equipment, and fitness.

ADVENTURE EXPEDITION ONE

Measures to prevent cold injury in older expedition members:

- Avoid exhaustion and limit exposure to the elements. Always have access to adequate shelter.
- Carry and wear adequate layers of clothing to stay warm and dry. When exerting yourself, avoid becoming wet through excessive sweating by adjusting your exertion level and clothing layers.
- Maintain adequate fluid and food intake (avoid consuming snow and ice-cold fluids if possible).
- Pre-expedition physical training and cold acclimatization.
- Avoid alcohol and unnecessary use of medication. Be aware of the effects of your essential medication.

Several physiological changes occur as we age that can adversely affect our adaptation to altitude, including changes in the oxygen transport in our lung alveolar membranes and changes in our hypoxic ventilatory drive. Many chronic diseases adversely affect our adaptation to altitude, including cardiovascular disease, pulmonary disease, diabetes, renal disease, and others. However, studies at altitude have shown that many elderly can still acclimatize well, particularly if they are physically fit and live at moderate altitude.

You should meet with your doctor to make sure you are well enough to exert yourself at altitude and to go over your chronic medications to see how they may affect your performance at altitude before your trip. Patients with significant heart or lung disease will be advised against exposing themselves to or exerting themselves at altitude. Other recommendations to prevent altitude illness in the elderly are similar to those for any age group but more conservative.

Avoid strenuous activity when you first ascend to altitude, particularly if you have a history of acute mountain sickness, cardiovascular disease, or lung disease. Avoid significant exertion for at least twelve hours after arrival at an altitude of 8,200 feet (2,500 meters). Limit your rate of ascent to no more than 1,000 feet (300 meters) daily and delay exertion at that new altitude for about twenty-four hours (schedule frequent rest days during ascent).

MEDICAL

Space limitations do not allow for an extended discussion of the ramifications of many of the other chronic diseases that can affect the elderly in the wilderness. However, a few words about medications in the elderly are important. As we age, we tend to need to take more medication and combinations of medication. Many of these medications can have interactions with each other and with our organ systems, which may increase or decrease their beneficial effects and/or side-effects. At the same time, the aging process affects the way our bodies absorb, bind, metabolize and eliminate medication. Because of these factors, the elderly should carefully review their medication with their physician at each visit, making sure that there are no unwanted interactions or duplications, and making sure that their medication regimen is as simplified as possible.

Examples of medication to avoid or use with an abundance of caution in the elderly:

Antihistamines (e.g. diphenhydramine or Benadryl) are commonly used to treat allergic symptoms and motion sickness and are also used as a "safe" sleep aid. However, in the elderly, clearance is reduced, and tolerance develops when used as a sleep aid. Additionally, there is an increased risk of confusion, increased risk of falls, dry mouth, constipation, and other negative effects.

Older adults have increased sensitivity to benzodiazepines (medicines like Valium) and decreased metabolism of long-acting drugs in this class. In general, all benzodiazepines increase the risk of cognitive impairment, delirium, falls, fractures, and motor vehicle crashes in older adults. The same holds true for other sedatives such as barbiturates.

Other sleep aids such as Ambien (zolpidem) have adverse effects similar to those of benzodiazepines in older adults (e.g. delirium, falls, fractures, increased emergency department

Adventure Expedition One

visits and hospitalizations, motor vehicle crashes) and they only minimally improve sleep!

NSAID (non-steroidal anti-inflammatory) medications like aspirin, ibuprofen, naproxen, and many others increase the risk of gastrointestinal bleeding or peptic ulcer disease in high-risk groups, including those aged more than 75 or taking other medication such as corticosteroids, anticoagulants, or antiplatelet agents. Upper gastrointestinal ulcers, gross bleeding, or perforation caused by NSAIDs occur in approximately one percent of patients treated for three to six months and in approximately two to four percent of patients treated for one year; these trends continue with longer duration of use. Adverse effects on the heart and kidneys also occur with NSAIDs. Patients are hospitalized and deaths occur every year from this class of medication, which many people erroneously consider completely safe.

Several other large categories of commonly used medication, such as antidepressants and antipsychotics can be dangerous to use in the elderly. Be careful, and discuss your medication use with your doctor.

On a climbing expedition, we were having dinner and preparing for our long summit climb, which was to begin at 11:00 p.m. with all of us climbing through the night, hoping to reach the summit by morning and then spend the following day descending. Our group leader announced at dinner that he was planning to take a sleeping pill so that he could nap for four hours or so before we got up to prepare for the climb. He reasoned that in the past the sleeping pill never affected him for longer than four hours, so he would be fine.

However, knowing the characteristics of the drug, its effects and metabolism, I explained to him that the drug

MEDICAL

would indeed still be affecting him, even if he didn't feel it was, and given his age (over 70), he was putting himself and the entire group at risk. He would have a higher risk of falling, with a potential resulting injury that would jeopardize summit day for everyone. And, to top it off, data shows that the sleeping pill he planned to take is minimally effective. Fortunately, he decided against using the medication. —*TW*

Common illnesses: colds and other respiratory symptoms

Viruses cause colds. Antibiotics designed to combat bacterial infections will do nothing for colds. There are many different cold viruses and this explains why we keep getting colds. Our immune system fights one off (and we develop immunity to that virus), but a few months later another variant comes along and we're sick again.

When we are young, we haven't been exposed to many of these viruses yet, so young children will normally have around six to ten colds a year. Because the illnesses may be clustered in the winter months, it seems like our kids are sick all the time. Later in life, our immune systems have seen much more, so we tend to get fewer colds each passing year—adults typically will have only two or three annually.

Healthcare professionals spend time every day explaining when to effectively use antibiotics . Antibiotics are not always needed to treat an infection. In fact, they are indicated in the minority of infections overall. There are several reasons for this. Your immune system is amazing and will clear many infections quickly and easily. Antibacterial drugs (antibiotics) only treat bacterial infections. They do nothing for infections caused by the other categories of "germs"—viruses, fungi, and parasites. There are antifungal drugs, a few antiviral drugs, and most parasitic infections are treated with specific drugs for those germs.

ADVENTURE EXPEDITION ONE

Inappropriate antibiotic use is rampant and has many downsides. The major problems include side-effects and allergic reactions that can be serious. Inappropriate use also promotes the emergence of antibiotic-resistant organisms, which has become an increasingly serious problem in recent years. Many people will swear that they need an antibiotic whenever they have a cold (caused by a virus). There's a saying in medicine that says, "If you take this antibiotic for your cold, you'll be better in seven days. If you don't, it'll clear up in about a week." Judicious use of such medication is critical.

There are several recommendations that will help lessen the miserable symptoms of a cold. If fever and aches (more common with other viruses such as influenza) or a painful sore throat are present, acetaminophen (Tylenol) or a non-steroidal anti-inflammatory drug (NSAID) such as ibuprofen (Motrin) will help.

Acetaminophen vs. NSAIDs

Over the years, I've fielded many questions about this. Which is better? Which is safer? It seems the advertising battle has been won by the makers of NSAIDs, but there are good reasons to recommend acetaminophen over NSAIDs. When it comes to relieving pain or fever, it seems the two categories are similarly effective, yet many people believe NSAIDs to be superior. Studies show that there is some marginal benefit to NSAIDs in reducing fever and menstrual pain, and acetaminophen is marginally better at relieving headache and arthritis pain [source: Cleveland Clinic health essentials].

When it comes to safety concerns, most people have heard a lot of negative media coverage about problems with acetaminophen toxicity and believe that NSAIDs are safer. But the facts are that acetaminophen is one of the safest over-the-counter medications in use. Rare problems have occurred in people who have exceeded recommended doses of acetaminophen or who have liver disease.

188

MEDICAL

On the other hand, there are tens of thousands of hospital admissions in the US annually for gastrointestinal bleeding due to NSAID use, and thousands of resultant deaths each year. The Arthritis, Rheumatism, and Aging Medical Information System (ARAMIS) has estimated that more than 100,000 hospitalizations and more than 16,000 deaths in the United States each year are due to NSAID-related complications. NSAIDs can also have adverse effects on patients with heart or kidney disease. An FDA report warns that if acetaminophen use were to be restricted, and consequently aspirin and other over-the-counter NSAID use increased in the United States, available data suggest that more people would die from aspirin and other NSAID-related gastrointestinal bleeding than those potentially spared from acetaminophen overdose liver toxicity. —*TW*

Currently, the best available treatment for the cough and runny nose of a cold is a combination decongestant and antihistamine medication taken orally. Use the older, sedating antihistamines rather than the new non-sedating ones, as they seem to work better. Throat lozenges (especially those containing menthol) can help with the sore throat or cough symptoms. Over-the-counter cough syrups containing dextromethorphan and guaifenesin have been shown to be no more effective than placebo for relief of coughs and are no longer recommended in young children because of their lack of effectiveness and demonstrated side-effects.

Warm fluids such as tea are soothing for coughs and sore throats. Honey has been shown to have a mild effect in reducing coughs, so add some honey in your tea. Codeine cough preparations have been used and promoted for decades (actually, heroin was thought to be a non-addictive and safe treatment for coughs in the late 1800s!), but it has frequent side-effects and offers no demonstrable effectiveness. Extra rest and fluids are a reasonable recommendation. As long as there is only minimal fever, muscle aches, and cough, a vigorous

ADVENTURE EXPEDITION ONE

physical schedule can be maintained without causing any harm or delaying recovery. Nasal decongestant spray or oral decongestant medications can help with a runny nose.

> Consider a word of caution about decongestant nasal sprays such as Afrin. Heed the warning on the package to not use for more than three days. Nasal tissue will quickly become habituated (think "addicted") to the medication. Suddenly, you find that your nose is swollen shut unless you take a few more sprays. When we see patients in this predicament, it can be difficult to get them to stop using the spray, but that is just what is needed to break the cycle. Nasal steroid sprays (like Flonase) can be used to help with symptoms while patients are breaking this "habit." —*TW*

Common colds usually last about ten days, with the first three days or so being the most miserable. It is not uncommon to have an irritating cough that persists for three to eight weeks or more but this does not mean that you need an antibiotic. However, there are times when an illness begins as a cold, but you develop a bacterial infection (such as pneumonia, bacterial sinus infection, bacterial middle ear infection) on top of the cold virus that can benefit from antibiotic therapy. The clue is usually that instead of beginning to feel better towards the end of the first week, you are feeling worse.

You may start to spike fevers five days into a cold, or start coughing up bloody sputum, or you may have a fever and ear pain, or feel chest pain in a discrete area that worsens with breathing or coughing along with shortness of breath. These can all be signs that you have developed a secondary bacterial infection on top of your cold.

Sometimes, expedition members will complain of cold-like symptoms that are due to exposure to the environment you are in. Very cold air has low humidity and is irritating to our airways, and a persistent dry cough is a common complaint in polar explorers and

MEDICAL

alpine climbers. One of the functions of our nasal passages is to warm and humidify inspired air, but extreme cold overwhelms this ability. Unfortunately, there isn't any genuinely effective treatment for this cough. It's possible to limit coughing by using a face mask to help warm and humidify inspired air.

Another common symptom that can be mistaken for a viral infection is cold rhinorrhea. This is an annoying persistent drip of clear thin fluid from the nostrils that occurs in some people in very cold environments. Long icicles will gradually grow from the nostrils. Both authors have personal experience with this. Symptoms can be lessened with a mask to warm inspired air, but it can get soaking wet or freeze to the face or beard, making repeated removal painful. There is a prescription nasal spray (Ipratropium or Atrovent) that can lessen the annoyance of cold rhinorrhea.

Treatment of pain

Most common pain such as headaches or musculoskeletal pain can be treated effectively with over-the-counter medications such as acetaminophen or NSAIDs (see the previous discussion for warnings/precautions). Many people prefer to use NSAIDs for musculoskeletal pain, thinking that inflammation is an important part of the cause of the symptoms and should be treated with an anti-inflammatory drug. However, acetaminophen is often just as effective (and as discussed above, much safer) in these situations. Try it first. Try to rest the affected area—if you have to keep moving, at least favor the area, or rest it with taping, splinting, or a sling if appropriate.

Once pain exceeds the level that these first-line drugs treat, what do you do? For example, an expedition member has a fracture. First, do not make the mistake of giving more than the recommended maximum doses of your first-line drugs (acetaminophen or a NSAID). You will not provide any additional pain-relieving effect, but you will succeed in providing more toxicity and side-effects. Splinting, elevation, and application of cold packs are an important part of your first-aid treatment and will help with pain.

ADVENTURE EXPEDITION ONE

If you need something more, you need to have a stronger pain medication in your kit. Usually, the next step is something like acetaminophen with hydrocodone (Vicodin) for this higher level of pain. Anything in this stronger category is a prescription drug and is subject to special controlled prescriptions under the authority of the DEA (drug enforcement administration). You will need to discuss obtaining these types of medication with your physician (who will hopefully be sympathetic to the needs of your expedition). Your doctor can go over when it is appropriate to use these more potent pain medications as well as the proper dosage and common side-effects.

Insomnia

Poor sleep is a common complaint on expeditions. This is not surprising because you are in a new, challenging environment; you may be sleeping on the ground or on ice; you may be sharing a cramped sleeping shelter; you are cold, or hot, or sweating, or itchy, or being tormented by insects. You may also be at extreme altitude and are being awakened by the irregular Cheyne-Stokes respiratory pattern. There may be dozens of reasons contributing to poor sleep. Medications to aid in sleep have been commonly used for decades, especially on climbing expeditions.

The current recommendation is not to take any of them.

It turns out that no matter what category of medication for insomnia is chosen, they all come up lacking in reasonable effectiveness. They all have problematic side-effects, some of which can be life-threatening to an expedition member in an extreme environment, such as a challenging climb at extreme altitude.

Rather than resort to ineffective and dangerous medication to help you sleep, you should simply sleep. Do everything that your common sense tells you will help. Avoid excess caffeine and alcohol, especially later in the day. Make your sleep environment as comfortable as possible—cool and dry is best. Use earplugs liberally to shut out wind noise or a noisy tent mate. Above all, remember that no one ever perished from lack of sleep.

192

MEDICAL

> Both on expeditions and while working long challenging hours in the hospital on very little sleep, sometimes for more than thirty-six hours, I can attest that you can continue to push on and function at a high level (although impaired) until your next opportunity to rest. You may actually be putting yourself at greater risk of an accident by taking a sleeping pill than by sleeping as much as you can naturally and then persevering. —*TW*

Common skin problems

Chafing and blisters from friction are an almost universal complaint on long expeditions. Besides the feet, problem areas include the groin, armpits, breasts, and nipples. Prevention by using well-tested socks and footwear and close, but not tight or loose-fitting, clothing is the first step. Lubricants (such as Runners Lube, Sportslick, Body Glide, or others) can be applied before going out for your day and can prevent problems. Similarly, applying tape or another product such as Moleskin or Band-Aid Brand Blister Pads to vulnerable areas can prevent problems.

What is the best treatment for blisters if you don't notice the problem in time to prevent them? Here's a favorite, time-tested amongst wildland firefighters. First, clean and disinfect your hands with soap and water if possible, or do your best to clean up, and then use an alcohol hand sanitizer. Put on latex gloves if available, especially to protect yourself if working on someone else. Clean the blister and surrounding area using a disinfectant soap or solution such as alcohol or Betadine. Small blisters can usually be treated without puncturing and draining. Leave them intact and dress with an antibiotic ointment and gauze as described below.

For large or obviously fragile blisters, sterilize the tip of a needle by soaking it for at least three minutes in a disinfectant solution or heating it until it glows red, then cools. Next, make a small puncture at the base of the blister. Leave the roof of the blister attached so it can continue to protect the skin. Use a gloved finger to gently push

ADVENTURE EXPEDITION ONE

the fluid out. Cut a hole the size of the blister in a piece of moleskin. Cover the blister with the moleskin so that the blister rests in the middle of the hole and the adhesive sticks to the skin around the blister. Apply antibiotic ointment liberally over the blister and cover with gauze and tape in place. Replace the bandage daily and check for signs of infection: heat, pain, and swelling on or around the blister, pus, red streaks radiating from the blister, or fever. Complete healing will take about ten days, but the soreness should improve rapidly over the next few days. Many firefighters have found that this treatment makes them comfortable and able to continue working almost immediately.

There are a few other skin problems that are common enough that expedition members should be ready to deal with them. Insect bites and stings can be uncomfortable but usually will heal well without complications such as infection. An over-the-counter cream containing one percent hydrocortisone will provide relief of local itching from bites such as mosquito bites and help avoid the repeated scratching that can lead to bacterial infection.

Other common skin problems include bacterial infections such as folliculitis, abscess, and cellulitis. Patients with superficial folliculitis usually have multiple small red bumps and pustules on a red base pierced by a central hair. They can be painful, itchy, or both. Usually, folliculitis will heal well by keeping the area as clean as possible and avoiding continued friction or overly-constricting clothing. An abscess is a more painful and serious local skin infection manifested by formation of a larger pustule. In order to heal, the pocket of pus needs to drain. This can be promoted by the application of warm compresses or soaks in warm (clean) water, which helps to thin the skin overlying the abscess. However, a deeper abscess may need to be drained by an expedition member who can perform an incision and drainage procedure (usually a doctor accompanying your trip or a doctor you seek out locally) followed by a dressing. An adequately drained abscess will not usually need treatment with antibiotics unless there is a significant amount of surrounding skin infection (cellulitis).

Cellulitis is a bacterial skin infection manifested by a patch of skin that is red, hot to the touch, and tender. The skin may also be broken

194

MEDICAL

and weep some fluid. A fever may be present. These infections may start with a break in the skin such as a scrape or an insect bite, but sometimes no break in the skin is apparent. Treatment includes resting and elevating the area if possible, application of warm compresses or soaks, and oral antibiotics that will eliminate the usual bacterial cause. Because of the widespread development of resistant organisms causing this (termed MRSA for methicillin-resistant *Staphylococcus Aureus*), the antibiotics recommended today are usually high-dose sulfamethoxazole-trimethoprim (Septra) or clindamycin (prescription medications).

Another common skin infection is a yeast infection (cutaneous candidiasis) that can cause red, irritated skin surrounded by red bumps at the outer edges. Common forms of this are candidal vaginitis (a common vaginal infection in women), candidal diaper dermatitis (diaper rash in infants), candidal balanitis (a yeast infection on the penis in men), and perianal candidiasis. Notice where this yeast loves to grow: dark, warm, moist areas of your skin. Treatment is to keep the area as dry as possible and use a local antifungal cream such as miconazole or clotrimazole (many other generic and brand names are available over-the-counter) or vaginal suppositories or cream in women. Even more conveniently, an oral medication, Diflucan (prescription medication) is now available and is recommended for your kit. A single oral dose of Diflucan usually clears a vaginal yeast infection in women much more conveniently and without the mess of topical creams.

Serious venomous injuries

Snakebites

First-aid recommendations for snakebites have changed through the years. No longer recommended is cutting, applying suction, or even tourniquets (although there are some experts who still feel that suction is worth doing in the first few minutes after the bite). It turns out that these methods do not remove any significant amounts of the dangerous venom, and tourniquet use has led to more, not less, tissue damage. Sucking on the bite wound with your mouth risks introducing a serious infection from the bacteria of your mouth.

195

It is best to keep the patient quiet and the bitten limb elevated gently above heart level, with any constricting jewelry or clothing removed, and get the patient evacuated to a medical facility that can provide the only effective treatment: antivenin. Minimize walking for the bite victim as much as possible. Fortunately, dangerous snakebites are not all that common, with about 2,000 venomous bites occurring annually and only about twelve deaths per year in the United States.

Worldwide statistics about snakebites are incomplete, especially in the developing world. It is thought that there are about two million venomous snakebites worldwide each year, resulting in an estimated 100,000 to 125,000 annual deaths. If a member of your party suffers a snakebite, there is a reasonable chance of no ill effects. A "dry bite" without envenomation can occur in a significant percentage of cases (50 percent in a coral snake, 25 percent from a pit viper such as a rattlesnake).

To summarize, the only treatment that really helps is antivenin, and this cannot be given in the field, so prompt evacuation to a medical facility is your best course of action.

Scorpion stings

Scorpion stings cause a wide variety of symptoms. The stings of most scorpions are a simple nuisance, with the majority of envenomations resulting only in a painful local skin reaction. Of the 1,700 or so scorpion species worldwide, only about twenty-five are considered medically significant, with stings capable of causing serious reactions, including neurologic, cardiovascular, and respiratory complications.

Of the naturally occurring species in the United States, only the Arizona bark scorpion (*Centruroides sculpturatus*) is medically important. Its venom affects nerve transmission and leads to a variety of neurologic symptoms. Antivenin alleviates symptoms in minutes but may have side-effects, especially when used in children. Without antivenin treatment, symptoms can last 24–48 hours. No scorpion-related deaths have been reported in the United States for over twenty years, but scorpion envenomations are a significant problem in other countries. Scorpion stings are especially a problem in the Sahel region of Africa, South India, the Middle East, Mexico, and South Latin America.

MEDICAL

The estimated number of scorpion stings worldwide is 1.2 million annually, leading to 3,250 deaths. In Mexico, one thousand deaths from scorpion stings occur per year. In general, scorpions are not aggressive. They are nocturnal creatures, hunting during the night and hiding in crevices and burrows during the day to avoid the light. Accidental human stings occur when scorpions are inadvertently touched while in their hiding places, with most of the stings occurring on the hands and feet. This is why it is commonly advised that you inspect and shake out your clothing and footwear before dressing in the morning.

Prognosis (the expected course of recovery) is dependent on many factors, including species of scorpion, patient health, and access to medical care. Most patients recover fully after scorpion envenomation. If the victim survives the first few hours without severe heart, lung, or neurological symptoms, the prognosis is usually good. A worse prognosis can be expected with the presence of severe generalized symptoms such as cardiovascular collapse, respiratory failure, seizures, and coma.

If an expedition member has severe symptoms shortly after a scorpion sting, prompt evacuation to a medical facility capable of providing the needed intensive care should be initiated. Meanwhile, keep the patient quiet and calm, keep the bitten extremity immobilized and below the heart to delay venom absorption, and provide any other supportive care that you can.

Spider bites

Although most spiders produce venom, the majority do not have fangs capable of delivering it through human skin. Black widow spiders are among the few spiders capable of causing a poisonous bite to humans. Black widow spiders usually bite when their web is disturbed or upon inadvertent contact in shoes and clothing. Most bites are felt immediately as a pinprick sensation at the bite site, followed by increasing local pain that may spread quickly to include the entire bitten extremity. The bite mark tends to be limited to a small puncture wound or a swollen red hive that often is associated with a halo.

ADVENTURE EXPEDITION ONE

The effects of the bite can spread and may eventually cause severe, widespread pain along with other symptoms such as vomiting and sweating. Rarely, dangerous and even fatal organ complications can occur. Treatment in the hospital involves wound care and treatment of such symptoms as muscular pain. An antivenin is available but is usually only used when symptoms are not relieved with safer medications because severe reactions to the antivenin can occur.

Recluse spiders (also known as a violin or fiddleback spider) have a brown, violin-shaped mark on the dorsum of the cephalothorax. The venom is toxic to cells and causes clots to form in small blood vessels, leading to more cell death around the bite site. There are eleven species of recluse spiders native to the United States, including the brown recluse spider (*Loxosceles reclusa*), as well as two introduced species, the Mediterranean recluse spider (*L. rufescens*) and the Chilean recluse spider (*L. laeta*).

Only *L. reclusa* and *L. laeta* have been confirmed to cause medically significant bites. Management initially involves local wound care and tetanus prophylaxis. These bites can go on to cause significant tissue loss, but the surgical care that may be needed is provided days or weeks later when the extent of the tissue loss becomes apparent. Antivenin and other treatments are still considered experimental and have not yet been shown to improve outcomes.

Bee stings

In the case of a bee sting, if the stinger is left in the skin, remove it promptly by scraping it away with something like a credit card or a knife edge. The idea is to avoid grasping the venom sac that is on the base of the stinger and squeezing even more venom into the skin as you remove the stinger. There is really no effective prompt treatment of the pain from a bee sting other than the application of cold packs. It is normal for the pain of a bee sting to be intense for the first hour or more, and the local swelling and redness to be present for three to four days. Over-the-counter pain medication such as acetaminophen or ibuprofen can help lessen the pain.

Warning signs of a more serious allergic reaction to a bite or sting include rapid onset of hives and itching on areas of the skin away

MEDICAL

from the site of the sting, rapid onset of difficulty breathing, wheezing, swelling in the throat (may be manifested by a hoarse voice or noisy breathing), or fainting (can be a sign of low blood pressure, a feature of anaphylactic shock). A serious allergic reaction is known as anaphylaxis and is a true medical emergency that can rapidly cause death.

Emergency treatment includes an injection of epinephrine (carry an epinephrine autoinjector) and a dose of antihistamines. Because a patient with anaphylaxis can initially improve and then worsen a few hours later (termed a biphasic allergic reaction), a second dose of epinephrine may need to be administered. Normally patients with anaphylaxis are kept under observation in the emergency room for a minimum of six hours because of this possibility.

Exotic diseases

In previous sections, we discussed some of the common hazards of expeditions in North America. What might you encounter in more exotic locations? This is a huge topic. It will be instructive to touch on some examples of exotic hazards you may face. As recommended throughout this book, do your own research so that you are familiar with what the regional hazards are and how you can best minimize your risk.

Non-North American infectious diseases

Viral infections

An important cause of non-North American exotic diseases are the major viral infections. Some of these cause what is called viral hemorrhagic fever and they include:

Yellow fever	Bolivian hemorrhagic fevers
Dengue	Ebola
Lassa fever	Marburg viruses
Argentine hemorrhagic fevers	Crimean-Congo hemorrhagic fevers

≈199≈

ADVENTURE EXPEDITION ONE

The term viral hemorrhagic fever is used to describe a (usually) severe illness affecting multiple organ systems of the body. A characteristic of all these infections is that the overall vascular system is damaged and the body's ability to regulate itself is impaired. These symptoms are often accompanied by hemorrhage (bleeding); however, the bleeding is rarely life-threatening. Humans are not the natural reservoir for any of these viruses.

Humans are initially infected when they come into contact with infected host animals (such as monkeys), or the virus is transmitted from the host to humans by vectors such as mosquitoes or ticks. The viruses are geographically restricted to the areas where their host species live. With some viruses, after the accidental transmission from the host, humans can transmit the virus to one another resulting in severe outbreaks with many fatalities (Ebola is a famous example).

Human cases or outbreaks of hemorrhagic fevers caused by these viruses occur sporadically and irregularly. The occurrence of outbreaks cannot be easily predicted. With a few noteworthy exceptions, there is no cure or established drug treatment for these infections. A few, like yellow fever, can be prevented with vaccines. Speak to your travel medical advisor for more information on the inoculation.

West Nile virus is one of several mosquito-transmitted viruses that can cause encephalitis (an infection of the brain) and is now native to the United States. West Nile virus causes a seasonal epidemic in North America, flaring up during the summer until the first frost. This virus has received significant media attention in the last few years. Other causes of viral encephalitis include tick-borne encephalitis, La Crosse encephalitis, Japanese encephalitis, and others.

Zika virus has quickly become a worldwide travel concern for women who are pregnant or sexually active and their male partners. Zika can be transmitted through mosquito bites, blood transfusions or sex, and most concerning is transmission from a pregnant woman to her fetus. Many people infected with Zika virus have no symptoms or only mild symptoms. Common symptoms include fever, rash, headache, joint pain, red eyes and myalgias (muscle pain). If symptoms occur, they can last for several days to a week. Fetal infection can cause devastating birth defects such as microcephaly (small and

MEDICAL

abnormal brain and head development), or other problems such as miscarriage or stillbirth. There is no treatment or vaccine to prevent Zika, so avoidance of exposure for women and their sexual partners is key. Areas at risk for Zika include multiple African countries, areas in Asia, the Pacific Islands, the Caribbean, Central America, South America and Mexico. For specific up-to-date information, please refer to a reliable web site such as the Center for Disease Control at https://wwwnc.cdc.gov/travel/page/zika-travel-information.

The best way to reduce your risk of infection with mosquito-borne viruses is to prevent mosquito bites. Use insect repellent, wear long sleeves, long pants, and socks or even stay indoors while mosquitoes are most active. Not all mosquitoes are most active at dusk, dawn, or at night. Some, like those that transmit La Crosse encephalitis, are most active during the daytime, so do your research and know the risks of the region you will be exploring. There are vaccines to prevent some of these illnesses, including Japanese encephalitis, which can be given before you travel. Again, see your travel medical professional who can provide up-to-date information tailored to your region of travel and medical history.

Some viruses cause hepatitis (an infection of the liver), and there are many lettered hepatitis viruses, including hepatitis A through E (most well-known are hepatitis A, B, and C). Another category is viruses that cause hepatitis as part of a more widespread infection, and examples include the Epstein-Barr virus and cytomegalovirus.

Hepatitis A is a more mild illness that is contracted through the fecal-oral route (usually by ingesting contaminated food or water). Hepatitis B and C can cause more severe illness and chronic infections and are transmitted by sexual contact, body fluid contact, IV drug use with contaminated needles or syringes, or via blood transfusion. Hepatitis A and B can now be prevented with vaccines given before exposure. Epstein-Barr virus, or EBV, is one of the most common human viruses in the world. It spreads primarily through saliva. EBV can cause infectious mononucleosis, also called mono, and other illnesses. Most people will become infected with EBV sometime during their lifetime and will have minimal or no symptoms.

ADVENTURE EXPEDITION ONE

Cytomegalovirus, or CMV, is a common virus that infects people of all ages. Over half of adults by age forty have been infected with CMV. Once CMV is in a person's body, it stays there for life and can reactivate. Most people infected with CMV show no signs or symptoms. However, CMV infection can cause serious health problems for people with weakened immune systems, as well as babies infected with the virus before they are born (congenital CMV).

Bacterial infections

There are several bacterial infections that are important for the traveler to be aware of. You likely recognize the last three of these bacterial names because our routine childhood vaccinations prevent them.

Typhoid fever
Meningococcal disease
Pertussis
Diphtheria
Tetanus

Typhoid fever

Typhoid fever is a life-threatening illness caused by the bacterium *Salmonella Typhi*. An estimated 5,700 cases occur each year in the United States. Most cases (up to 75 percent) are acquired while traveling internationally. Typhoid fever affects more than twenty million people worldwide each year. Typhoid fever is common in most parts of the world except in industrialized regions such as the United States, Canada, western Europe, Australia, and Japan. Areas of risk include all of the developing world, East and Southeast Asia, Africa, the Caribbean, and Central and South America.

Salmonella Typhi lives only in humans. Persons with typhoid fever carry the bacteria in their bloodstream and intestinal tract. In addition, a small number of persons, called carriers, recover from typhoid fever but continue to carry the bacteria (Typhoid Mary is a historic and famous example). Both ill persons and carriers shed *Salmonella Typhi* in their feces. You can contract typhoid fever if you eat or drink something that has been handled by a person who is

MEDICAL

shedding *Salmonella Typhi* or if sewage contaminated with *Salmonella Typhi* bacteria gets into the water you use for drinking or washing food. Therefore, typhoid fever is more common in areas of the world where handwashing is less frequent and water is likely to be contaminated with sewage.

Once *Salmonella Typhi* bacteria are ingested, they multiply and spread into the bloodstream. Persons with typhoid fever usually have a sustained fever as high as 103°F to 104°F (39°C to 40°C). Other symptoms include weakness, stomach pains, headache, or loss of appetite. In some cases, patients have a rash consisting of flat, rose-colored spots. Diagnosis is by having samples of stool or blood tested for the presence of *Salmonella Typhi*. Typhoid fever is treated with antibiotics. Follow-up testing is important to ensure that you are not continuing to carry and shed the bacteria.

Two basic actions can protect you from typhoid fever: avoid risky foods and drinks and get vaccinated against typhoid fever. However, because the vaccines are not completely effective, watching what you eat and drink when you travel continues to be important after you have been vaccinated. Avoiding potentially contaminated foods will also help protect you from other illnesses, including traveler's diarrhea, cholera, dysentery, and hepatitis A.

Meningococcal disease

Meningococcal disease can refer to any illness that is caused by the type of bacteria called *Neisseria meningitidis*, also known as meningococcus. These illnesses are often severe and include infections of the lining of the brain and spinal cord (meningitis) and bloodstream infections (bacteremia or septicemia). The symptoms of meningitis include sudden onset of fever, headache, and stiff neck. Additional symptoms commonly include nausea, vomiting, photophobia (increased sensitivity to light) and altered mental status (confusion). The symptoms of meningococcal meningitis can appear quickly or over several days. Typically, they develop within three to seven days after exposure.

Another outcome of meningococcal infection is bloodstream infection, called septicemia or bacteremia. Septicemia is the more

ADVENTURE EXPEDITION ONE

dangerous and deadly illness caused by *Neisseria meningitidis* bacteria. When someone has meningococcal septicemia, the bacteria enter the bloodstream and multiply, damaging the walls of the blood vessels and causing bleeding into the skin and organs. Symptoms may include fever, fatigue, vomiting, cold hands and feet, cold chills, severe aches in muscles, joints, chest, and abdomen, rapid breathing, diarrhea and, in the later stages, a dark purple rash. Meningococcal septicemia is very serious and can be fatal in as little as a few hours. In non-fatal cases, permanent disabilities can include amputation of toes, fingers, or limbs or severe scarring as a result of skin grafts. Meningococcus bacteria are spread through the exchange of respiratory and throat secretions (e.g. by living in close quarters, kissing). Meningococcal disease can be treated with antibiotics, but quick medical attention is extremely important. The best defense against meningococcal disease is to keep up to date with recommended vaccines.

Pertussis

Pertussis (whooping cough) is an acute infectious disease caused by the bacterium *Bordetella pertussis*. In the 20th century, pertussis was one of the most common childhood diseases and a major cause of childhood mortality in the United States. Before the availability of the pertussis vaccine in the 1940s, more than 200,000 cases of pertussis were reported annually. Since the widespread use of the vaccine began, incidence has decreased by more than 75 percent compared with the pre-vaccine era. However, since the 1980s there has been an increase in the number of reported cases of pertussis. In 2012, the last peak year, over 48,000 cases of pertussis were reported. The disease is caused when pertussis bacteria attach to cilia, which are microscopic hair-like structures on the cells lining our respiratory tract, produce toxins that paralyze the cilia, cause inflammation of the respiratory tract and interfere with the clearing of lung secretions.

Symptoms of pertussis usually develop within five to ten days after being exposed, but sometimes not for as long as three weeks. Pertussis has a mild onset with catarrhal symptoms (mucus build-up in the nose and airways) that are indistinguishable from those of a

MEDICAL

more minor cold. The cough, which is intermittent at first, becomes paroxysmal—it comes in explosive fits. In typical cases, paroxysms terminate with a whooping sound on inspiration (hence the common name, whooping cough) and vomiting can follow the cough.

Paroxysms of coughing, which may occur more at night, usually increase in frequency and severity as the illness progresses and typically persist for two to six weeks or more. The illness can be milder and the characteristic "whoop" may be absent in children, adolescents, and adults who were previously vaccinated. After paroxysms subside, a nonparoxysmal cough can continue for two to six weeks or longer. Unvaccinated or incompletely vaccinated infants younger than twelve months of age have the highest risk for severe and life-threatening complications and death. In infants, the cough may be minimal or absent, and apnea (breathing suddenly stops) may be the only symptom. Pertussis can be treated with antibiotics and the incidence lessened by vaccination.

Diphtheria

Diphtheria once was a major cause of illness and death among children. The United States recorded 206,000 cases of diphtheria in 1921, resulting in 15,520 deaths. Starting in the 1920s, diphtheria rates dropped quickly due to the widespread use of vaccines. Between 2004 and 2015, only two cases of diphtheria were recorded in the United States. However, the disease continues to cause illness globally.

In 2014, 7,321 cases of diphtheria were reported worldwide to the World Health Organization. Overall, 5–10 percent of people who contract diphtheria will die, with higher death rates (up to 20 percent) among persons younger than five and older than forty years of age. Before there was a treatment for diphtheria, the disease was fatal in up to half of cases. When the bacteria that cause diphtheria attach to the lining of the respiratory system, they produce a toxin that can cause weakness, sore throat, fever and swollen glands in the neck.

The toxin destroys healthy tissues and within two to three days the dead tissue forms a thick, gray coating (pseudomembrane) that can build up in the throat or nose. This pseudomembrane can cover tissues in the nose, tonsils, voice box (larynx), and throat, making it very hard

205

to breathe and swallow. The toxin may also get into the bloodstream and cause damage to the heart, kidneys, and nerves. Diphtheria treatment involves giving diphtheria antitoxin to stop the toxin produced by the bacteria from damaging the body and by using antibiotics. The best prevention is to be sure your vaccines are up-to-date.

Tetanus

Tetanus is unique among the vaccine-preventable diseases because it does not spread from person to person. The bacteria are usually found in soil, dust, and manure and enter the body through breaks in the skin—usually cuts or puncture wounds caused by contaminated objects. Tetanus is uncommon in the United States, with an average of twenty-nine reported cases per year from 1996 through 2009. Nearly all cases of tetanus are among people who have never received a tetanus vaccine, or adults who don't stay up-to-date on their ten-year booster shots.

Tetanus is a disease that occurs when *Clostridium tetani* spores enter the body through a wound or breach in the skin and germinate in the presence of anaerobic (low-oxygen) conditions. Toxins are produced and spread through the body via the bloodstream and lymphatic systems. Toxins act at several sites within the central nervous system, including peripheral motor nerve endings, spinal cord, and brain, and in the sympathetic (or autonomic) nervous system, which controls our organs' automatic functions.

The typical signs and symptoms of tetanus are caused when tetanus toxin interferes with the release of certain neurotransmitters, which leads to unopposed muscle contraction and spasm. Seizures may occur, and the autonomic nervous system may also be affected. The disease is characterized by painful muscular contractions, primarily of the jaw and neck muscles, and less prominently of trunk muscles. A common first sign suggestive of tetanus in older children and adults is abdominal rigidity, although rigidity is sometimes confined to the region of injury.

History of an injury or apparent site of entry may be lacking. Tetanus is a medical emergency requiring hospitalization (usually intensive care), immediate treatment with tetanus immune globulin, a tetanus vaccine booster, agents to control muscle spasm, and aggressive

MEDICAL

wound care and antibiotics. The incubation period ranges from three to twenty-one days and usually is about ten days. In general, the further the injury site is from the central nervous system, the longer the incubation period. A shorter incubation period is associated with more severe disease, more complications, and a higher chance of death.

<u>Malaria</u>

Malaria is another illness that expedition participants need to be aware of. It is relatively uncommon in North America but causes a large burden of disease worldwide. The parasites infect successively two hosts: female Anopheles mosquitoes and then humans. In humans, the parasites grow and multiply first in the liver cells and then in the red blood cells. In the blood, successive broods of parasites grow inside the red cells and destroy them, releasing daughter parasites ("merozoites") that continue the cycle by invading other red cells. These blood stage parasites are responsible for causing the hallmark symptoms of malaria—episodic fevers, anemia, and rupture of blood cells.

When certain forms of blood stage parasites ("gametocytes") are picked up by a female Anopheles mosquito during a blood meal, they start another, different, cycle of growth and multiplication in the mosquito. After ten to eighteen days, the parasites are found (now termed sporozoites) in the mosquito's salivary glands. When the Anopheles mosquito takes a blood meal on another human, the sporozoites are injected with the mosquito's saliva and start another human infection when they parasitize the liver cells. Thus, the mosquito carries the disease from one human to another (acting as a vector). In contrast to the human host, the mosquito vector does not suffer from the presence of the parasites.

Complications of malaria can include severe anemia due to hemolysis (destruction of the red blood cells), hemoglobinuria (hemoglobin in the urine), acute respiratory distress syndrome (ARDS), an inflammatory reaction in the lungs that adversely affects oxygen exchange, abnormalities in blood coagulation, low blood pressure, acute kidney failure, hyperparasitemia, where more than five percent of the red blood cells are infected by malaria parasites, and abnormalities in our bodies' acid and blood sugar balance.

ADVENTURE EXPEDITION ONE

After repeated attacks of malaria, a person may develop a partially protective immunity. Such "semi-immune" persons can often still be infected by malaria parasites but may not develop severe disease, and frequently lack typical malaria symptoms. In areas with high *P. falciparum* transmission (most of Africa south of the Sahara), newborns will be protected during the first few months of life by maternal antibodies transferred to them through the placenta. As these antibodies decrease with time, these young children become vulnerable to disease and death by malaria. If they survive repeated infections to an older age (two to five years) they will have reached a protective semi-immune status. This is why in high-transmission areas, young children are a major risk group and are targeted preferentially for malaria control interventions.

The toxic factors that are released stimulate our immune systems to respond by producing substances that act to produce fever and shaking chills, along with influencing the other symptoms associated with malaria. One of the most serious human symptoms caused by malaria occurs when *Plasmodium falciparum*-infected red blood cells adhere to the blood vessel walls and do not freely circulate in the blood. When these clumps of infected red blood cells develop in the vessels of the brain it is believed to be a factor in causing the severe disease syndrome known as cerebral malaria, which is associated with high mortality.

There is an interesting relationship between the genetic blood disorder sickle cell and the malaria parasite. *P. falciparum* malaria has been a leading cause of death in Africa since ancient times. Persons who have the sickle cell trait (heterozygotes, meaning they carry only one of the pair of the abnormal hemoglobin gene) are relatively protected against *P. falciparum* malaria and thus enjoy a biologic advantage. It is thought that this is why the sickle cell trait is more frequently found in Africa and in persons of African ancestry than in other population groups.

MEDICAL

First described by Hippocrates, a severe illness marked by fever and the passage of dark urine was again recognized and described in West Africa in the early 1800s. Most of the patients died within a few days. The illness was given the name blackwater fever in 1884. Blackwater fever is a complication of malaria infection in which red blood cells burst in the bloodstream (hemolysis), releasing hemoglobin directly into the blood vessels and into the urine (causing very dark urine, hence the name), frequently leading to kidney failure and causing a high mortality rate. Even with treatment, the mortality remains about 25 to 50 percent.

Blackwater fever is most prevalent in Africa and Southeast Asia. Individuals with increased susceptibility, such as nonimmune immigrants or individuals who are chronically exposed to malaria, are more prone to this complication. Blackwater fever seldom appears until a person has had at least four attacks of malaria and has been in an endemic area for six months.

The most probable explanation for blackwater fever is an autoimmune reaction caused by the interaction of the malaria parasite and the use of quinine for prevention of malaria. Blackwater fever occurs in patients who suffer heavy parasitization of red blood cells with *Plasmodium falciparum*. People with certain red cell abnormalities such as glucose-6-phosphate dehydrogenase deficiency are particularly prone to developing it.

Blackwater fever is much less common today than it was before 1950 because quinine plays a role in triggering the condition, and this drug is no longer commonly used for malaria prophylaxis. Quinine, however still remains an important drug (in combination with others) for the treatment of malaria.

Toxoplasmosis

At any time, it is estimated that 30 to 50 percent of the worldwide population carries this infection. Three principal routes of transmission typically infect people: foodborne, animal-to-human (zoonotic), or mother-to-child (congenital). Toxoplasmosis is not passed from person-to-person, except in instances of mother-to-child (congenital) transmission and more rare circumstances such as blood transfusion or organ transplantation.

A woman who is newly infected with Toxoplasma during pregnancy can pass the infection to her unborn child (congenital infection). The woman may not have symptoms, but there can be severe consequences for the unborn child, such as diseases of the nervous system and eyes, making it critically important for pregnant travelers to avoid this exposure.

Kittens and cats can shed millions of Toxoplasma oocysts in their feces for as long as three weeks after infection. An infected cat that is shedding the parasite in its feces contaminates the litter box, and if the cat is allowed outside, it can contaminate the soil or water in the environment as well. People then can accidentally swallow the oocyst form of the parasite, such as after cleaning a cat's litter box or accidental ingestion of oocysts in contaminated soil (e.g. not washing hands after gardening or eating unwashed fruits or vegetables from a garden) or by drinking water contaminated with the Toxoplasma parasite.

Eye disease from Toxoplasma infection can result from congenital infection or infection after birth. Eye lesions from congenital infection are often not identified at birth but occur in 20 to 80 percent of infected persons by adulthood.

River blindness (onchocerciasis)

In addition to visual impairment or blindness, onchocerciasis causes skin disease, including nodules under the skin or debilitating itching. Worldwide onchocerciasis is second only to trachoma as an infectious cause of blindness. The World Health Organization (WHO) estimates that at least 25 million people are infected with the offending parasite, *O. volvulus* worldwide; of these people 300,000 are blind and 800,000 have some sort of visual impairment.

Schistosomiasis

After malaria and intestinal helminthiasis, schistosomiasis is the third most devastating tropical disease in the world, being a major

MEDICAL

source of disease and death for developing countries in Africa, South America, the Caribbean, the Middle East, and Asia. More than 207 million people, 85 percent of whom live in Africa, are infected with schistosomiasis, and an estimated 700 million people are at risk of infection in 76 countries where the disease is found, as their agricultural work, domestic chores, and recreational activities expose them to infested water.

Globally, 200,000 deaths are attributed to schistosomiasis annually. The disease is due to immunologic reactions to Schistosoma eggs trapped in tissues, and the symptoms and signs depend on the number and location of eggs trapped. Initially, the inflammatory reaction is reversible. In the latter stages of the disease, it is associated with deposition of scar tissue, resulting in organ damage that may be only partially reversible.

High altitude

Individuals vary in their ability to acclimatize to high altitude, and this ability seems to be genetically predetermined. Some will adjust quickly without discomfort, others will experience symptoms of acute mountain sickness (AMS) but then recover and are able to continue to ascend, and yet others will fail to acclimatize even with gradual ascent spread over weeks.

The tendency to acclimatize well or to become ill during a climb seems to be consistent in individuals on repeated climbs given that the ascent rate and altitude reached are similar. Many factors affect the incidence and severity of AMS, such as the rate of ascent, altitude attained (especially altitude of sleep), duration of exposure to altitude, and possibly the amount or intensity of exercise undertaken at altitude.

The most important and least understood variable is the underlying susceptibility of the individual. Few people experience significant symptoms below 7,000–8,000 feet (2,100–2,400 meters), whereas most unacclimatized persons ascending to 10,000 feet (3,000 meters) or higher experience at least a few symptoms. Individuals with a history of altitude illness may tolerate ascent better if the rate of ascent

ADVENTURE EXPEDITION ONE

is slowed or if they spend a day or two acclimatizing at an intermediate altitude. In some studies, women had more symptoms than men.

Aerobic and strength training do not improve your physiologic acclimatization to altitude. However, training for exertion at altitude is important in order to improve your ability to perform work effectively at altitude. To maximize your performance, train at an intermediate altitude (above about 6,000 feet or 1,800 meters) for ten to twenty days before you leave for your expedition in order to both improve fitness and maximize acclimatization.

The mechanisms that our bodies use to acclimatize to high altitude are varied and complex. Successful initial acclimatization seems to mainly protect against altitude illness of all types and improve sleep. Longer-term acclimatization over a period of weeks will improve aerobic exercise ability. When you descend for even a few days, you again become susceptible to altitude illness, especially high-altitude pulmonary edema (HAPE), on re-ascent. However, the improved ability to perform work at altitude persists for weeks.

Upon exposure to altitudes of about 5,000 feet (1,500 meters), the lower oxygen pressure stimulates our respiratory system to move more air through our lungs. This increased hypoxic ventilatory response seems to be genetically determined and is the first physiologic adaptation we make when exposed to altitude.

An immediate result of this increased ventilation is a drop in the carbon dioxide content of your blood, which causes complex compensatory changes in the way your renal system adjusts the pH of your blood. The combination of these two physiologic acclimatization mechanisms causes your ventilatory pattern to reach a maximum after about four to seven days at altitude and then will continue to adjust with each successive gain in altitude. These changes in your renal function, which improves your adjustment to altitude, cause an initial fluid loss. Also, cold air has lower humidity, causing increased fluid losses as we climb. These increased fluid losses at altitude through your lungs and kidneys are some of the reasons that good fluid intake is recommended when climbing.

Your circulatory system responds to altitude with increased output, thereby pumping more blood through your lungs to pick up the

MEDICAL

scarce oxygen and then delivering it to your tissues. Several changes also occur in your blood that helps us at altitude. First, a complex change in your blood chemistry shifts the affinity of your red blood cells' hemoglobin for oxygen, ultimately causing more oxygen to be delivered to your tissues at altitude.

Another slower but important acclimatization mechanism is that lower blood oxygen stimulates the release of a hormone called erythropoietin, which stimulates bone marrow production of more red blood cells, thereby increasing the amount of oxygen that your circulatory system can deliver to your tissues at altitude. Finally, there is evidence that the density of the capillaries (the very tiny vascular structures in your tissues where oxygen exchange occurs) in human tissues actually increases after about three weeks at altitude.

Some symptoms are normal at altitude and are simply due to the physiologic processes that are occurring during acclimatization. Hyperventilation and/or a feeling of shortness of breath (dyspnea) occurs on exertion but there should be no shortness of breath at rest (this is a sign of more serious trouble such as HAPE—see below). Increased urination and awakening many times at night (sometimes to urinate—a good reason to use a "pee bottle" in your tent), as well as periodic breathing, is to be expected. Periodic breathing is a normal phenomenon at altitude and is most prominent during sleep. It is characterized by periods of successively deeper breaths followed by a period when breathing temporarily stops (apnea). The duration of apnea is commonly three to ten seconds but may be up to fifteen seconds.

This period of apnea causes a feeling of distress or even panic, and it is common to feel that you need to sit up and gasp for air. Periodic breathing (also known as Cheyne-Stokes respirations) occurs in everyone above their personal altitude "threshold." It may lessen slightly with acclimatization but does not go away until you descend. It becomes more pronounced with ascent but interestingly is not associated with altitude illness. It is reassuring to know that this is a universal symptom and is a normal response to altitude.

Periodic breathing worsens problems with insomnia at altitude, but sleep problems are also thought to be due to lower oxygen levels in the brain (cerebral hypoxia). Acetazolamide (Diamox) 125 mg taken orally about one hour before bedtime acts as a respiratory stimulant and helps to reduce periodic breathing and can improve sleep. If needed, this should be continued until the trekker has descended below the threshold elevation where periodic breathing became troublesome. As discussed earlier, other sleeping pills should be avoided at altitude.

Many physical problems and symptoms are associated with the ascent to altitude. Some of these are merely an annoyance while others are life-threatening. The serious altitude problems are usually divided into three major syndromes: acute mountain sickness (AMS), high-altitude pulmonary edema (HAPE), and high-altitude cerebral edema (HACE). Other problems can occur, such as impaired sleep, swelling (edema) of extremities and high-altitude retinal hemorrhage. Finally, the effects of ascent to extreme altitude can be more risky for certain special populations. A discussion of various preventative and acute treatments for high altitude problems is included below but, as always, these specific treatments need to be discussed with your personal physician during your expedition preparations, tailored to your individual medical needs, and should never be administered by untrained persons.

Swelling of hands and feet (peripheral edema) and facial edema are common at altitude. If this is an isolated symptom without other symptoms of AMS it is not considered serious and is not a reason to interrupt your ascent. It commonly worsens with ascent and is more common in women than men. It resolves rapidly with descent. Acetazolamide (Diamox) can help lessen the swelling but is only necessary if this symptom is troublesome.

MEDICAL

The immune system is impaired at extreme altitude and climbers to these regions have learned that infections are more common. They are more difficult to clear and more resistant to antibiotics unless the climber descends to a more moderate altitude to recover.

Sore throats and chronic coughs are nearly universal in expedition members who spend at least two weeks at altitudes over 18,000 feet (5,500 meters). It is thought that these problems are not due to infections but are a result of chronic exposure to the very dry, cold air at altitude. The chronic cough can be so forceful and spasmodic that rib fractures can occur, a disabling problem in extreme climbers. Response to antibiotics is poor and most climbers resign themselves to tolerating the symptoms until descent, which seems to be the only thing that improves the symptoms. There seems to be some benefit from inhaling steam (this can be done while melting snow for drinking in the tent). Using a balaclava or similar face mask to warm inspired air and trap some moisture can also help with these troublesome symptoms.

A minor, common and humorous effect of altitude is high-altitude flatus expulsion (HAFE). Colonic gas passes at increased rates at altitudes of about 10,000 feet (3,000 meters) and above. Tent-mates should exercise patience and understanding when this annoying and universal event occurs.

A common but sometimes frightening event at high altitude is high-altitude retinal hemorrhages (bleeding in the back of the eye), occurring in anywhere from 36 percent of climbers at 17,500 feet (5,300 meters) to as many as 79 percent in expedition climbers at extreme altitudes (24,700 feet or 7,500 meters). Fortunately, most retinal hemorrhages do not cause symptoms of significant visual loss and go unnoticed by the affected climbers. The exception is when these hemorrhages involve the macula, the central part of the retina that we use for most of our visual tasks. Most high-altitude retinal hemorrhages heal with no adverse visual effects. A history of high-altitude

ADVENTURE EXPEDITION ONE

retinal hemorrhages does not necessarily preclude subsequent trips to high altitude.

AMS

Acute mountain sickness (AMS) is defined by its symptoms, but the exact cause of AMS is still unknown. Cerebral edema (brain swelling) may play a role. Symptoms of AMS occur in nearly everyone if ascent is too rapid. A marked variability in symptoms is characteristic of AMS. Although some experience only minor inconvenience, for others, the symptoms are incapacitating. The symptoms of AMS include the presence of a headache and at least one of the following symptoms during a climb:

- Loss of appetite
- Nausea or vomiting
- Fatigue or weakness
- Dizziness or lightheadedness
- Difficulty sleeping

> Dehydration is a common cause of non-AMS headaches. If a member of your climbing expedition has a headache, it is reasonable to try having them drink a liter of fluid and take a mild pain reliever (aspirin, acetaminophen, or ibuprofen). If the headache goes away completely, it's not likely to be AMS.

Assessing the rate of ascent is an important part of managing AMS. At what elevation has the patient slept during their ascent? Did they fly into a high airstrip, or walk in from low elevation? Trekkers on their way to Everest who fly into a high airstrip (Lukla at 9,400 feet or 2,900 meters) have twice the incidence of AMS as trekkers who walk in from the lowlands (Jiri at 6,300 feet or 1,900 meters). Have they exceeded the usual recommended 1,000 feet (300 meters) sleeping elevation gain per night? At what elevation were symptoms first experienced?

MEDICAL

Denial is extremely common. Many trekkers with obvious AMS will blame their headache on something else. Trekkers who have walked for eight hours uphill with a backpack will believe that it is normal that they are not hungry. People who have saved and planned for their trip of a lifetime have a great deal invested in remaining well enough to achieve their goal. Many people fear being left behind or holding up the group until they become so ill that the fact that they are suffering from serious AMS is apparent. This group dynamic likely explains why serious altitude illness (HACE, HAPE) is more common in trekkers who are part of an organized group.

Slow, gradual ascent with adequate time for acclimatization provides the best protection from AMS. Once symptoms of AMS occur, additional time for acclimatization before ascending further usually is the only treatment needed for mild AMS. If symptoms worsen despite additional time for acclimatization and mild pain relievers (acetaminophen, aspirin, or ibuprofen or another non-steroidal anti-inflammatory (NSAID) medications), descent to a lower altitude (especially sleeping altitude) is needed.

A descent of 1,000 to 3,000 feet (300 to 900 meters) usually is sufficient to improve symptoms. Supplemental oxygen (usually only carried by groups attempting extreme altitudes) also effectively relieves symptoms of AMS. Maintenance of adequate fluid hydration is important since symptoms of dehydration may be similar to those of AMS, but excessive or "over" hydration does not prevent AMS and should be avoided. Once patients are completely symptom-free they have acclimatized at the current altitude and can resume continued gradual ascent.

The drug most extensively used for the treatment and the prevention of AMS is Diamox. For AMS prevention, Diamox 125 mg twice daily is usually effective, while 250 mg twice daily is recommended for treatment of established AMS. Smaller doses may be effective in some people. Starting Diamox one day before ascent and continuing for a couple of days while at altitude is recommended for prevention. Diamox also reduces the amount of troublesome periodic breathing at night.

> If you have a sulpha-drug allergy, consult your doctor before taking, as Diamox may cause an allergic reaction.

Another drug that has been used in AMS extensively is a corticosteroid, dexamethasone. For prevention, it is given at a dose of 2 mg every six hours or 4 mg every twelve hours. For treatment of AMS, the usual recommended dose is 4 mg every six hours. Prolonged use (more than ten days) is not recommended. If you feel that you or someone on your team will need this drug, discuss it with your personal physician.

> Warning: High doses of corticosteroids are reserved for very high-risk situations or severe cases of AMS complicated by cerebral edema (HACE). As discussed below, this is a serious and life-threatening situation and you will need emergency medical expertise.

The over-the-counter herbal supplement ginkgo biloba has been investigated for the prevention of AMS, primarily due to its low incidence of adverse effects. Although early studies were promising, more recent ones do not support the use of ginkgo biloba. In a couple of studies, ginkgo biloba was no better than a placebo in the prophylaxis of AMS. Therefore, the main drugs used for treatment remain acetazolamide and dexamethasone.

Portable hyperbaric treatment bags (e.g. the Gamow bag) simulate descent to a lower altitude. These bags are effective for treating AMS, although they are rarely needed unless AMS is complicated with high-altitude cerebral or pulmonary edema and the patient's ability to walk needs to be improved before safe descent can be achieved.

MEDICAL

The serious forms of AMS cannot be ignored. Several years ago, a photographer who was working with an expedition at altitude on the Tibetan Plateau developed serious symptoms of acute mountain sickness. He was (properly) evacuated to a lower altitude where his symptoms promptly improved. The tragedy occurred when he convinced other team members to allow him to re-ascend rapidly by helicopter to the altitude he was evacuated from so that he could resume his work. He was found dead in his tent the next morning.

HAPE

High-altitude pulmonary edema (HAPE) is a serious and potentially life-threatening manifestation of altitude illness. The reported incidence ranges from 0.1 percent (skiers traveling to 8,200 feet (2,500 meters) in Colorado) to 4.5 percent at 14,000 feet (4,300 meters) among trekkers in Nepal. On Denali (Mt. McKinley) in Alaska, the incidence is as high as 20 to 33 percent. Children appear to be more susceptible than adults. Males are more likely to develop HAPE than females, but the reasons are unclear.

The first symptoms of HAPE usually occur one to three days after arrival at altitude. In adults, these symptoms commonly occur after exercise and consist of coughing, shortness of breath, chest tightness and fatigue. In approximately half the cases, these symptoms are associated with the other typical symptoms of AMS (headache, loss of appetite, nausea or vomiting, fatigue or weakness, dizziness or lightheadedness, and difficulty sleeping).

Initially, the cough is dry, but thin, clear, yellowish or blood-tinged sputum is later produced. Fatigue may be the first symptom to occur, even before shortness of breath develops—manifesting as the inability of the affected individual to keep up with the pace of the group. The team member with HAPE can appear blue (cyanosis) and have a fever as high as 101°F (38.5°C); a higher fever creates suspicion of pneumonia. A healthcare professional doing an exam will likely find neck veins that are not distended (the opposite is present

ADVENTURE EXPEDITION ONE

with pulmonary edema caused by heart failure) and rales over the mid-chest (a crackling noise heard when listening to the lung sounds). Heart and respiratory rates are increased. A pulse oximetry measurement will show a significantly lower reading compared with healthy team members at the same altitude.

A form of HAPE known as re-ascent HAPE or re-entry HAPE occurs in acclimatized individuals who descend to lower altitude and then re-ascend. In these cases, individuals usually spent three to five days to as many as ten to fourteen days at lower altitude before returning to higher elevations. For unknown reasons, these individuals have an increased likelihood of developing HAPE.

The most important treatment for HAPE is immediate descent to lower altitude. Descent results in dramatic symptomatic improvement. Often, a descent of only 1,000–3,000 feet (300–900 meters) is necessary. Early descent, before HAPE becomes severe, potentially can save more lives than any other treatment. Use of supplemental oxygen reduces pulmonary artery pressure and improves symptoms; however, sufficient quantities of oxygen are rarely available under field conditions.

The most commonly used drug for HAPE is nifedipine. Remember that even if treatment with medications is available, it should not delay early and rapid descent. Portable hyperbaric bags (e.g. a Gamow bag) work by simulating descent and have been used to stabilize and improve the victim so that they can descend more safely. Nifedipine and phosphodiesterase-5 inhibitors (drugs like Viagra) are useful in preventing HAPE among susceptible individuals. The best treatment for HAPE remains prevention by gradual ascent and early recognition of HAPE symptoms.

HACE

High-altitude cerebral edema (HACE) is an extremely dangerous form of altitude sickness caused by swelling in and around the brain. The hallmark is a change in mental status and/or ataxia (unsteady walking or uncoordinated limb movements) in a person at altitude. Without prompt treatment, further neurologic deterioration and death are likely. HACE is considerably less common than HAPE and

MEDICAL

AMS, with prevalence thought to be 0.5 to 1.0 percent. Many cases of HAPE occur without coexisting HACE but, conversely, most cases of HACE have coexisting HAPE. Whether males are more likely to develop HACE than females remains unclear, although more cases of HACE in males have been reported by some researchers.

Signs and symptoms of HACE may progress rapidly (within twelve hours) from mild symptoms to coma but typically this progression occurs more slowly. Often the symptoms of HACE begin at night, occasionally resulting in the onset of coma during sleep so that the climber cannot be awakened in the morning. Most cases of HACE occur after individuals have been at altitude for several days. HACE may be lethal if not recognized and promptly treated; thus, early recognition and treatment is crucial.

The hallmark symptoms to watch for are a change in the level of consciousness or the onset of ataxia (unsteady gait). If you see these symptoms, the situation requires immediate action—descend! Along with plans for an immediate descent, treatment includes giving supplemental oxygen, if available, along with dexamethasone 8 mg initially and then 4 mg every six hours thereafter. Early use of a hyperbaric bag (i.e. Gamow bag) may relieve symptoms and make descent easier but should not be considered a substitute for descent, especially because recovery often requires ten or more days, even with treatment at low altitude.

It is not uncommon at extreme altitudes, such as in the Himalayas, to have an expedition member who is found in the morning in a comatose state. Information will be limited to knowing the ascent profile and some second-hand information on whether the team member appeared ill the day prior. It will be difficult to determine whether the ill climber has HACE, HAPE or a combination of both, or even another medical emergency such as stroke (which can occur at extreme altitudes without warning signs or the presence of other risk factors in otherwise healthy trekkers).

ADVENTURE EXPEDITION ONE

So what to do? Your team's goal is to try to improve the ill trekker to the point that he or she can once again walk, so your team can more easily evacuate them to a lower altitude (immediate descent is always the goal in altitude emergencies because it is the factor that can improve the situation most reliably). The best approach is to treat the patient for both HACE and HAPE. Your team will need a member with enough medical training to administer drugs by injection. Never try to give medications by the oral route in a comatose patient—you risk aspiration (causing foreign materials to enter the airways rather than the stomach).

Dexamethasone 8 mg given as an injection, nifedipine 10–20 mg sublingual, and ideally also give oxygen at 4 liters/minute, and hyperbaric treatment for one hour with a portable device such as a Gamow bag. Hopefully, at the end of this hour, the patient is alert and more information can be obtained from them. Further treatment can then be carried out with oral medication and fluids, and the ill team member assisted to a lower altitude as rapidly as possible.

High-altitude deterioration

The highest permanently inhabited town in the world is La Rinconada, a mining village of over 7,000 people in southern Peru at an altitude of up to 16,732 feet (5,100 meters). Above this approximate altitude, the ability to acclimatize is outstripped by a chronic deterioration in physical condition and health. Miners in Peru have found from experience that they can perform work at higher altitudes than this but need to return to a lower altitude for sleep in order to remain healthy. This deterioration is more rapid the higher one ascends. Once in the "death zone," above 26,200 feet (8,000 meters), death can occur in a matter of days without supplemental oxygen.

Extreme climbers employ strategies to reduce their risk by minimizing their time spent in this zone. Lassitude may take over, so that simple life-sustaining tasks, such as melting snow for water, may

MEDICAL

become too difficult to accomplish. Death may result from dehydration, hypothermia, or neurologic or psychiatric dysfunction. Loss of body weight is a prominent feature of high-altitude deterioration. An acute organic brain syndrome, which includes impaired judgment and even frank psychosis that can threaten survival has been reported in as many as 35 percent of climbers above 23,000 feet (7,000 meters).

> One of climbing's greatest tragedies is partly a story of high-altitude deterioration. A prolonged storm in the summer of 1967 kept seven members of a group of climbers pinned down, two in a wind-battered tent and five in a snow cave near 20,000 feet (6,100 meters) on Denali. The storm raged for more than seven days, and winds were at times estimated to be 300 mph high on the mountain—conditions humanly impossible to descend in.
>
> Trapped at altitude in these extreme conditions, lassitude, along with hypothermia and dehydration, gradually gripped the men hunkered in their shelters. When a break in the weather finally came and allowed a window for escape, others who had been trapped lower on the mountain barely had the strength to descend to safety. High on the mountain, none of the seven could muster the strength and will to crawl out of their tent and cave and descend. Rescue crews later found three bodies of the seven who died high on the mountain. None of the bodies were ever recovered and brought down. The disaster is chronicled in James Tabor's *Forever on the Mountain*.

Changes in our blood-clotting mechanisms occur at altitude that make climbers more prone to various serious medical problems, the most worrisome including stroke (caused by blood clots blocking blood flow to a part of the brain) and deep vein thrombosis (or thrombophlebitis), when clots in the large deep veins of the legs or pelvis form—these can suddenly travel to the lungs, causing pulmonary embolism.

ADVENTURE EXPEDITION ONE

Pulmonary embolism can further impair the already compromised oxygen uptake in our lungs and acutely reduce the oxygen available to our tissues and, if severe enough, can rapidly cause incapacity and death, as illustrated by the below account of Art Gilkey on K2. The exact reasons for these increased risks are not completely understood but thickening of the blood from a combination of acclimatization and dehydration, prolonged cold exposure, and prolonged weather-imposed inactivity may all play a role.

In the summer of 1953, at the age of forty, the legendary mountaineer Charles Houston assembled a team of amateurs for the third American assault on K2. The team also included Bob Bates, George Bell, Bob Craig, Dee Molenaar, Tony Streather, Pete Schoening, and Art Gilkey.

After the long approach to the second-highest mountain in the world, they forced their way up the Abruzzi Ridge to roughly 25,000 feet (7,600 meters), where they were pinned down by a massive storm. After nine days, the team members were finally able to climb out of their tents. As Art Gilkey emerged, he fell face down, unconscious. Examining Gilkey, Houston (a physician) realized he had thrombophlebitis and was at risk of pulmonary embolism. At sea level, this condition is extremely serious; at 25,000 feet, it is virtually a death sentence.

Despite the nearly hopeless situation, the team was not going to abandon Gilkey. The team made an initial attempt to move him down the same route they had ascended—which ended when they realized the entire slope was about to avalanche. Craig and Schoening proposed lowering Gilkey down a rocky ridge to the east.

Houston made the alternative suggestion that the rest of the party descend while he remained with Gilkey until the weather improved and they could return. The team rejected the idea of splitting up, even though it meant getting most of the group

Medical

into a safer position. The team waited another day for the weather to improve, Gilkey's condition worsened and Houston determined that clots had indeed moved into Gilkey's lungs, making the situation even worse. The next morning, with the storm raging again, they wrapped Gilkey in one of the tents and launched their rescue effort—at the most extreme altitude ever attempted at that time.

By mid-afternoon, they'd moved their stricken teammate to within reach of an ice shelf. To reach it, they would have to haul him across a steep gully, beneath which the ice fell off steeply all the way to the glacier thousands of feet below. Schoening stationed himself above Gilkey on the slope and belayed Molenaar and Gilkey by using his ice axe as an anchor.

The plan was to pendulum Gilkey across the gully. The accident that nearly killed them all started when George Bell, who was also standing above Gilkey, fell and accelerated out of control down the slope. Ultimately, five men entangled in the ropes ended up rocketing down the slope until the strain fell on Gilkey—who was connected by a single rope to Schoening.

What occurred next is the most legendary ice axe arrest in mountaineering history. Schoening leaned into his axe (which fortunately was driven deep into the snow behind a large rock) and braced himself for the impact of the group fall. The axe and rope held. For the next five minutes, Schoening was able to hold all six men. This would have been remarkable anywhere, but it was miraculous at extreme altitude.

When they all came to a halt, Bell was lying precariously close to the drop, Molenaar was bleeding from a gash in his thigh, and Houston lay crumpled at the edge of the drop to the glacier below, unconscious. While the rest of the team struggled to right themselves, Bates climbed down to Houston, who began to regain consciousness. Bates had to struggle to force the concussed Houston to understand where he was and climb back up to the relative safety of the group.

225

ADVENTURE EXPEDITION ONE

> The priority now was to get the injured to shelter. Gilkey was anchored securely to his position in the gully with two ice axes while the others moved to the other side of a rocky rib to set up a tent. Houston, Bell, Schoening, and Molenaar climbed inside, then the least injured two men returned for Gilkey. When they got back to the gully, the anchoring axes were gone and Gilkey had disappeared. An avalanche had apparently torn through the chute and taken him with it to his death.
>
> The next morning, after a horrendous night, the team continued climbing down to safety through a tangle of rope fragments, a broken ice axe shaft jammed in the rocks, and some blood streaked rocks. Four days later, the seven survivors stumbled into base camp, grief-stricken by the loss of their friend. The porters erected a cairn dedicated to Gilkey on a prominent point of rock 200 feet above the glacier floor, where it still stands.
>
> (Described in Chapter 8 of Jim Curran's *K2 The Story of the Savage Mountain*)

Chronic medical problems and altitude

Some individuals who are on your expedition team may have special medical problems. Ascent to high altitude by persons with an underlying cardiac disease, pulmonary disease, and sickle cell anemia deserve special mention. Unacclimatized people with <u>coronary artery disease</u> may develop increased symptoms of angina (chest pain resulting from inadequate blood flow to meet heart muscle demands) following ascent to altitude because of an increase in cardiac work levels, as well as some vasoconstriction (narrowing) of the coronary arteries that feed the heart muscle.

Some heart rhythm problems may worsen after rapid ascent to altitude, even without underlying coronary artery disease. Studies show that ascent to altitudes of 10,000 feet (approximately 3,000 meters) has little direct effect on myocardial ischemia (inadequate oxygen delivery to the heart muscle tissue) but may increase cardiac symptoms

MEDICAL

by increasing heart rate and blood pressure during moderate exercise, which increases the work the heart is doing.

In a large survey of trekkers in Nepal, no deaths from cardiac disease were reported, although several individuals required evacuation for cardiac problems (hence you can anticipate an increased risk of needing to arrange for evacuation if you travel to altitude with a team member who has coronary artery disease). Other studies conducted at moderate altitudes in the Colorado Rocky Mountains among unacclimatized elderly individuals suggest a relatively low risk. With sufficient time for acclimatization, patients with coronary heart disease are likely to experience decreased symptoms because of a lowering blood pressure. With long-term exposure to altitude, coronary artery disease mortality rates in these individuals are actually reported to be lower than those observed at sea level.

What about people with chronic lung disease at altitude? Shortness of breath occurs in everyone, including those without heart or lung disease, after ascent to altitude. Even at sea level, patients with <u>chronic obstructive pulmonary disease (COPD)</u> are frequently limited by impaired lung mechanics and shortness of breath (dyspnea). Because of the increased ventilatory requirements of exercise at altitude, patients with COPD can expect to experience a worsening of their symptoms during exposure to altitude. One study concluded that patients with mild or moderate COPD without cor pulmonale (high blood pressure in the pulmonary artery system) actually tolerate altitude exposure well as long as the adequate time for acclimatization is allowed. People with COPD who are living at altitude, as opposed to visitors, develop cor pulmonale more frequently and have an increased mortality rate when compared to similar patients living at low altitude.

The lower oxygen levels at altitude cause effects that raise pulmonary artery pressure in visitors to high altitude. Therefore, in people with already elevated pulmonary artery pressures, from diseases such as idiopathic pulmonary hypertension, ascent to altitude results in even higher pulmonary artery pressures. These patients are likely to experience additional symptoms, such as fatigue, shortness of breath, or fainting. An increase in supplemental oxygen or the use of drugs to help lower the pulmonary arterial pressures may be helpful in improving

Adventure Expedition One

symptoms at altitude. Prior to traveling to high altitude, persons with idiopathic pulmonary hypertension should consult a physician familiar with altitude problems who can evaluate the potential risks.

Asthma

Asthma is a common disorder affecting many young, active individuals; therefore, a significant number of trekkers to altitude will have asthma or reactive airways. The dry, cold air often encountered at high altitude may cause bronchoconstriction (constriction of the smaller airways, which worsens symptoms of wheezing). However, at altitude, the air also contains fewer allergens, which are often the most problematic trigger for asthma. As a result, many people with asthma report doing as well or even better at high altitude than at lower elevations.

The reduced barometric pressure at altitude results in decreased air density, so the air we are moving in and out of our lungs is less viscous and therefore easier to move. Thus, even though the ventilatory demands of activity at high altitude are greater, this reduced air density at least partially compensates. Patients with asthma who want to travel to high altitude can be encouraged to do so, but they should bring an adequate supply of their medication and pay attention to their respiratory symptoms. As always, it is advisable to meet with your doctor and discuss this first.

Sickle cell disease

Sickle cell disease is a common, genetically mediated disorder of hemoglobin, the large molecule in our red blood cells that carries oxygen and releases it to our tissues. Individuals with sickle cell disease can have significant problems that make the ascent to high altitude inadvisable. Under conditions of hypoxia, the red blood cells in these individuals become deformed and take on the shape of a sickle, causing blood viscosity to increase, cells to clump together more readily, and circulation through our capillaries to become blocked. Major symptoms of this sickle cell crisis include bone pain and splenic infarction (splenic tissue dies from blocked blood flow, causing severe abdominal pain).

MEDICAL

Approximately six to eight percent of African-American people in the United States carry at least one abnormal hemoglobin gene. Most of these individuals have the sickle cell trait and are largely asymptomatic, while a few have the far more severe condition, sickle cell anemia. Those with sickle cell anemia probably already know about their disease, but those with only the sickle cell trait may be unaware of the problem and, therefore, may travel to high altitudes and experience problems unexpectedly.

Because exposure to hypoxia (lower oxygen levels) at high altitude may precipitate a sickle cell crisis in patients with sickle cell anemia, these individuals should not attempt to travel to higher altitudes. Even the modest hypoxemia associated with airline travel may precipitate symptoms in susceptible individuals. Because of this, supplemental oxygen is often provided to individuals with sickle cell anemia during aircraft flights.

Travel by commercial airline is generally safe for patients with the sickle cell trait; however, rarely they may experience symptoms during airplane flights. Similarly, those with the sickle cell trait generally tolerate altitudes of 8,000 to 10,000 feet (2,440 to 3,050 meters) without difficulty, although a few may become symptomatic. Although most persons with sickle cell disease are of African-American ancestry, the sickle cell trait, and even sickle cell crisis, may occur in other ethnic groups.

Cold injuries

Our bodies have complex systems in place that regulate our body temperature within a relatively narrow range. We generate heat through metabolism of food and the metabolic activity of our tissues, and we can mount increased heat generation through increased muscular activity. We conserve heat through a complex system that is controlled by the hypothalamus in our brain and primarily involves our skin and vascular system, which preferentially shunts blood flow away from our peripheral extremities where more heat can be lost, and toward our central organs to preserve life.

ADVENTURE EXPEDITION ONE

These systems of heat generation and conservation operate within a narrow range. The normal diurnal variation in our body temperature is only 1°C (1.8°F). Our behavioral response to thermoregulation is of utmost importance: what we choose to wear, the shelter we seek, our strategy to stay dry, fire starting, etc. We do have an acclimatization response to cold, so training for your cold-weather expedition by exercising in similarly cold environments for about three weeks, if possible, should be part of your preparation.

Cold injuries can be divided into localized injury to a body part (e.g. frostbite) or a generalized drop in body temperature (hypothermia).

Hypothermia

Hypothermia is defined by a core body temperature decrease to 35°C (95°F) or less. The causes of hypothermia are either primary or secondary. Primary, or accidental, hypothermia occurs in healthy individuals inadequately clothed and exposed to severe cooling. Accidental hypothermia can be further divided into immersion and non-immersion cold exposure. The high thermal conductivity of water leads to the rapid development of immersion hypothermia. Although the rate of heat loss is determined by water temperature, immersion in any water less than 16°C (60.8°F) may lead to hypothermia within minutes. In secondary hypothermia, another illness predisposes the individual to accidental hypothermia.

Secondary hypothermia occurs because of an acute failure of thermoregulation; shivering does not usually occur as it normally should in these patients. Alcohol causes many cases, resulting in cutaneous vasodilation (blood vessels dilate in and under the skin), loss of shivering, hypothalamic dysfunction, and lack of concern regarding the environment. Other medical factors that predispose an individual to secondary hypothermia include the following: endocrine diseases (e.g. hypothyroidism, pituitary insufficiency, Addison's disease, diabetes mellitus); cardiovascular diseases (e.g. myocardial infarction, congestive heart failure, vascular insufficiency); neurologic diseases (e.g. cerebrovascular accident, head injury, tumor, spinal cord injury, Alzheimer dementia); some drugs (e.g. phenothiazines, barbiturates, antidepressants); pancreatitis (inflammation of a large gland in the abdomen, the pancreas); cirrhosis (chronic liver scarring); and hypoglycemia (low blood sugar).

230

MEDICAL

Hypothermia has effects on multiple organ systems. Initially, the metabolic rate increases, with more rapid heart and respiratory rates, increased muscle tone, constriction of peripheral blood vessels, and generation of maximal shivering. With continued core temperature drop, the metabolism progressively declines, with loss of the shivering response (and further loss of core heat), slower heart and respiratory rates, and subsequent build-up of carbon dioxide. The shivering mechanism stops at around 31°C (87.8°F). The heart rate drops to half its normal rate at 28°C (82.4°F), and the force of heart contractions decreases. The risk of ventricular fibrillation (an ineffective and fatal heart arrhythmia if not promptly corrected) increases at body temperatures below 28°C (82.4°F). Cerebral metabolism decreases 6 to 7 percent per 1°C drop in temperature, which results in a declining level of consciousness.

The symptoms of hypothermia vary depending on the severity of the cold injury. In mild hypothermia, symptoms are often vague and include dizziness, fatigue, joint stiffness, nausea, and pruritus (itching). The skin is pale and cool as a result of peripheral vasoconstriction. The person may exhibit lethargy, flat affect (flat emotional state), impaired judgment, and mild confusion progressing to motor incoordination, ataxia (unsteady walking), and slurred speech.

In severe hypothermia, mental status is further impaired, leading to hallucinations, stupor, and even coma. Heart arrhythmias are common with moderate hypothermia and characteristic changes can be seen on the ECG. The patient may appear clinically dead, with no peripheral pulses, fixed and dilated pupils (dilated pupils that do not react to shining a light in the eyes), and stiff posturing with arms and legs extended. Cardiac standstill (heart stoppage) usually occurs at 20°C (68°F), but survival has been reported with core temperature as low as 15°C (60.8°F).

The general principles of treatment for hypothermia in the field are to:

1. Prevent further heat loss
2. Rewarm the body core temperature
3. Avoid precipitating ventricular fibrillation (primarily by the gentle handling of the cold teammate).

ADVENTURE EXPEDITION ONE

The application of these principles depends primarily on the resources available in the field. The person should be moved into a tent or other dry shelter for protection from the wind. Wet clothing should be removed. Insulation, such as a sleeping bag, should be placed under and over the patient, who should not be allowed to stand or sit and whose head should be covered. A well (warm) teammate should take off outer insulating clothing and join the ill teammate between the insulating layers. A fire should be built or a stove lit. No fluids should be given by mouth until the patient is alert and can drink on their own. If possible, the patient should be transported to the hospital in an ambulance heated to 30°C (86°F).

Severe hypothermia is defined as a core temperature less than 28°C (82.4°F) and should be recognized as a life-threatening emergency. If the patient is not breathing, ventilation should be initiated with a bag-valve mask ventilator or a pocket mask connected to a humidified, heated oxygen delivery system (obviously you are not likely to have this in the field). If a slow weak pulse is present, do not perform cardiac compressions (CPR) because this may precipitate ventricular fibrillation.

To avoid inappropriate chest compressions, it is recommended that prehospital personnel examine the patient for a full minute before diagnosing pulselessness. If the patient is pulseless, external cardiac compressions with ventilations (CPR) should be initiated unless the exterior chest wall is frozen and not compressible. Cardiopulmonary resuscitation should continue until the patient is evaluated and treated in the hospital.

The traditional dictum that should be followed is that patients with severe hypothermia should not be considered dead until they are "warm and dead." Even with a prolonged cardiac arrest, resuscitation is possible. Many physicians who are specialists in hypothermia believe that patients with severe hypothermia should not be rewarmed in the field, but, rather, kept in a "metabolic icebox" until in a hospital setting in which physiologic monitoring and advanced life-support equipment are available. The exception to this rule of continuing resuscitation efforts is when the team reaches the point of exhaustion or when continued field resuscitative efforts will endanger other team members.

232

MEDICAL

Frostnip and frostbite

Local tissue-freezing injuries are termed frostnip and frostbite. The mildest form of peripheral cold injury is frostnip, which tends to occur in peripheral body structures (nose, ears, hands, feet), where blood flow is most variable and at risk in the cold. Frostnip commonly occurs in skiers exposed to fast-moving, very cold air. Simple warming either by pressure from a warm hand or by placing the hand in the armpit is sufficient treatment. Generally, no serious damage is seen until tissue freezing occurs.

More consequential local cold injuries may be divided into freezing (frostbite) and nonfreezing (chilblains and immersion foot) injuries. During frostbite, ice crystals many times the size of individual cells form from the available fluid outside the cells, producing dehydration within the nearby cells. The cell content becomes hyperosmolar (has a higher salt content because of the water loss to the ice crystals), and toxic concentrations of electrolytes may cause cell death. A reversal of this process occurs during thawing of frozen tissues.

After tissue thawing, vasodilation (dilation of blood vessels) and leakage from capillaries occur, causing tissue edema. Alternating freeze-thaw cycles worsen the vascular injury and lead to tissue death from inadequate circulation (ischemic infarction).

Several days after the injury, frostbite can be classified into four degrees of severity, first-degree being the least severe and fourth-degree the most severe, involving complete necrosis with gangrene and loss of the affected part. However, many clinicians do not favor this classification of frostbite into four degrees of severity, because assessing the full extent of tissue injury is difficult in the immediate setting.

A simpler classification divides frostbite injury into two types: superficial or deep. Superficial frostbite (first- and second-degree frostbite) involves the skin and subcutaneous tissues. The skin is cold, waxy white, and non-blanching (does not blanch with applied pressure). The frozen part is anesthetic but becomes painful and flushed with thawing. Edema develops and clear bullae (large blisters) appear within the first twenty-four hours.

Deep frostbite (third- and fourth-degree frostbite) involves the muscle, tendons, neurovascular structures, and bone, in addition to

ADVENTURE EXPEDITION ONE

the skin and subcutaneous tissues. The frozen part is hard, woodlike, and anesthetic. It appears ashen-gray, cyanotic, or mottled and may remain unchanged even after rewarming. Edema develops, but bullae (large blisters) may be absent or delayed. Bullae, if present, are filled with hemorrhagic (bloody) fluid.

Initially, as the tissue is freezing, the team member experiences discomfort or pain. This progresses to numbness and loss of sensation. Upon inspection, the frozen tissue is white and anesthetic. Favorable signs include some warmth, normal color, and some sensation.

Several factors can predispose to cold injury. For example, frostbite occurs at more mild temperatures in patients with pre-existing arterial disease. In addition, people with black ethnicity have an increased susceptibility to frostbite. Finally, it has been demonstrated repeatedly that a person who previously suffered frostbite is more prone to develop cold injury in the same body part than an individual with no prior frostbite injury.

Several principles of frostbite treatment are universally accepted. If possible, remove the patient from the cold environment. Treatment should not be attempted in the field if a hospital is available within a short distance or if there is a risk that the extremity will be refrozen. Once the rewarming process has begun, weight-bearing on the affected part is almost certain to result in additional injury. Traditional treatments such as rubbing the frostbitten part with snow or exercising it in an attempt to hasten rewarming have been shown to be harmful and should be avoided. Also, contrary to the popularly-held belief that it is not harmful, walking some distance on frostbitten feet can result in tissue fracture and should be avoided if possible.

The preferred initial treatment for frostbite is rapid rewarming in a water bath at a temperature of 39–42°C (102.2–107.6°F). If prompt evacuation is not possible, rewarming can and should be performed in the field. The rewarming bath ideally should be large enough so that the frostbitten part does not rapidly reduce the temperature of the water. The temperature of the bath is monitored carefully as the bath cools. Additional hot water is added to the bath only after the extremity is removed from it. After hot water is added, the bath is stirred and the temperature retested before the extremity is reintroduced.

MEDICAL

Rewarming is continued until the frostbitten tissue has a flushed appearance, demonstrating that circulation is re-established. This rewarming procedure usually takes 30–45 minutes. Because rewarming is painful, strong narcotic painkillers are often required. After rewarming, the injured extremity is cleaned, dressed, and immobilized and protected from any subsequent freezing injury. Be careful that dressings are not constricting because the injured tissue can be expected to swell, often dramatically, after rewarming. Further treatment and tetanus prophylaxis will be continued after evacuation to a hospital.

> The most dramatic case of frostbite I was involved in treating during my career in emergency medicine occurred in a nine-year-old boy. He was the passenger in a small plane that crashed into deep snow in the mountains, killing everyone else on board. He kept his wits and stayed in the plane wreckage, pulling out whatever clothing and other insulating materials he could in order to keep warm.
>
> However, it took some days for rescuers to find and reach him, and by then the combination of cold, dehydration, and lack of food had caused severe hypothermia and frostbite. He was rapidly transported by air to our emergency department before thawing his frozen extremities in a controlled setting.
>
> When we first examined him, he was alert, but his legs were frozen solid to the touch up to his mid-thighs, so we were worried that he would lose both legs. Amazingly, when his severe frostbite finally matured, his necessary amputations were at the mid-foot level, demonstrating that with proper care, the amount of tissue damage can end up being much less than it first appears. —*TW*

The effects of frostbite can persist for years or be permanent. Patients feel abnormal amounts of pain when their affected hands or feet are exposed to cold and have an abnormal sensory perception of vibration, cold, and warmth. Other persistent symptoms include whiteness and cold sensation in the affected digits.

ADVENTURE EXPEDITION ONE

Frostbite is such a common problem on expeditions to cold environments that detailed recommendations for prevention are worth reviewing. Dress to maintain general body warmth, which will help protect your extremities. Pay particular attention to protecting your face, head, and neck, because these areas can be the source of a tremendous amount of heat loss. Eat plenty of appealing food, which helps with heat generation, and maintain good hydration. At low altitudes, polar explorers have found that including generous amounts of fat in the diet is helpful. At high altitudes, fats are more difficult to digest and the diet should include a higher proportion of carbohydrates. When possible, avoid climbing in extreme weather conditions or during the night when the cold is most severe.

Avoid tight clothing, particularly on the hands and feet. Avoid perspiring in extreme cold—ventilate, remove some clothing, or slow down your pace to avoid becoming wet from perspiration. Be fastidious about keeping hands and feet dry. Carry extra dry socks to change into and be very careful about continuing to wear your boots during periods of inactivity. Wear mittens instead of gloves in extreme cold. Mittens generally keep hands warmer and allow for thumbs to be moved and fists held in the palm of the mitten intermittently for warming. If mittens need to be removed temporarily to perform a task, use glove liners (and mitten leashes to avoid loss of a mitten in the wind). If you will need to touch a metal piece of equipment such as a camera, cover the metal parts ahead of time with tape to provide some insulation.

Be very careful about handling bare metal or fuel in extreme cold. The freezing point of white gas is $-70°F$, and its rapid rate of evaporation can cause skin injury very quickly. Keep toenails and fingernails trimmed closely. Avoid washing your hands, feet, and face too frequently—your tough, weather-beaten skin will be more resistant to frostbite. When a teammate becomes thoroughly chilled, it takes several hours of warmth and rest to recover. Don't allow them to venture out too soon. Avoid drinking alcohol or smoking in cold environments, they will make you more susceptible to cold injury. If a team member suffers frostbite or another cold injury, keep them calm. Panic always complicates the situation and can cause more sweating, which is detrimental to warming them.

MEDICAL

Severe cold injury to the eyes can occur if the eyes are not protected from strong wind by the use of goggles. The corneal injury is initially painful and debilitating, with excessive sensitivity to light, spasm of the eyelids, and excessive tearing similar to the ultraviolet injury known as "snow blindness." If severe, this injury can result in permanent opacification of the cornea, requiring a corneal transplant.

Chilblains

Chilblain, also known as pernio, represents a more severe form of cold injury than frostnip and occurs after exposure to nonfreezing temperatures and damp conditions. This condition is characterized by a chronic, recurrent vasculitis, which is a skin lesion caused by inflammation of the blood vessels in the skin. Chilblain is manifested by red-to-purplish raised bumps usually on more vulnerable areas such as the distal extremities and face. Blisters, erosions, or ulcers (areas of skin loss that leave a "hole") are sometimes seen. It more often affects young and middle-aged women and is associated with some chronic medical disorders, especially Raynaud phenomenon.

The chilblain lesions usually heal in one to three weeks, but they may recur in some individuals. Treatment involves minimizing chronic cold exposure if possible, local heat, gentle massage, and lubricants to keep the skin supple. Drug therapy with Nifedipine (Procardia) has been used to reduce the pain and speed the resolution of the lesions. Nifedipine is thought to help by improving blood flow through the inflamed dermal blood vessels.

Trench foot

Immersion foot, or trench foot, a disease of the sympathetic nerves and blood vessels in the feet, is observed in shipwreck survivors, soldiers, and expedition members whose feet have been wet and cold, but not freezing, for prolonged periods. It can occur at temperatures near or slightly above freezing and is usually associated with dependency and immobilization of the lower extremities and constriction of the limb by shoes and clothing. Immediate symptoms include numbness and tingling pain with itching, progressing to leg cramps and complete numbness.

ADVENTURE EXPEDITION ONE

Initially, the skin is red; later, it becomes progressively pale and mottled and then gray and blue. The soles of the feet are wrinkled and very tender to touch. The progression of immersion foot has three stages:

- The first phase (termed prehyperemic), lasts for a few hours to a few days, during which the limb is cold, slightly swollen, discolored, and possibly numb. Pulses can be difficult to feel.
- The second phase (termed the hyperemic phase), lasts two to six weeks. It is characterized by bounding, throbbing circulation in a red, swollen foot.
- The third phase (or posthyperemic) lasts for weeks or months. The limb may be warm, with increased sensitivity to cold. The injury often produces a superficial, wet gangrene whereas severe frostbite produces a dry, mummification gangrene that looks very different.

Management of immersion foot includes careful washing and air-drying of the feet, gentle rewarming, bed rest, and slight elevation of the extremity. Improvement occurs within 24–48 hours, while the injury usually completely heals in one to two weeks. Early physical therapy is helpful. The patient should be warned that the previously injured area is more susceptible to repeat injury if re-exposed to similar conditions. The key to prevention of immersion foot injury is keeping the feet dry for at least eight hours per day.

Heat illness

Heat illness includes minor illnesses, such as heat edema, heat rash (i.e. prickly heat), and heat cramps, as well as the serious and life-threatening problems, heat syncope and heat exhaustion. Heat stroke is the most severe form of heat-related illnesses and is defined as a body temperature higher than 41.1°C (106°F) associated with neurologic dysfunction.

Exertional heat stroke is the most concerning problem and generally occurs in young individuals who engage in strenuous

MEDICAL

physical activity for a prolonged period of time in a hot environment. There is another form of heat stroke, nonexertional heat stroke, which affects sedentary elderly individuals, persons who are chronically ill, and very young persons. Nonexertional heat stroke occurs during environmental heatwaves and is more common in areas that do not typically experience periods of prolonged hot weather.

Despite wide variations in ambient temperatures, we normally can maintain a constant body temperature by balancing heat gain with heat loss. When heat gain overwhelms the body's mechanisms of heat loss, the body temperature rises, potentially leading to heat stroke. Excessive heat actually affects the biochemical make-up of our cells, causing proteins, phospholipids, and lipoproteins to break down and, on a larger scale, leading to cardiovascular collapse, multiorgan failure, and, ultimately, death.

The exact temperature at which cardiovascular collapse occurs varies among individuals because coexisting disease, drugs, and other factors may contribute to or delay organ dysfunction. Full recovery has been observed in patients with temperatures as high as 46°C (114.8°F), and death has occurred in patients with much lower temperatures. Temperatures exceeding 41.1°C (106°F) are generally catastrophic and require immediate aggressive therapy.

The most devastating case of heat stroke I treated during my career in emergency medicine actually started out as a trauma case. During a hot summer day, a construction worker was brought in by ambulance after falling off a roof. While working to stabilize him, we noticed how hot his skin felt to the touch. One of the nurses then reported that his core temperature was 42.8°C (109°F). The paramedics were able to find out that he had actually been working inside the attic of the house, where temperatures were likely approximately 66°C (150°F). Unfortunately, despite aggressive and intensive care, he succumbed to multi-organ failure. —*TW*

Under normal physiologic conditions, heat gain is counteracted by a commensurate heat loss. This is orchestrated by a structure deep in the brain, the hypothalamus, which functions as our body's thermostat, controlling our body temperature through mechanisms of heat production or heat dissipation, thereby maintaining body temperature in a narrow normal range.

Thermosensors located in the skin, muscles, and spinal cord send information regarding the core body temperature to the anterior hypothalamus, where the information is processed and appropriate physiologic and behavioral responses are generated. Physiologic responses to heat include an increase in cardiac output and blood flow to the skin, which is the major heat-dissipating organ; dilatation of the peripheral venous system; and stimulation of the sweat glands to produce more sweat. The skin can transfer heat to the environment mostly through radiation and evaporation.

Radiation is the most important mechanism of heat transfer at rest in temperate climates, accounting for 65 percent of heat dissipation, and clothing can modulate it. At high ambient temperatures, evaporation, which refers to the conversion of liquid sweat to a gaseous phase (water vapor), becomes the most effective mechanism of heat loss. The efficiency of evaporation in dissipating heat depends on the condition of the skin and sweat glands, the ambient temperature, humidity, air movement, and whether or not the person is acclimated to hot temperatures.

Evaporation becomes inefficient when the ambient humidity exceeds 75 percent and is less effective in individuals who are not acclimated. For example, non-acclimated individuals can only produce one liter of sweat per hour, which on evaporation only dispels 580 kcal of heat per hour, whereas acclimated individuals can produce two to three liters of sweat per hour and can dissipate as much as 1,740 kcal of heat per hour through evaporation.

Acclimatization to hot environments usually occurs over seven to ten days and enables individuals to reduce the threshold at which sweating begins, increase sweat production, and increase the capacity of the sweat glands to reabsorb sweat sodium, thereby increasing the efficiency of heat dissipation. When heat gain exceeds heat loss, the

MEDICAL

body temperature rises and the progression of heat illness begins. As heat illness progresses, the normal sweating mechanisms are eventually overcome, and the victim will have hot, dry skin.

Heat stroke affects the genders equally. Infants, children, and elderly persons have a higher incidence of heat stroke than young, healthy adults. Infants and children are at risk of heat illness due to inefficient sweating, a higher metabolic rate, and their inability to care for themselves and control their environment. Elderly persons are also at increased risk of heat-related illnesses because of their limited cardiovascular reserves, pre-existing illness, and use of medications that may affect their fluid status or sweating ability. In addition, elderly people who are unable to care for themselves are at increased risk of heat stroke because of their inability to control their environment.

Exertional heat stroke is a leading cause of injury and death in high school athletes; approximately two-thirds of such cases occur in August and involve football players, often those who are obese or overweight. Lack of acclimatization is a major risk factor for exertional heat stroke in young adults.

Predictors of a poor outcome from heat stroke include an initial temperature measurement higher than 41°C (106°F), or a temperature persisting above 39°C (102°F) despite aggressive cooling measures, coma duration longer than two hours, and other factors. When therapy is delayed, the mortality rate may be as high as 80 percent. However, with early diagnosis and immediate cooling, the mortality rate can be reduced to 10 percent. Mortality is highest among the elderly population and patients with pre-existing disease.

Prevention involves adequate acclimatization prior to your expedition, access to adequate fluid replacement during exertion in a hot environment, proper clothing that allows for rapid and efficient sweat evaporation, and limiting exertion in a hot environment when humidity is high. In addition, it can be helpful to apply additional cooling measures to the head and neck, such as a wet bandanna or an ice pack held within a hat or bandanna. There is an outdated notion that you should "train" yourself to require less fluid in a hot environment by depriving yourself of adequate amounts of water. This is wrong-headed, leads to no beneficial acclimatization, and in fact is likely to increase your risk of heat-related illness. Stay well hydrated!

Heat cramps are often considered a more mild form of heat illness. They typically occur in athletes who compete for long periods in the heat and can be prevented with adequate hydration and dietary salt intake. Heat cramps are brief, intermittent but excruciatingly intense muscle contractions. They can occur by themselves without more serious heat illness, but heat cramps commonly accompany heat exhaustion, occurring in about two-thirds of cases. Treatment of heat cramps includes fluid and salt replacement and resting in the shade or another cooler environment. Salt tablets are sometimes not tolerated well, and it is best to replace salt and fluids together with something like a sports drink. These formulations also contain an easily absorbed sugar that improves their taste and helps with the ability of the body to absorb needed electrolytes.

Injuries in remote location

Contrary to popular belief, injuries in wilderness areas are usually not due to exotic causes such as wild animal attacks, rock climbing accidents, poisonous bites or stings, etc. More commonly, injuries are suffered during more mundane activities such as hiking, running, swimming, and driving to your destination. It may sound odd, but probably your best insurance against an injury on your expedition is a seat belt and an airbag en route.

Accidents, by definition, involve unforeseen events and therefore cannot be prevented reliably. You can and should minimize the risk of injury with careful preparation, planning, problem anticipation, and training, as well as the careful execution of the trip once underway. Once on your expedition, often the most consequential decisions you make will involve when to stop to rest, eat, and hydrate. Often a trip-ending and even dangerous injury will occur when you push yourself past the point of exhaustion. A misstep when you are exhausted late in the day can cause a badly injured ankle that will jeopardize the remainder of the expedition for the entire party, now focused on evacuating you to safety.

MEDICAL

Careful planning for your trip lays the foundation for safety. Research the weather, trail conditions, best times to travel, and predictable hazards on your route. Review your equipment checklist carefully and never go into the wilderness with untested or unfamiliar equipment. Plan alternative routes and emergency evacuation routes at several points on your planned line of travel. Create a realistic activity timeline and ask these questions:

- Can your group really be expected to average twenty miles a day at that elevation or in those weather conditions?
- What is your alternative plan when the weather forecast ends up being wrong?
- Can you shelter comfortably or at least safely bivouac?
- Has the group budgeted adequate time so that you can weather the storm and not be forced to travel in the teeth of it?
- What injury hazards will your team predictably face? (For example, trail runners or hikers on rough terrain risk trip-ending ankle and foot injuries. Whitewater kayakers risk shoulder dislocations, etc.)
- Will your entire group commit to reducing the risk with adequate footwear, ankle-strengthening training, and vigilance while on the trail?
- Will your group prepare with proper strength, endurance, and technique training to minimize the risk of injury?
- If the risk is high enough that you can still anticipate the problem, will your group members seek special training so that the problem can be more safely treated in the field if it occurs?
- If you are climbing, is the rate of ascent planned properly in order to minimize the risk of altitude sickness and allow for adequate acclimatization?
- What are your treatment and descent plans? (Even with that proper planning, someone in your group may end up not being able to acclimatize and will suffer serious altitude illness.)

Your preparation will involve physical, mental, and equipment issues. Many remote destinations will not have the same health and

ADVENTURE EXPEDITION ONE

hygiene standards that you are used to, and we have already covered many of those issues. Expect and plan for health and hygiene standards that are lacking and have a plan for how you will respond in an emergency. As discussed, physical preparation involves being highly physically fit for your planned expedition, and at your peak health when you depart. Then, on the expedition, do all you can to maintain that peak health with good hygiene practices, safe and nutritious food and water, and adequate rest periods.

On remote expeditions, a much higher level of medical self-sufficiency will be required of your group. If you (or a key expedition member) need additional medical training, plan adequate time and resources for this before your trip. You may want to look into an organization such as the National Outdoor Leadership School (www.nols.edu), which offers wilderness medical training at several different levels. Just reading a book on wilderness first aid is a far cry from actually having to stabilize and evacuate a teammate who is ill or injured. Hands-on training and experience will help you perform calmly and effectively in the stress of a critical situation.

Essential tips on wound care and closure in the field

One of the most common injuries dealt with in emergency medicine are wounds. There are some key tips on proper care of these injuries. The first task is to clean the wound. There is no point in trying to close a dirty wound. If you do, you are almost guaranteed an infection. The optimal way to clean a wound is to first clean the surrounding skin. This can be done very effectively with soap and water and/or an antiseptic solution like povidone iodine. Once the surrounding skin is clean, the interior of the wound is best cleaned by irrigation with a forceful stream of clean water. If you are in the field, it is best to make sure the water you use is first adequately disinfected and purified, either by boiling, adequate filtering, or chemical treatment with iodine or chlorine. We usually perform the irrigation in the emergency room with a syringe and an 18-gauge

Medical

needle, but you will need to improvise in the field. The forceful stream helps to dislodge and remove debris and bacteria that can cause wound infections.

If you cannot remove all visible dirt from the wound, then you are better off not closing the wound. Simply leave it open, apply a clean dressing (which you will plan on changing daily), and let the wound heal slowly on its own (this is called healing by secondary intention). If deep, the wound will heal with a wider scar, but with less chance of infection, and this is the main goal.

When you can get the deep gaping wound completely visibly clean, then you can consider closing it. Small wounds that are not gaping do not need to be closed. Simply protect those with a dressing. Tissue adhesives have revolutionized wound closure in the emergency room. Dermabond® is the medical product used in hospitals, and it is made of a cyanoacrylate adhesive that has been tested extensively on wound treatment. In the field, you may need to make do with another form of cyanoacrylate that you are carrying in your kit.

The key here is to not get any glue inside the wound. It will defeat your purpose by gluing the tissues apart and is very difficult to remove! Removal may require soaking in mineral oil for long periods of time. The proper technique of closing a wound with adhesive is to hold the wound edges together with your gloved fingers a short distance from the edges (maybe a quarter of an inch) and apply the tissue adhesive to the skin surface. Sometimes it will be necessary to use your fingers to apply traction along the long axis of the wound in order to bring the edges together. Keep the edges carefully together so that no glue runs into the wound and allow approximately ten seconds for a thin coat to dry, then apply another coat, let it dry, and then a third.

Once the adhesive is dry, carefully release the wound edges and make sure they stay together. If your gloved

ADVENTURE EXPEDITION ONE

finger is stuck, it usually can be carefully rolled off the glue without disturbing the wound. The adhesive acts as its own dressing and additional protective dressings are often not needed.

Don't apply an antibiotic ointment over the adhesive—it may break down the glue. If you are dealing with a wound with many irregular edges (a "stellate" laceration), closure with adhesive will not usually work, and you are better off applying a dressing. If large or cosmetically important, these complex or stellate lacerations usually need to be sutured in the emergency room. If you are looking at a wound that is more than you can deal with in the field, clean and dress the wound and make plans for evacuation to a medical facility where definitive care can be provided. A key part of wound care is to provide tetanus prophylaxis. Hopefully, all of your team members took care of this before your expedition. —TW

Mental preparation is all about having the confidence that you are well prepared for the challenges you will face and that the trip planning has been comprehensive and complete. Confidence is well founded when you know that you have the skills and experience necessary to handle the situations you will face without exceeding your limits. Adventure is about pushing personal limits and enjoying the experience of performing well in a particular environment. Be aware of your teammates' levels of comfort and expertise with self-rescue and in their ability to aid others in an emergency. Team leaders must be ready and willing to take charge and make decisions to carry out your emergency plan when needed.

Equipment needs to be complete, proper, tested, and organized. Backup systems should be planned for critical pieces of equipment. Critical decisions will be made during the planning process about what you will bring and how much.

If every ounce of weight is critical, your planning process will necessarily involve difficult decisions about what to leave behind and how

MEDICAL

you will be able to continue the expedition without that piece of gear. Think through ways to improvise with what you have. If you cannot carry splinting materials, what can you use to improvise a splint for an injured teammate until you can get them out to a medical facility? For example, you can use extra clothing for padding, natural materials such as wood or equipment such as ski or tent poles for rigidity, and strips of cloth to secure your splint. A backpack can be dismantled to provide padding, fabric, and straps for splinting, or it can double as a half-bivouac sack. Extra clothing, a padded hip belt, or closed cell foam along with other materials can be fashioned into a system to stabilize an injured neck (improvised cervical collars have a bad reputation, but if this is all you have, and if done carefully, it is better than nothing).

Simple soap and clean water are perfectly adequate to clean a wound before applying a dressing, so you may not need to carry another specialized wound-cleaning solution. Duct tape can be used for many equipment repairs but also can serve to secure splints or bandages and cover hot spots before blisters develop. You should always have a plan for shelter if you have to spend an unplanned night out in bad weather. Do you have a bivy sack, a way to dig a snow cave, an insulating pad, and extra clothing? Keep a gear checklist and coordinate equipment with other team members so that there is not duplication, equipment is compatible, and critical pieces of equipment are not forgotten or broken.

Finally, anticipate problems. Discuss and agree on the route and schedule, with adequate time for weather delays built in. Your group needs a leader, and each expedition member's fitness, abilities, and special capabilities in a rescue or emergency situation should be assessed and utilized. Has everyone had appropriate immunizations and preparation to handle their personal medical problems on the expedition? Is everyone on the same page in terms of hygiene, safe water and food, and illness prevention? Do you need to train as a group for special rescue situations such as crevasse rescue or avalanche rescue? It goes without saying that it does no good if the only trained team member is the one stuck in the crevasse or buried in the avalanche.

ADVENTURE EXPEDITION ONE

Several ways to construct an emergency litter out of available materials have been described. A continuous loop system (also known as a daisy chain, cocoon wrap, or mummy litter) has been described in Paul Auerbach's extensive textbook *Wilderness Medicine*. First, a climbing rope is laid out on the ground in a continuous loop, with the loops turning side to side from head to foot. A tarp is laid on the rope, then foam pads (your sleeping pads), then stiffeners such as skis, tent poles, tree branches, canoe paddles, etc.), then more foam pads. The injured victim is then placed (with more adequate padding such as a sleeping bag) on the system. The tarp is folded around the victim and then secured by fashioning the rope loops into a daisy chain, being careful to take up slack in the rope to keep the patient secure in the litter system. Other emergency litter systems have been improvised from backpack frames, kayaks, canoes, or snowshoes.

Previous sections discussed injuries that occur in severe environments such as high altitude or extreme cold or heat. For most wilderness activities, traumatic injuries are the most predictable medical issue. Members of your team will have varied medical knowledge, capabilities, and resources, but it is the severity of the injury and the environment that your expedition is in that will most influence the outcome. Complex medical interventions are impractical, even impossible, in remote areas. Therefore, management of a severely injured teammate will focus on stabilizing and expeditiously evacuating them.

The first priority in this emergency is to control yourself and the situation. It is normal to feel anxious during an emergency, but your anxiety for the injured victim should not be transmitted to the victim or other team members. It is natural for the most highly trained medical member of your team to take over leadership of medical care of the victim, but the team leader should continue to lead the evacuation efforts. Control the situation to ensure the safety of the victim

MEDICAL

and the other team members who will be helping in the rescue. An already complex situation will become worse if another teammate is injured or killed in the rescue effort. Assess and mitigate continued dangers right away. For example, the victim may need to be moved (carefully!) before the luxury of stabilizing their spine if they are in a position where they cannot breathe, or they or rescuers are in danger from an immediate hazard (such as continued rock fall or fire). An efficient evacuation requires that all team members continue to be able to function at maximal mental and physical efficiency.

Backcountry rescuers will tell you that it takes a minimum of six healthy rescuers to evacuate an injured party on a stretcher over rough ground. Therefore, if your party is small, a wise early decision will be to send for help. If electronic communication is not possible, send someone for help and have them carry the communications equipment so that they can call for help as soon as they can (for example, from a nearby high ridgeline). Have someone stay to care for the victim, make sure that their location can be accurately pinpointed, and ensure that the party going for help knows the most efficient route and will not become lost. Protect the injured victim from further environmental hazards.

Hypothermia remains an important contributor to poor outcomes in trauma, so it is critical to keep the injured warm and dry. Erect a shelter and move them into it. Use extra clothing, insulating pads, sleeping bags, or any other equipment (such as a pack) to improvise. If you cannot move to avoid continued small rock fall hazards, shield the victim with a helmet and eye protection.

Improvised carry systems

Many techniques to carry an injured victim who can still sit up and assist with their own evacuation have been described.

Ski pole carry: Two carriers with ski poles, ice axes, or tree branches can stand side-by-side wearing backpacks. They extend the poles between them, supported by the backpack straps, and the victim sits on the poles (padded by other

Adventure Expedition One

material) and stabilizes him/herself with arms over the rescuer's shoulders. This technique requires a wide trail.

Split-coil seat: A coiled climbing rope or webbing is used to support a victim in piggyback fashion on the rescuer's back. The weight can be distributed between two rescuers side-by-side if the trail is wide.

Backpack carry: Holes are cut in a backpack to allow the victim to be supported, again piggyback style, on the rescuer's back.

Three-person wheelbarrow carry: This is an efficient system for long carries over rough terrain. Two rescuers stand side-by-side and the victim wraps his/her arm over their shoulders, while the rescuers lock arms and support the victim's back. A third rescuer is in front supporting the legs. This serves to distribute the weight of the victim over three rescuers and thereby reduces fatigue. Rope or webbing can be improvised to fashion a seat to support the victim's weight, or a sling to support their ankles.

Nonrigid litters can be fashioned out of various materials and used to move a non-critically injured patient. You need to be confident that there is no spinal injury! These can be fashioned from tree branches or skis with blankets, life jackets, backpacks, or sturdy parkas with rope suspended between. Be creative! The context of the situation should always be taken into account. We must improvise to do whatever we can, even if it is medically suboptimal, to rescue a teammate. A resourceful approach to problem-solving combined with some ingenuity could save a life.

Once these initial priorities and decisions are dealt with, you have more time to assess and stabilize the injured. We cannot go over all the details of trauma care here, but it is important that you deal with major life-threatening problems properly. In trauma care, the ABCDE priorities of care have been traditionally taught. You need to carefully examine and talk to the injured teammate and make these assessments and interventions quickly.

MEDICAL

ABCDE trauma management

Airway

First priority is to assess the airway, and simultaneously keep the neck (cervical spine) stabilized in a neutral position. Clear the airway and position the patient so that they can breathe well. For example, you may need to gently, while maintaining their spinal alignment, turn them to their side so that they can clear vomit, blood, or secretions from their throat.

Breathing

Patients need to keep moving air through their airway. Remove any constricting ropes or clothing and position them so that they can breathe. If they are initially unconscious and not breathing, you may need to assist them with mouth-to-mouth or by using a portable mask if your team carries one.

Circulation

Circulation is next. The main priority in the field is to control bleeding. Direct pressure over the bleeding site is still the best field technique. Remember to carefully check the patient's back and the back of their head for bleeding wounds that need attention. A person can lose a surprisingly large amount of blood from a scalp wound. If direct pressure does not control profuse bleeding from an extremity, a tight tourniquet applied proximal to the bleeding site may be needed.

Disability

D reminds you to do all you can to reduce the risk of disability. As much as is practical, stabilize the entire spine. If you cannot, it may be best to wait for more help (unless you must continue to self-rescue). If a limb is badly deformed from a fracture, and the distal part is pale or anesthetic, in order to improve blood flow it may be necessary to gently move the limb to a more normal position and splint it.

ADVENTURE EXPEDITION ONE

Environment

E is for exposure and environmental control. You need to keep the victim warm, but you can carefully move or temporarily remove clothing to make sure you have not missed something that you need to deal with, such as that bleeding wound on the back. Clean and dress any major wounds, splint any obvious fractures, continue to keep the patient warm, calm, comfortable, and safe.

- Now that you have a more complete idea of the injuries, formulate your evacuation plan.
- Do the injuries warrant evacuation?
- Or is it safest for the injured teammate to be treated in the field for more minor injuries and continue?
- If evacuation is needed, will it be best accomplished by land, water, or air?
- Air evacuation is not always the best answer.

The surrounding environment may make air evacuation too dangerous. Sometimes a combination of moving by foot, then ground vehicle, and finally air transport is the best option. Work with your available resources, be creative, and make wise decisions.

Years ago, two of my kayaking buddies took on a new, challenging whitewater run. An accident occurred and one friend, Hank (not his real name) sustained a severely displaced and unstable ankle fracture on the right, and a severe sprain of the left ankle. He was unable to walk and there was only one healthy teammate available to help. Their location was in a steep rugged canyon without road access for miles; it was near sunset and they had no equipment for an overnight bivouac. They decided that the best option was self-rescue.

Hank painfully stuffed his badly injured legs back into the boat and continued downriver. I don't know many others

MEDICAL

who are tough enough to do what Hank did, but he managed the severe pain, despite a few more miles of very challenging whitewater. He was even knocked over once and had to stay in his boat and roll up in order to safely continue, a maneuver that puts a lot of pressure on your ankles! They reached the takeout as it was getting dark. They still needed help hauling Hank from the river's edge up a steep bank to the road. Fortunately, another person was relaxing by the river and was able to assist. After a long night, surgery at the hospital, and months of recovery, Hank has healed and continues to enjoy the outdoors. —*TW*

Once you are out to a medical facility, your tough decisions are not over. Is the local facility really capable of dealing with the treatment of these injuries? If not, after stabilization, you will need to work with the local medical staff to evacuate to a more capable medical facility. There are medical facilities around the world you will not want to have orthopedic surgery at. Once you are stabilized, insist on travel to a better facility. These decisions can be difficult to make on the fly, so your planning and research before the trip is critical to help with decision-making during the crisis.

One of the most famous (and one of my favorite) stories that illustrates an amazing self-rescue and the difficult decision-making that can follow an injury is the story of Joe Simpson and his climbing partner, Simon Yates, detailed in the riveting book *Touching the Void* (which has also been made into a movie). The pair was climbing Siula Grande (a peak of 20,814 feet or 6,344 meters) in the Peruvian Andes in 1985 in very difficult conditions when Joe suffered a serious fall and injury. Both climbers knew that they would not likely both survive getting off the mountain, but they stuck together and worked

253

ADVENTURE EXPEDITION ONE

> at getting down for as long as possible before another disaster separated them and led to an unimaginable ordeal before Joe made it to safety, literally on the very edge of death.
>
> The point Joe's survival story illustrates that is relevant to our discussion is this: where should you be cared for after a serious injury? Joe was ultimately evacuated (partly on the back of a mule) to a Peruvian hospital where he was appropriately stabilized and treated. However, he had a complex fracture requiring specialized surgical and rehabilitative care. Most of us would prefer to defer that part of our care, if at all possible, until after transport to an excellent hospital closer to home. —*TW*

Finally, should you consider recruiting someone with more advanced medical training to join your expedition? It has been fairly common for large climbing expeditions who are tackling extreme altitudes where serious medical problems can be anticipated to include an expedition doctor on the trip. This can entail additional expense and require the inclusion of additional equipment and supplies. In return, this strategy can improve the overall safety of the group. In a smaller group, or one taking less risk, smaller amounts of supplies will be needed in the first-aid kit. Climbing doctors have accompanied climbing groups to more moderate altitudes and have been able to carry the necessary high-altitude emergency treatment drugs in a reasonably sized first-aid kit in their personal pack. A larger group climbing to extreme altitudes will need more supplies and equipment, such as oxygen bottles and a Gamow bag, dramatically complicating the logistical planning.

The ideal background for this medical team member is a physician specializing and experienced in emergency medicine, with an interest in expedition and wilderness medicine. You may want to recruit a nurse or paramedic with similar experience and interest. Finally, at a minimum, make sure a few team members are trained and comfortable in wilderness first aid. The National Outdoor Leadership School is a great place to start. Oxther organizations, such as Boy or Girl Scouts or the American Red Cross, also provide first-aid training.

254

MEDICAL

Numerous search and rescue and mountain safety organizations offer training in outdoor and mountain rescue and first aid. Finally, (usually local) governmental organizations offer advanced training for emergency medical technicians (EMTs) and wilderness emergency medical technicians (WEMTs).

> During an off-trail crossing of the Sierra that involved strenuous ascents and steep descents, sometimes through thick brush at altitudes of about 10,000 feet (3,000 meters), one of our team of three, Mike, became ill. At first, we all felt his symptoms were from the altitude. However, he became worse instead of better when we dropped down to 6,000 feet (1,800 meters), so we suspected some other cause.
>
> By the sixth day, he developed additional symptoms consistent with an acute coronary syndrome (chest tightness with exertion, nausea, shortness of breath) and worsened to the point that even with us carrying his gear, he couldn't walk slowly enough to avoid developing chest pain. We had no ability to call for help from the remote and steep canyon we were in. We had to formulate a workable plan to get him evacuated to a hospital before something worse happened. This was a situation where a subscription satellite device such as Garmin's InReach® would have been a huge help.
>
> It was mid-afternoon, so our plan had to unfold quickly. Because we had no ability to communicate when separated, we decided to hike slowly as a group with Mike not carrying any load until we found a place to camp that was also accessible by helicopter. Fortunately, we promptly found a suitable site and quickly erected a shelter. I stayed with Mike to have him rest and keep him fed, hydrated, and comfortable, while the other member of our team, Mark, packed a light pack and quickly hiked up the canyon to a ranger station more than five miles away. Fortunately, the ranger station was manned (the ranger was planning to leave the next day for a five-day trek and the station would have been unmanned).

ADVENTURE EXPEDITION ONE

> Mark carried a detailed map with our position marked, written GPS coordinates, and my medical notes about Mike's condition. Despite some communications challenges caused by a malfunctioning repeater, the ranger was able to get a helicopter dispatched in time to evacuate Mike before dark. The helicopter pilot did an amazing job of balancing one strut of the craft on the sloping granite above the steep river in order to drop off two Parkmedics to stabilize Mike and then pick him up with the same "hotload" technique. Mike has recovered and is doing well. —*TW*

First, you should organize your personal medical kit and then work on a more extensive kit for the group. An important factor to consider is the risk of accidental separation from the rest of the group. There are things that you should keep on your person in case of a fall, or swamping, or another accident that not only separates you from your group but also separates you from your pack. These basic supplies can be kept in cargo pockets or a small hip pack and will enable you to self-treat more minor wounds, signal for help, and help protect you from the elements.

Always with you gear list:
- Identification
- Hat and sunglasses
- Small pack of bandages and tape
- Knife or other sharp blade
- Bandanna or triangular bandage
- Signaling devices— whistle, signal mirror
- Map and compass
- Lighter or waterproof matches
- Thin nylon cord
- Poncho and/or space blanket
- Energy bar

(adapted from Auerbach, Paul, editor, *Wilderness Medicine,* 4th edition, St. Louis, Mo., 2001)

MEDICAL

In-pack personal gear:

- Water and water purification system
- Personal first-aid and hygiene supplies
- Prescription medications in waterproof container
- Selected over-the-counter supplies: acetaminophen, Loperamide (Imodium AD), hydrocortisone cream, antifungal cream, sunscreen, antibacterial ointment, DEET insect repellent

(adapted from Auerbach, Paul, editor, *Wilderness Medicine*, 4th edition, St. Louis, Mo., 2001)

Team medical kit

Wound care supplies:

- Irrigation syringe with 18-gauge needle (for washing out wounds with purified water)
- Povidone-iodine solution and/or alcohol pads (for cleaning the skin surrounding the wound)
- Wound closure strips and tincture of benzoin (adhesive for the closure strips)
- Wound closure glue (Dermabond or cyanoacrylate)
- Moleskin
- Antiseptic towelettes
- Cotton-tipped applicators
- Non-latex gloves
- Antibiotic ointment (triple antibiotic, Neosporin, etc.)

ADVENTURE EXPEDITION ONE

Bandaging materials:
- Adhesive cloth tape
- Bandaids
- Gauze 4 × 4 sterile dressing pads
- Nonadherent sterile dressing (xeroform gauze, Vaseline gauze)
- Elastic bandage wraps (Ace wraps)
- Gauze bandage roll
- Trauma dressing

Over-the-counter supplies:
- Sunscreen and lip balm
- Hydrocortisone cream 1 percent
- Antifungal cream (Tinactin, Clotrimazole, Lotrimin, Lamasil, etc.)
- Pain relievers: Acetaminophen and Ibuprofen (see text for discussion of relative advantages/disadvantages)
- Antihistamine: Diphenhydramine
- Ranitidine (antihistamine and stomach acid blocker)
- Antacid (Maalox or Mylanta—chewable tabs rather than liquid)
- Antidiarrheal: Loperamide (Imodium AD)
- Rectal glycerine suppositories
- Saline eyewash
- Glucose paste

MEDICAL

Miscellaneous equipment:

- Scissors
- Forceps
- #11 scalpel blade
- Sterile 18-gauge needle (for wound irrigation, blister drainage, and splinter removal)
- Thermometer
- Temporary dental filling (Cavit)
- Temporary splinting material (SAM splint) and/or air-stirrup ankle brace
- Triangular bandage and safety pins
- Plastic resealable bags to keep supplies dry and organized

(adapted from Auerbach, Paul, editor, *Wilderness Medicine*, 4th edition, St. Louis, Mo., 2001)

In addition to these basic supplies, additional supplies can be carried if your expedition will include a member with more advanced medical training. In addition, some specialized supplies should be included for expeditions in unique environments or at high risk.

Advanced medical equipment for major expeditions at risk of serious injury/illness:

(As with any piece of equipment, the inclusion of each item should be considered individually based on your risk assessment and weight/space limitations. Use of this equiment requires advanced medical training and expertise.)

- Oropharyngeal and nasopharyngeal airway equipment
- Cricothyrotomy set-up
- Thoracic vent set-up
- Ophthalmoscope with fluorescein strips

ADVENTURE EXPEDITION ONE

- Backup glucometer and oral glucose preparation (diabetics on the trip should be carrying their own set)
- Oxygen
- Stethoscope
- Pulse oximeter
- Mechanical suction device
- Incision and drainage kit
- IV solution and administration sets
- Needles and syringes

(adapted from Auerbach, Paul, editor, *Wilderness Medicine,* 4th edition, St. Louis, Mo., 2001)

Medications for high-risk expeditions (requiring medical training and prescription):

General use:

- Antibiotics (a selection is required based on likely cause of infection. Recommended are ciprofloxacin, ceftriaxone (injectable), azithromycin, trimethoprim/sulfamethoxasole, clindamycin, metronidazole. Others may be selected for travel in certain regions.)
- Ondansteron (Zofran®) for vomiting
- Beta-agonist metered dose inhaler (albuterol) for asthma or anaphylactic reaction
- Ophthalmic anesthetic
- Epinephrine autoinjector (individuals needing this know how to use it and should be carrying their own set on person)
- Oral corticosteroid
- Narcotic oral pain medication (Vicodin®)
- Narcotic pain medication patch (Fentanyl® for severe pain when unable to give oral pain medication)

MEDICAL

For expeditions to high altitude:
• Acetazolamide • Corticosteroid (such as Decadron, both oral and inject-able, for HACE) • Nifedipine (for HAPE) • Pulse oximeter • Gamow bag and accessories for large expeditions • Oxygen for expeditions to extreme altitudes
For expeditions at risk of snow blindness:
• Ophthalmic cycloplegic (such as cyclopentolate 1 percent) to help with pain from snowblindness • Ophthalmic corticosteroid-antibiotic combination (such as Maxitrol) for short-term use in snowblindness (must first do fluorescein stain exam to rule out herpetic keratitis). (adapted from Auerbach, Paul, editor, *Wilderness Medicine*, 4th edition, St. Louis, Mo., 2001)

For other specialized expeditions, you will want to consider additional equipment or medications to help with the risks you anticipate. For example, expeditions to very cold environments should carry additional hand and/or foot warmers and ensure that clothing and shelter are available to assist an expedition member who is suffering from frostbite or hypothermia. Another example would be an exploratory whitewater expedition that would want to carry additional equipment to assist a teammate who suffers a near-drowning accident, such as a CPR Microshield or Pocket Mask. If there is the risk of avalanche, additional gear for avalanche safety and search and rescue should be included (Avalanche backpacks, Life-link ski/probe poles, avalanche beacons, shovels, and, by far the most efficacious when someone is buried, avalanche search dogs).

261

ADVENTURE EXPEDITION ONE

In addition to all of these equipment items, your most important device will be your evacuation and communication plan. When an accident occurs that is critical or otherwise exceeds your group's ability to self-rescue, how will you call for help? In some areas, a cell phone is adequate if you get a reliable signal and can keep it charged (and working in extreme cold!). For a more remote trip, your group may need to invest in a satellite phone or a more sophisticated radio system (such as for an open-water trip) in order to be able to put out a distress call. Accurate navigation is always critical when a medical emergency occurs. Whether you will self-rescue or you call for help, your location needs to be known and communicated. Do not leave on your trip without knowing how to use your map and compass and your GPS device.

> My closest call occurred when I was caught in a sudden storm at 13,900 feet (4,200 meters) on one of the Cascade volcanoes. Conditions rapidly deteriorated from mild temperatures and blue sky to sustained 100 mph winds, -11°C (12°F) real temperature, and whiteout visibility. I couldn't see my feet for the next eight hours of daylight while I descended. My communications gear mistake: I did not keep my cell phone warm. It does no good to be where you get a good signal if the phone is so cold it won't even turn on. I learned to take my phone out of my pack and carry it inside my jacket to stay warm in case of emergency. —*TW*

Careful planning and preparation for potential medical problems on your expedition will reduce risks and will improve the chances that an ill or injured teammate will be able to continue travel with your group. When a more serious emergency occurs, your careful planning will help to keep your team calm and the injured teammate more safe and comfortable while rescue is carried out.

Stay safe out there.

262

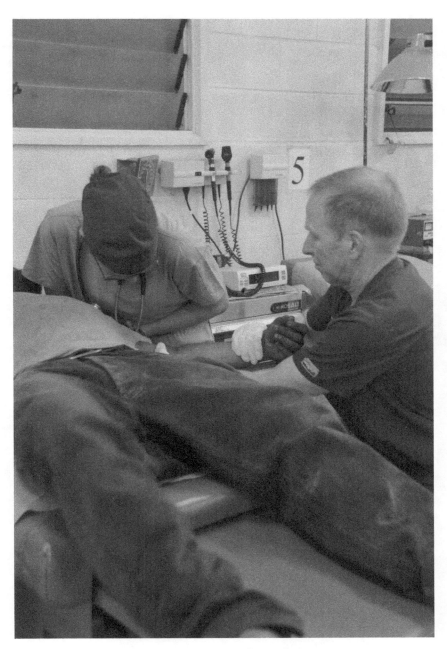
Terry repositioning an elbow dislocation.

PART NINE

A Full Expedition Day

Antarctica

<u>The morning</u>
   My watch alarm goes off at 6:00 a.m. I've been awake for thirty minutes already but I force myself to stay in my sleeping bag, moving as little as possible. Every minute of rest means I'll be able to ski another twelve miles today.
   Although my mind wants to remain in bed for another half hour, I know that's a mistake. A half hour of sleeping in costs me three-quarters of a mile of travel. Over three months of sleeping in a half an hour, that's an entire sixty miles lost. I remind myself that expeditions have failed simply because teams have slept in too often.
   Another reason I linger is the need to have a bowel movement. Since I'm eating 6,000 calories per day and most of it is fat, my digestion has been in overdrive mode for a month. I pull my boot liners from my sleeping bag and stuff them into my Norwegian boots. They've been drying in my sleeping bag overnight aided by my body heat. I prevent the water bottles from falling out of my sleeping bag, as it's −50°F and overcast with a 20 mph wind outside. If I leave them out for any longer than necessary, they'll chill and freeze before I can drink them later today.

A Full Expedition Day

While I'm putting my boots on, I turn my sleeping bag inside out and spread it out. This allows the bag to air out and dry from my body moisture. The times I failed to do this, my bag is colder the next night. It makes a noticeable difference in my sleeping comfort.

I drag my shell pants into the bag and put them on over my thin wool long underwear—it's too cold to squat inside the tent in just long underwear. I grab a single packaged wet wipe and put it into my pocket to warm it up. I roll around into a sitting position while still enveloped in the sleeping bag and pull off my down booties one at a time and slip my feet into the ski boots. I move carefully to prevent the steel buckles from puncturing anything.

Unzipping the tent door and fly, I step over the zipper to avoid damaging it and take a squatting position on the ice platform I built last night. I make sure to pull my clothing down far enough not to soil myself. Even the slightest mistake here is a potential disaster. There is no way to launder clothing here and the chance of infecting myself from fecal residue is high. Hiding in the tent's vestibule, I assume the position over the toilet pit. I remove my thin glove liners and stuff them into the top of my shirt fingers first while leaving the wrists hanging out. This keeps the fingers warm while preventing the gloves from slipping down my shirt into the toilet pit.

Using the chunks of ice I prepared last night, I clean up. The trick is to wipe fast enough to prevent frostbite without going too fast. Antarctic ice is like sandpaper if used too aggressively. I drop each piece into the makeshift toilet hole inside the vestibule. Once the ice is clean, I roll forward into my tent to relieve the burn in my legs. I tear off only two squares of toilet paper to finish the job and then clean my hands using alcohol sanitizer. It chills my fingers, so I stuff them inside my pants until the burning stops, then put the liner gloves back on to prevent my skin from splitting. I put the down booties back on and stuff the boot liners into armpits of my jacket to keep them warm.

I use my titanium spork to chisel off chunks of butter using the snow shovel as a cutting board to avoid stabbing or cutting myself. A laceration can be fatal here. Should I cut a major blood vessel, I'll likely die before help arrives. I never, ever cut toward my legs, hands, or anything else. Each butter chunk goes into my mug, followed by

265

ADVENTURE EXPEDITION ONE

a pre-measured mix of a cup of granola, three heaped tablespoons of cane sugar, and a cup's worth of whole fat powdered milk. I pour a hot chocolate packet into my other mug with a lid. Pulling the somewhat hot water thermos from its cocoon of ski poggies (ski pole hoods) and gloves, I pour the water into both mugs. The water is sixty degrees but steams. Though cool, the water burns my tongue, as my body is used to polar temperatures. The spoon freezes to my tongue several times while the cereal turns into an icy slush. In minutes the hot chocolate is cool. Everything in snowy locations takes longer. By the time I'm done eating, the food and drink are cold.

I have used the last of the hot water to make tea that allows me to swish the hot chocolate out of the cup. Once finished with the teabag, I have squeezed the water into the cup and drunk it. The teabag now becomes my sponge for a morning bath. This is the only way I can clean my skin. It is cold and unpleasant but prevents even less pleasant skin problems.

This breakfast mixture causes me to have a second bowel movement. There is little warning from the high-fat diet—it hits fast. The process is the same as before, but I use the semi-frozen wet wipes after the ice but before the two squares of toilet paper. I have little spare paper for emergencies, so everything is measured out exactly. I pack the remaining ice over the toilet hole to prevent contamination and not leave a surface mess.

My toes are usually cold from swapping boots, so I put my feet into my sleeping bag. At the same time, I pull out the ski boot liners and place them back into my jacket to warm them up along with my heavy gloves. Fifteen minutes before I leave the tent, I also put the actual boots in my jacket to warm them up. If I start with cold feet in the morning, they stay miserably cold all day. With my feet in the sleeping bag, I drain the air mattress and pack my gear. I load the sleeping bag into its stuff sack but leave the top hanging out.

To load the sled, I drag it into the vestibule. This awkward process keeps me from freezing while standing still in the cloudy −65°C (−86°F) wind chill. I load the sleeping bag at the front of the sled. I take five chugs of water to rehydrate, then test each water bottle for leaks, and then place all five one-liter water bottles into waterproof

A Full Expedition Day

bags. These go into the semi-unstuffed sleeping bag. Without this insulation, the bottles will freeze shut and possibly turn to solid ice.

A few minutes before I step out, I also put on my double-layer goggles to warm them up. If I put them on and immediately step out, they instantly fog and blind me. I pull out the warm heavy gloves from my jacket, put them on with the safety (idiot) cords, put on the towing harness over my shirt, and put my jackets on top. This assembly process allows me to adapt to daily temperature changes without removing the harness. Changes in cloud cover, wind speed, and hills make a huge difference in temperature. Overheating and sweating guarantees hypothermia, invites frostbite, makes clothing constantly cold, and makes me nauseous. Also, the harness squashes the jacket insulation, creating cold spots.

I shove the sled out, make sure the tent vents are unzipped, and hide in the vestibule. Mildew has formed inside the tent from food crumbs and occasional melted snow. I use a tiny bit of hand sanitizer to kill the mildew and brush food particles out with a bike brush from the tent every morning to keep things sanitary.

Crawling out, I partially zip up the door and completely zip the fly. The wind shoves me around and I immediately start cooling down. I clip carabiners to the sleds and upwind the tent guy lines. The sleds provide a minor windbreak and prevent the tent from blowing away should I lose control. I loosen the guy lines but don't dig the stakes out, pull the tent poles out of one side, and let the tent deflate. If the tent's vents are zipped, deflation takes forever, making me colder.

I always face downwind while handling the shovel. High winds can easily flip it up and hit me in the face. I also never pry with the shovel, as the ice is hard and cold temperatures make metal brittle. This shovel broke earlier in my expedition and I had to repair it. I pull out the downwind stakes and nest them, wrapping the guy lines around them. If I don't, they tangle and make pitching the tent nearly impossible in severe weather.

Burrito-rolling the tent with the poles still inside the sleeves, I lie on the tent while being extremely cautious not to damage anything. I only have two spare poles. With the tent rolled, I pull the remaining tent stakes with the same procedure as the downwind ones. I strap the

ADVENTURE EXPEDITION ONE

rolled tent to the sled bag. Only then do I relax. Should I damage the tent, poles, or lose the tent in the wind, my expedition and life are at risk. Using the ski pole tips to chip ice out of the boot binding holes, I clip into my skis as quickly as possible. The quicker I am on my skis, the less my feet chill. When my feet grow too cold while breaking camp, I step on the skis for a moment to warm my feet. It's amazing how much difference standing on the skis instead of the ice makes.

Checking around for any dropped items, I clip the harness to the sled traces (rope), put my gloves into the ski poggies, and drag the sleds forward ten feet. I look back to make sure once more that I haven't dropped anything (it's happened), and begin my first 75-minute towing session.

<u>While ski-towing</u>

I adjust my speed so I never have to stop for a breather. Every stop causes me to lose mileage and is demoralizing. This is similar to mountain climbing. I adjust my pace to avoid overexertion. Even though traveling slow is annoying, stopping and starting is worse. Travel efficiency is everything in polar travel.

Traveling toward the pole from Hercules Inlet means the sun will be at my back from nine a.m. to six p.m. Should I have made the return trip, I would have needed to switch schedules. The radiation is intense and will cause second-degree burns on any exposed skin.

To navigate, I use a globally balanced compass. One that is tuned for North America would be difficult to use. The magnetic declination starts at 39° at Hercules Inlet (80° latitude) and drifts to 45° near the pole. A compass with an adjustable declination is key to avoiding mistakes. I hold my compass mid-chest and take a sighting, look up and select prominent sastrugi or clouds, then drop the compass while still looking at my target and ski away. Should I look away even for a moment after sighting or skiing, I invariably lose the target. It all starts to look the same. The technique requires constant concentration. After a month of travel, I become obsessed with traveling straight. During whiteout conditions, navigation becomes even more challenging. I have mounted the compass on a Delrin harness attached to my chest, freeing my hands.

268

A Full Expedition Day

When I ski, I time myself to the minute. To do this, I keep my analog watch on the inside of my wrist. It's much easier to use a ski pole to lift my glove to see the time. This technique is easy, efficient, and only distracts me for a second. This position allows me to easily reseal my glove and jacket. It's difficult to check time with my watch on the outside of my wrist with heavy jackets. The top-of-wrist position always exposes my skin, causing me to stop to prevent frostbite.

Digital watches turn dark at a steep viewing angle with polarized goggles or glasses. GPS watches are nearly useless. They require constant charging and the LCD becomes sluggish in the extreme cold. An analog watch can be checked with a half-second glance. Digital requires a much longer look. Some explorers keep a watch on a necklace but I would worry that it would snag or become lost.

When stopping for breaks, I chug five full gulps of water, eat my food, then chug water five more times. This volume generally keeps me hydrated. If I'm not conscious of how much water I drink on breaks, I end up parched half-way through a towing session. To compensate I would have to drink much more water on the next break, causing me to have to stop for a pee break, slowing me down even more. It took time to figure out the exact amount to drink while having one liter of water remaining at the end of the day. The experience is like running a precise machine. It requires constant attention. After my last drink, I always wipe water off the bottle threads and tap out the water from the lid. Even the tiniest bit of water can freeze the lid shut before the next break. Often the water freezes on the threads while drinking. It's important to remove the ice, as it can damage the plastic threads and cause leaks.

My bars and food freeze during the day. However, crunching them up when warmed the night before makes eating them possible. Breaking a tooth would be an unpleasant prospect. It's important to choose food that can be eaten while frozen solid.

My breaks are no longer than fifteen minutes, as I end up shivering violently. I keep them to ten minutes when possible and even then I freeze. It isn't worth pulling out an extra jacket to put on because I could lose it in the wind, plus pulling it from and putting it back in

269

ADVENTURE EXPEDITION ONE

the sled takes time. Instead, I just choose to freeze. It is tough to deal with but ends up being more efficient.

I try to film myself in action as much as possible, though not nearly enough. Two of the three camera batteries I have brought are generics—a huge mistake. In warm conditions, they worked the same as the originals. In cold conditions, they haven't lasted.

Stopping the moment I feel a hotspot is important. Keeping my feet dry, cool, and unblistered makes all the difference. It is dangerous to completely pull off my boots and socks while in extreme cold with strong wind. What I do is sit on my sled and create a pocket inside my down parka inside the sled. I untie my boot on the downwind side of the sled, pull my foot out, and immediately stuff it inside the parka. This keeps my toes from freezing. It is awkward but it prevents frostbite. Even the slightest bunching or pill on a sock causes debilitating pain. A subtle change in my gait can hurt my legs, back, and hips while towing three hundred pounds. I fix the socks and reverse the process, moving as quickly as possible. I have left the ski attached to my other foot the whole time. My goal is not to stand directly on the ice until setting up camp.

I haven't developed blisters or lost skin on the bottom of my feet. The pairing of Wright® socks and mid- to heavy-weight Smart Wool® socks is working perfectly. This combination effectively gives me three socks, eliminating friction. I find pulling the heavy sleds chafes my Achilles and heel so I have applied Band-Aid Tough Strips® on the heels of both feet. They're superior to duct tape, as they breathe and stick for over ten days if I don't snag or adjust them after sticking them on. They're a critical part of my kit. I've seen horrid pictures of the bottom of people's feet completely missing all the skin because of sweaty feet from overexertion or using vapor barrier liners. Keeping my feet dry makes all the difference.

It's important to prevent any foot infection. I mark all of my socks 'L' and 'R' and keep them on that foot. Should I develop athlete's foot, the infection will be contained to one foot. This technique helps minimize the spreading of problems.

Keeping my goggles from fogging requires constant attention. If I even become slightly warm, they will fog from evaporating

A Full Expedition Day

perspiration. That means I have to stay annoyingly cool the whole time. I add heat by speeding up for a moment or adjusting my jacket. I never breathe into my goggles to clear them. That only creates an icy film. At times when my goggles fully ice up from breathing into my face mask, I substitute glacier glasses to keep going. These ice up almost immediately, too. What I do is hang them slightly off my face so I can only see my feet and compass. It requires careful attention not to develop snow blindness while doing this. The few times I go outside without my goggles or glasses, I use both of my arms to block the snow and sky to create a viewing slit. It feels silly but I never injure my eyes.

In complete whiteouts, I waggle my head back and forth to try and develop a sense of the landscape. Without shadows, humans cannot see obstacles when everything is white on white. I found that if I shift my head back and forth like a snake, I could pick up subtle shading variations and see the landscape. Although it is annoying and distracting, I avoid countless holes while skiing essentially blind.

Preventing polar thigh and stomach takes some work. This is a condition where skiers develop severe chilblains, leaving large open sores ripe for infection. I know about the problem, so I create my own polar thigh guards (I've seen other explorers wear skirts) and use a fleece jacket around my waist to prevent stomach chilblains. I never develop chilblains because of that precaution. Once they develop, there's almost no way to get rid of them until I warm up for days. They won't heal just sleeping overnight in a sleeping bag.

In the event that I need a bowel movement while skiing, I have to prepare as early as possible. Without a tent, exposing myself in −56°C (−70°F) wind chill invites frostbite and chilblains. The moment I realize this is going to happen, I set up my sleds as a windbreak. Then, with my shovel, I dig a hole deep enough to squat in out of the wind. Depending on the ice consistency, I sometimes have to move my sleds to find softer snow. I make sure to cut and then lift the snow rather than prying, to prevent breaking my shovel. Also, I pile the snow chunks within arm's reach, as I use them to clean up. I quickly learn to stow my toilet paper where I can find it easily. I have to be careful to avoid letting the roll and its bag blow away in the wind and prevent it from falling into my waste. Every

271

chunk of ice is used for exactly one wipe and then tossed as far as possible to avoid contamination. The rest of the procedure is the same as in the morning.

I leave my heavy outer gloves on so that if I have a wiping mistake, it is easier to deal with by cleaning them with snow. Liner gloves are too absorbent and holding ice with bare hands guarantees frostbite. Avoiding spreading germs is key to staying healthy. Again, I only use two squares of toilet paper at the end of the process. I only stay with my pants down for the minimum time possible while making sure I am completely clean. I develop eraser-sized chilblains on my hips and bum from the exposure but nothing worse.

The technique of hiding in a pit works so well that sometimes I think the wind has stopped as there is nothing to indicate wind (flags, trees, etc.). That is, until I raise my head up into the 40 mph wind, being nearly blown over every time. Digging the hole takes effort but it saves me every time.

Setting up camp

After stopping at six p.m., I position the sleds to create a blockade and attachment point for the tent. The wind is rarely less than fifteen miles per hour, more than enough to blow the tent away. I first test the snow to see if it is soft enough for tent stakes and digging. The ice needs to have the consistency of styrofoam, solid enough to hold structure, but not any harder. Only then do I disconnect my skis. Since the ice drains heat out of my feet, I only have so long while standing on ice before they are searing from the cold conduction.

Once I have found a good spot, I drive the stakes straight into the ice, careful not to bend them, and clip carabiners from each sled to the stakes. I then unroll the tent and clip the upwind main guy lines to the carabiners. The door is always downwind. Lying on the tent, I push the poles into place. While holding the center guy line I step off the tent. It immediately pops into shape, often dragging the sleds and me until the stakes stop the motion. I have tried to stake out the whole tent bottom and then slide the poles in, but they flail around in the wind. Others have had tent poles smash them in the face, shattering their goggles. This is also why I prefer a tunnel to a dome tent design.

A FULL EXPEDITION DAY

Pitching a dome tent alone in windy conditions is extremely difficult as a soloist, and tough as well with a team.

As soon as I have the tent staked out and taut, I transfer my camping supplies into the tent. I keep everything in large waterproof bags, preventing loss of small, important items. It also makes loading and unloading fast. As soon as everything is in the tent, I pull the sleeping bag and down-filled air mattress out of their stuff sacks. This allows the down to expand while I finish building my camp. I also place the water bottles back into the sleeping bag to prevent freezing while I am outside.

I use my shovel to build a wind blockade. Even though it is extra work, it makes a significant difference in tent warmth and also reduces wind noise. I pile the chunks up to six feet thick and as tall as the tent. On stormy days, the wind will turn the blocks into a solid aerodynamic mass, allowing most of the wind to blow over rather than on the tent. On extreme wind days, the wind tears apart most of the snow block wall.

During strong wind days, I seal the entire tent fly with snow blocks. Although others suggest not doing this, I find it prevents spindrift snow from filling up the gap between the fly and tent. This powdery snow would solidify, weigh the tent down, and add an hour to breaking camp the next day. Once I have the tent secured, I fill the vestibule with snow chunks for water. It takes a sizeable mound of snow to make five liters of water.

Once I have piled the snow and built the berm, I double-check the tent stakes and guy lines. Often the tent shifts, causing the lines to droop. I make adjustments so the tent is snug but not overly tight. If it's too tight, the seams can tear. If it's too loose, the whipping action shreds edges and allows the guy lines to abrade the connection points. At this temperature, constant yanking can also break the stake attachments.

Before I hop into the tent, I inspect the bottom of my sleds and re-wax my skis. Polar snow is coarse. It's similar to skiing on sand. It's so cold that the snow doesn't melt from the pressure. The friction from the harsh snow scrapes off the wax, increasing drag and slowing me down. If I skip waxing for two days, I can feel the difference. It is

273

ADVENTURE EXPEDITION ONE

tough to apply cold-weather wax with a cork to melt it into the skis but the effort always made a nine-hour ski day easier.

By the end of setting up camp, my hands and feet are cold. I jump into the tent, zip up the door, and nestle into the sleeping bag to warm myself up. I sit on my foam Z-Rest® so I'm not sitting on the ice. Once in the tent, I set about working on several priorities. I place the satellite phone, GPS, and camera into my jacket or pants to begin warming them up.

Handling the stove

Handling the stove and fuel requires careful attention. Topping up the fuel bottle with white gas requires extreme care. Any fuel spilled on human skin can cause instant frostbite from the rapid evaporation. A fuel frostbite injury ended an Arctic expedition in 2017 in the first days of the expedition. Using gloves to handle fuel is dangerous because they'll soak up the gas and then be exposed to open flame, a sure recipe for disaster. For all the risks of frostbite, bare hands are the best.

Another risk is poisoning from spraying or spattering fuel on the ice chunks meant for water. I carve a small spot right next to the tent when I fill my small fuel bottle from 1.5 liter storage bottles through a funnel. When these plastic bottles run low, I transfer fuel into them from the one-gallon steel cans. I only do this on clear, low-wind days, away from the tent, to eliminate the risk of a large spill on any of my gear. Others have destroyed their satellite phones and sleeping bags from fuel spills. I dig a small hole and pack the bottle in with the loosened ice chunks. The bottles never tip and I avoid contaminating the snow. I use light waterproof gloves for the large transfers, as the steel can is too cold without gloves.

It is important to watch the pot water level at all times. Too little water and the snow will sponge it up, allowing the pot to scorch. Too little snow and I waste time by not getting the most out of my stove. The key is to take a quick peek into the pot

A Full Expedition Day

to make sure all is going well. After some time, I have learned how long to go between checks based on the temperature, snow density, and wind.

Lighting the stove is a dangerous activity. I know from *North to the Pole* (Steger and Schurke) that Will Steger's Arctic dog team suffered from fume and carbon monoxide nausea until they started warming up their fuel bottles in $-70°F$ temperatures. A fume-induced headache and nausea are miserable. Although one should never use a stove inside a tent, there is no choice in polar and high mountain environments. Standing outside in a $-90°F$ wind chill isn't an option. I have safely run the stove inside the tent in the worst weather.

I coat the fuel pump O-ring with lip balm, as well as the metal rod that inserts into the pump. It's easy to damage the pump to fuel hose O-ring and cause a dangerous fuel leak. The lip balm makes inserting the rod easy. I use an MSR XGK Expedition Stove®. Only stoves that run the fuel line through the flame can be used due to the cold and altitude. The South Pole atmospheric altitude is 11,000 feet (3,350 meters).

I have brought two backup pumps and a complete backup stove. Should they fail, I might die from dehydration before help arrives. I don't want to risk my life and a six-figure expedition on a twenty-dollar plastic pump.

My two-liter pot has a heat exchanger to improve heat transfer and reduce fuel usage. The stove is wrapped with heavy aluminum for the same purpose. I use a flint and steel to light the stove. It's the only fire starter I know of that's not affected by cold or altitude. I have brought a spare flint and steel, plus four lighters and a few packs of matches. Many things can be overcome but the inability to light the stove would terminate my expedition.

It is important to have the stove on some sort of stove board. This is important to reflect heat back to the stove. More importantly, it allows me to pick up and throw the stove out in

ADVENTURE EXPEDITION ONE

case of a fire. The board also prevents snow from melting and tilting the stove and boiling water over. I used a double-stacked aluminum basting pan. It was squashed by the end of the expedition but it's the lightest option available. It also allows me to keep the fuel bottle off the ice, improving stove performance.

I don't use fuel paste to ignite the stove. Instead, I turn on the fuel and allow some to spatter into the cup, and then shut it off. This keeps flare-ups to a minimum. Sometimes it takes one strike and other times twenty with the flint and steel to ignite the stove but it always works. The moment the fuel ignites, I turn the fuel back on to a low level. The goal is to avoid any flare-ups. They can set the tent on fire and generate a blast of carbon monoxide. All the while doing this, I keep the upper door zipper and both tent vents completely open to allow fumes to escape.

After a few days on the expedition, I learned that I have to completely unzip the top zipper and stick my head out of the tent until the fumes clear. The fumes are stomach-churning and I soon found they could give me a headache for the rest of the night. I can't unzip the door from the bottom because it prevents the stove from operating properly and allows snow in. While sticking my head out, I hover over the stove, so I have to avoid flare-ups. I hold the door open as wide as possible during start-up with my arm out of the way of any flame columns until I can stick my head out to breathe. Even though heat escapes the tent, I would rather deal with cold than carbon monoxide poisoning. This has killed people in their tents . Even after the flame is blue, it takes time for the fumes to dissipate.

Before lighting the stove, I place the pot on my shovel and add an inch of water to prepare for snow melting. This prevents snow sublimation—that is, having the ice turn to steam, bypassing the water stage. The pot can scorch, warp, and even crack from the tremendous heat without water. I have to finish my ski day with at least a liter of water to start

A Full Expedition Day

the melting process and also to rehydrate myself while I wait. I've made the mistake of having no water at the end of the day on other expeditions. Coaxing water out of snow takes patience and extreme care. After making this mistake once, I decided I would rather be a bit dehydrated than have no water to start melting snow.

I never put the pot on the snow as it sticks and then drops into the flame, extinguishing it. I learned this the hard way. Instead, I use the shovel as a pot holder. It's the safest place to put a blazing hot pot, too. All my outer gear is synthetic, which will easily melt from hot metal or flames.

Although this seems like a laborious discussion about the stove, handling it safely is everything. A mistake can be costly or lethal. Imagine the disaster of passing out from carbon monoxide or burning a tent down in a five-day polar storm.

Boiling the water but not allowing heavy steam to form requires constant attention. For pot handling, I used my light waterproof gloves. Burns from a hot pot or boiling water is painful. The moment the water boils, I take the pot off, pour the water into a Nalgene® bottle, set the pot back on the stove, and put the lid back on to avoid letting heat and steam out.

The reason to avoid boiling steam is three-fold. One is avoiding fuel waste. The water isn't going to be any hotter after it starts boiling. Second is to prevent the steam from icing the tent. Every time I allowed steam to form, I end up being extra cold from the steam converting to water and then ice on me. That steam also penetrates down coats, ruining the insulation quality of the down. The third reason is to prevent tent zippers from icing shut.

ADVENTURE EXPEDITION ONE

Every time I fill a Nalgene®, I wipe water off the threads to prevent the lid from freezing shut and to avoid leaks. I don't put the Neoprene sleeve on the bottle until after I fill it. The reason I do this is that invariably some water will dribble down the side, soaking the Neoprene that will then turn to ice, defeating the insulation. Every time I then tilt the bottle sideways to check for leaks from ice build-up. Should there be a leak, I open the lid, wipe off the residual ice and try again until there are no leaks. Nalgene® bottles are tough but not invincible. Half-way through my expedition, one of the lids completely fails. It is ice-free but it keeps leaking. I have brought one spare lid for just such an emergency.

Electronics

I place the first hot water bottle of the night into a small waterproof silicone nylon bag, seal it, and insert it into my sleeping bag to keep it warm. This is why checking for a leak is critical. Storing them in the sleeping bag is the only way to prevent the bottles from freezing. This hot water bottle also allows me to warm my electronics. I load the satellite phone, satellite transponder, camera, and GPS into a sealable plastic bag, place it on the hot water bottle, then drape the sleeping bag over the bundle.

No matter how long I have the satellite phone inside my parka, the LCD is sluggish and the battery won't hold up well. The boiling water bottle trick warms the phone up to 60°F. Charging the battery when warm extends the runtime, too.

While the stove melts ice, I prepare the solar panels. Initially, I tied them to bamboo poles outside but the wind blew them around. Should the panels be damaged, I can't charge my satellite phone to make my daily calls. This would terminate my expedition because it is too dangerous to be on the ice without communications.

I have brought a small multimeter with me to diagnose electrical problems. With some experimentation, I have figured out that if the two panels are connected in parallel, they will maintain the voltage between the tent and outside fly. The tent has to be facing in the correct direction and there can be absolutely no clouds, even high

A FULL EXPEDITION DAY

thin ones. If conditions are good, there is enough current to maintain the phone-charging circuit. Should the voltage drop from poor placement or cloud cover, the phone acts up and has to be reset by removing the battery. Satellite phones are touchy. Now that I have figured this configuration out, I can charge all of my devices even when there are 50 mph winds outside. If cloud cover is thin and winds are light, a rare condition, I place the panels outside for better efficiency. Charging every evening is important because there can be stretches of complete overcast for a week, preventing any type of charging.

It is important that I call my support company exactly on time. There is only a ten-minute window to make the call each night. The stove is loud enough to make hearing difficult, so I have to be done with it before my call. Add flapping tent noise in strong winds to that of a running stove and hearing is nearly impossible. Being efficient with camp activities like melting water makes a significant difference in how stressful the evening is.

Only when my satellite phones are fully charged will I charge my camera. The phones are far more important and I have back-up camera batteries. I only transmit a GPS point to my tracking company once the transponder is warm, extending its battery life, too.

The Nightly Routine

Once each pot of water has boiled, I follow the same filling procedure and keep them in the sleeping bag. My goal is not to use the stove in the morning at all, by doing the work at night. I also have a thermos to keep the water extra-warm for a morning hot chocolate and to help make breakfast more palatable.

After the electrical system is set up, and between loading ice into the hot water pot, I prepare food for the next day. The rule is to randomly grab a daily ration bag from the sleds. If I make a conscious choice, I know I will start eating the food I prefer most. That would be a mistake, as I would subconsciously leave the least desirable food until the end, the toughest part of the expedition. This would cause stress, so I force myself never to look at the daily ration bag.

279

ADVENTURE EXPEDITION ONE

I use the second bottle of hot water for my dehydrated dinners. Using a food thermos, I pour the food in and quickly add the hot water. Every second that the container is open makes my food that much colder by the time I eat it. It is important to fill the water to near the top. If not, the dehydrated food will remain crunchy and cold. Stirring the powder with the titanium spoon is the only way to prevent dry dust globs. Shaking doesn't eliminate them.

When I pull the dinner out of the gallon bag, I put the next day's food bars into my jacket. After an hour, they are somewhat thawed. I crunch up the contents but leave them in the wrapper. The next day, I can tear open the wrapper and eat the tiny chunks. As the food bars freeze solid, having bite-sized bits makes it possible to melt them in my mouth. All food bars to be eaten the next day have to be crunched up, except for the shortbread cookies.

I use my watch to time ten minutes before eating. Any longer and the food starts to cool down. I have to balance eating with keeping up with ice melting. The food starts off tongue-burning hot. By the time I finish, it is lukewarm. Every time I add ice to the water pot, I close the food thermos. This prevents spills and also keeps it warmer. Although it seems inefficient to open and close the lid, leaving the container open means a colder dinner. Avoiding a spilled container prevents lost calories, a mess, tent contamination, and mildew growth.

I have learned the food thermos needs to be cleaned daily. Any food product with a cream or milk base causes the food thermos to smell bad the next evening. Even though the air is −40°F, solar radiation heats up the sled bag, keeping the food remnants in the thermos warm. I use snow chunks to scrape out the food scraps then pour in hot water, shake it, and drink the water. I make one more cleaning pass with snow. The thermos never smells bad after following this procedure.

After eating but while the snow is still melting, I inflate my down-filled air mattress to 90 percent capacity. Any fuller and it is too stiff for sleeping. Any less and the nightly cooling leaves me pressed against the ice. I use every moment to do something so I can go to sleep at 10 p.m., every night. If I stay up later, I am tired in the morning, which affects my skiing. Being disciplined makes a big difference in how I perform.

A Full Expedition Day

Every day I inspect all of my equipment for frays, tears, or any other sign of wear. This allows me to save my boots, as the soles have begun to separate. Using Seam Grip® as a glue and a broken aluminum bracket as a clamp, I repair my boot. I use JB Weld® to repair the epoxy coating of my skis. After stumbling on countless sastrugi, the metal edges chew through to the ski's wood core. Should they warm up slightly, absorbing any water, the freezing action will expand the wood and destroy the skis. Seams in my sled bag straps began to tear, so I re-sew them, preventing worse damage. I spend up to an hour every evening checking and repairing gear.

Once I have made my satellite phone calls, cleaned up my cooking gear, and made daily repairs, I stow all my equipment. I want to minimize time wasted in the morning when I am cold and groggy. It is much easier to prepare at night compared to being cold coming out of a warm sleeping bag.

Every night I film myself talking about the day. This helps record my thoughts and feelings beyond my journal. The footage will be handy for the documentary film, too. Once I have finished all my tasks, I change into sleeping clothes. This helps keep my bag cleaner and me warmer. I crawl into my sleeping bag full of bottles, electronics, boot liners, the day's socks, and the next morning's clothing. This dries things out at night and gives me warm clothes in the morning.

Every night I write in my Rite in the Rain® Journal using my Fischer Space Pen® while in my sleeping bag. When the pen starts skipping from extreme cold, I warm the tip on my tongue. I activate my warmed GPS inside my sleeping bag, write down the position, and immediately turn it off. The AA lithium batteries have only lost twenty-five percent of their charge after three months of use by being stingy. I always lie inside the bag to write. This keeps me warm and reduces negative emotions.

The silicone earplugs and eye mask I brought along make a huge difference in my sleep. When I first started, I used neither and was constantly tired from the noise and light. Once I used them every night, I felt refreshed in the morning. Foam earplugs hurt my ears after a few hours from the pressure, plus they are unsanitary after a few uses without a shower. I prefer silicone earplugs because I can clean them off.

ADVENTURE EXPEDITION ONE

I do my best to sleep at 10 p.m. If I stay up until 11 p.m. working on repairs, I am fatigued the next day. Being rigorous about my schedule keeps me on track. Even if I can't fall asleep, I force myself to lay still and rest.

During the night, I use a pee bottle. Instead of rising up, I lie on my side, keeping most of my body in the sleeping bag. This reduces chill, enabling me to resume sleeping faster. I also keep the eye mask partially on, minimizing light exposure, which improves my sleep. When I finish, I close the lid, open the tent zipper, hold the container outside, open the lid, and pour it out. This eliminates the need to keep the contents warm by stowing the container in my bag. Many explorers have suffered from sleeping bag urine stench. Although the technique is slower, I never suffer a spill. This also keeps the bottle threads dry, reducing the number of times the bottle freezes shut. I always keep it in the same place on a coat, making finding it easier.

Other notes

One of my favorite meals on my Antarctic expedition was freeze-dried lasagna. Although it was tasty, the cheese froze to the container and spoon, requiring extra effort to clean. Before leaving, test all food in a freezer to see how difficult cleaning will be. It's a significant annoyance and food-poisoning risk.

Try reading a digital top-of-wrist-mounted watch with all of your polar gear on and tied up. Time yourself to see how long it takes you to reseal your gloves, and then try the bottom of the wrist technique.

Mildew formed in the tent side-pocket where I stored my titanium food spork. I learned that I had to leave it sitting on a bottle to prevent ingesting potential toxins.

Avoid using a knife whenever possible. One Antarctic explorer was cutting cheese, had the knife slip, and sliced his hand. He was fortunate he didn't cut an artery. He could have bled to death before he was rescued. The accident ended his expedition.

Repackaging food makes a huge difference in weight. Placing each freeze-dried meal in a sealable plastic bag saved three pounds in dehydrated packaging beyond the food thermos.

A Full Expedition Day

Test your brand of toothpaste. I found only Colgate® doesn't freeze in extremely cold temperatures. Even then it needs to be warmed up before use. Other brands freeze solid. Make sure to keep the toothbrush clean and dry and remember to floss. Three months of poor dental hygiene can result in painful trouble.

Putting my socks and boot liners on the sunny side of the tent during the evening helped dry them out. I even saw steam rising from the solar radiation. I kept both in my sleeping bag at night and they were always dry in the morning. It felt like sleeping on a junk heap, but the dry and warm clothes made it worth the annoyance.

One explorer I met suffered food poisoning from salami. During the day, if the sun was out and there was no wind, solar radiation heated the sled bags. The sun was strong enough to melt ice on the tent, causing a minor mildew problem. After two weeks, I noticed my salami looked as though it had thawed and frozen several times. Fearful of food poisoning, I ditched it. The other explorer ignored the warning sign and ate the meat, then spent a full day vomiting.

I ate eight ounces of butter a day, equivalent to two sticks. They went rancid in the last two weeks of my expedition from solar radiation. Now, I pile snow on the sled bags every evening to prevent this problem. My shortbread cookies even melted from the radiation in −40°C (−40°F) temperatures.

Food psychology plays a big role in success. For humans, accepting whatever is served is less stressful than choosing. This assumes you can tolerate all the food you brought. If not, you made a huge mistake. You'll discover after weeks that you will prefer one thing to another. This subtle desire can build into morale-crushing stress.

Avoid scrimping on generic camera and electronics batteries. I have never found an off-brand that works well in extreme cold. They cause more frustration and problems than the few dollars they save.

Bring new fuel pumps on every expedition and test them before leaving. North Pole expeditions should have five pumps. I've met people who had to abandon their Denali attempt because their only fuel pump broke. They're inexpensive compared to the cost of an expedition.

283

ADVENTURE EXPEDITION ONE

Make sure to lace up your boots with your foot flexed up as high as possible. I injured my Achilles on an Arctic expedition by lacing my boots with my toes pointed outward while sitting in my tent. Put your foot on a rock, push down, and then tie. This gives the right amount of room to let your feet flex. Only tie your boots with toes pointed outward while traveling downhill to prevent toe injuries. Once you reach the flats or uphill, loosen the lace tension again.

Women have to urinate while squatting without assistance from a device (pee funnel), as it will freeze instantly. The best technique is to simply hide downwind of the sled. For men—face downwind. Do note that if the wind is strong, your urine stream will blow back on you. This is unavoidable. However, it's usually so cold at that point that it freezes the moment it strikes your shell pants and blows off. Keeping yourself clean and dry requires constant care and effort. Also, having gloves with safety (idiot) cords to draw onto your wrists prevents loss. It's common for people to lose gloves to the wind. I never had a loss, as I treated every glove removal with the utmost care. I knew I'd lose fingers if I lost a glove. I took my time.

Should you become extra chilled from clouds, a change in wind speed, or temperature, there are a few options. The Greenlandic Sirius patrol advises pinwheeling your arms at least thirty times for finger coldness. Any less and your fingers won't warm up. The same applies for foot and toe coldness. Kick the ground as many times as you can stand. It's unpleasant but it does work.

Kicking and pinwheeling is not practical while skiing, though. What I used was the focused mental technique of thinking about the hottest places or baths I've ever experienced. (Think Japanese onsens or Hungarian hot spas.) I kept thinking about those while still skiing. It was extremely difficult to do and required exhausting concentration. With effort, I could cause my hands and toes to sweat. I only had to stop a few times on the whole expedition to add layers when the temperature dropped too quickly for me to adapt. Normally unzipping or zipping up a jacket an inch or two, at the most, makes the difference between comfort, overheating, or freezing.

I coated the sides and back of my wool boot liners with Gorilla duct tape. If they aren't armored, they'll wear through. This happened

A Full Expedition Day

to another explorer. Regular duct tape doesn't stick well at all in polar temperatures. Only Gorilla Tape® seemed to work. It's so sticky that handling it began ripping apart my skin, so I used the pliers on my multitool to start a tear.

I preferred a snub to needle nose multitool for this reason. I never pried or twisted too hard with the tool, as I've seen others break theirs. In the extreme cold, the metal becomes brittle.

It's tempting when a zipper is frozen to yank on a zipper pull in order to break through the ice. Don't do it. Once that zipper fails in 80 mph winds, you're in trouble. The year before me, a team nearly burned their tent down by using a flame to melt the zipper. They damaged their tent. Never, ever use flame on any tent part.

Instead, use one of your boiling hot water bottles as an iron. With gloves on, pour boiling water into a Nalgene® but leave the Neoprene sleeve off. Press the Nalgene® against the zipper, just above the zipper pull. In a few moments, the ice will melt and steam. Unzip the door as you run the bottle upward. You'll lose heat in the tent but you'll be free. Once the zipper is open, do not close it back up. It can refreeze. Instead, use your snowbrush or toothbrush to brush the ice off. Clean every inch of the zipper, as one patch of ice can start the freezing process all over again.

Should the zipper freeze while the stove is putting out yellow flames (poisonous fumes), you'll be trapped in a gas chamber. In a pinch, you can put your mouth on the zipper next to the pull and exhale forcefully. The ice will momentarily melt so you can work the zipper loose. You'll be adding more ice to the problem but the door will be open. There's a chance of frostbite on your lips using this last-resort technique. Again, brush all the ice off every zipper tooth once it's open. Flex the zipper back and forth to chip up the ice.

Aaron skiing alone across Yellowstone at −30° F.

PART TEN

Return And Recover

Depending on the length of the expedition, you may need some significant recovery time. You may find it shocking or claustrophobic to be in a large room. The smell of concrete, grass, and gasoline can be jarring. If you set out on an expedition lasting a month or longer, plan on needing some beach time. Immediately returning to work may be more difficult than you think.

This is especially important if your expedition was solo. Being alone for a significant amount of time can affect you as strongly as prison solitary confinement. Humans are social creatures. Even though natural soloists can handle solitude, avoid underestimating the effect it will have on you.

If you have media or sponsor appearances, make sure to have someone coach you. Although you may think you look good on television, it's possible you don't. This is especially true if you have never been televised before. Practice what you're going to say to eliminate stumbling phrases like "umm." They'll make you look unprepared. This can possibly harm future efforts to secure sponsors.

Once you return from an expedition, you will find people want to know all about the experience. After that wears off, be prepared for the "What's next?" question. This is especially true if you complete a major expedition lasting more than a month. It can be difficult for

ADVENTURE EXPEDITION ONE

people to understand that you may have had your fill. Be patient with yourself and other people.

Should you have set a first or a record, consider sharing your experience through a book or film. Hopefully, you thought about this during the planning stages of your expedition. If you failed to record enough media and written material, you may struggle to produce what you planned to.

For video documentaries, for some reason, it often feels like you have filmed countless hours of footage. Yet, when you return home, there is less usable media than you envisioned. Did you write in a journal every day, documenting the dramatic as well as the mundane?

After three days of any travel, details become lost. When you are working hard trekking, the details disappear even more quickly. Often, the last thing you want to do is write in a journal or make video notes when you are dead tired, it's forty degrees below zero, and you can't keep your eyes open. Resist the temptation to put your documentation off until tomorrow. You'll find a week has passed and you can't remember which camp was which.

If you plan to write a book about your experience, enlist help. Often, writing a book is a tougher endeavor than any expedition. The distractions are endless. If you don't focus your efforts, years may pass and the book may never be completed. The same happens for documentary films. If you don't budget significant time for these, they will never come to fruition. There are countless resources on how to create films and write books. Visit a writing or film-making group to find help in making a lasting account of what you accomplished.

Be aware that you may be a subtly different person for a while when you return to your family. Being under physical stress for a long time may cause your family interactions to change. If you were on a solo expedition of significant length, remember that you have been in solitary confinement. This can seriously affect how you interact with people.

Make sure to be open and communicate with your family. You do not want your expedition experience to negatively impact your home life. Ideally, you will return to civilization a stronger and more confident person. The value of your experience can be immeasurable and it might take months or even years before you realize the benefits.

Closing

After you have returned to your normal life, the experience of your first expedition will stay with you for life. It may completely change you. You may become happily addicted to pursuing the next challenge. Hopefully the experience will strengthen you, improving your life in a dramatic or subtle way. Often, you will find yourself unconsciously changed by the experience. Some swear they'll never undertake such a trip again. The reactions are as varied as the people.

However you end up afterward, know that you had the courage to embark on an expedition. So often people talk about it but never commit. You will now have abilities that you, perhaps, never knew you had. Whatever the case may be, the authors hope that the experience was positive and that this text helped you along your journey.

Happy expeditioning!

Eating cups of butter for energy on a long expedition.

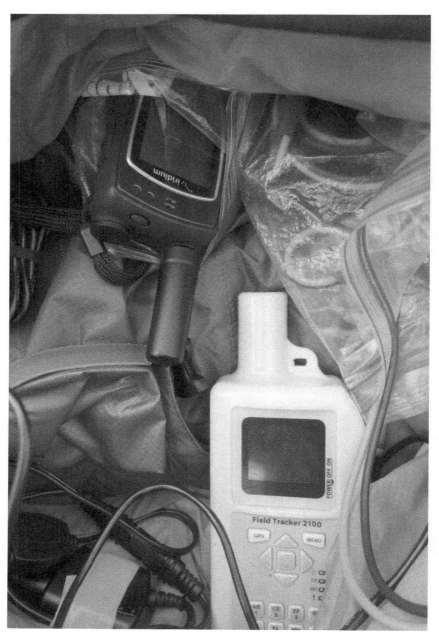
Satellite technology is required for remote communication.

PART ELEVEN

Survival List

The survival items in the below list are based on multiple sources. Consider each as you plan and train for your expedition. Keep them in mind when considering important factors in any survival situation.

1. Attitude and the will to survive. This rates above everything else. You can be dead in seconds without this.
2. Oxygen. Without it, you'll be dead in four minutes.
3. Core temperature maintenance. You'll be dead in half an hour if you let your core temperature drop too low.
4. Positive self-talk. Without this, you may not survive the day.
5. Work with what you have. Focus on what's available, even garbage, rather than worrying about what you don't have.
6. Protection from the elements, animals, injury, toxins. Not managing these items can reduce your survival to hours if things go wrong.
7. Shelter. This ties into #3 and #5. It can mean minutes to days without it.
8. Water. You won't survive much beyond three days without it.
9. Food. You may last a month without it in good conditions.
10. Fire. The warmth and psychological boost are incalculable.

The position of where fire fits into this list is arguable. It can be used for core temperature maintenance, assuming you're able to start a substantial enough fire to do anything for you. Fire can also be useful to sterilize water and cook food. However, fire isn't necessary for any one of these items. For survival shows, it's one of the primary focuses for the drama rather than the utility. The physical warmth and psychological boost can make the difference between life and death, though. In polar regions and some desert regions, building a fire is impossible without fuel that you've brought with you.

Cooking in a tent is dangerous but necessary in extreme locations and during raging storms.

Alone in the Arctic on an expedition.

PART TWELVE

Selected Resources

Books:

Auerbach, Paul. *Wilderness Medicine*. St. Louis: Mosby, 4th ed., 2001.
Blumenfeld , Jeff. *You Want to Go Where?* New York: Skyhorse Publishing, 2009.
Boy Scout Handbook. Boy Scouts of America; 13th edition, 2016.
Boy Scout Field Book. Boy Scouts of America, 4 edition, 2004.
Butcher, Tim. *Blood River: A Journey to Africa's Broken Heart*. New York: Grove Press, 2008.
Callahan, Steven. *Adrift: Seventy-six Days Lost at Sea*. Boston: Houghton Mifflin Company, 1999.
Curran, Jim. *K2 The Story of the Savage Mountain*. Seattle: The Mountaineers, 1995.
Dansercouer, Dixie . *Polar Exploration*. Cumbria, UK: Cicerone, 2012.
Grann, David. *The Lost City of Z*. New York: Vintage Books, 2009.
Graydon, Don and Hanson, Kurt, eds. *Mountaineering: the Freedom of the Hills*. Seattle: The Mountaineers, 6th edition, 1997
Humphreys, Alastair. *Microadventures*. London: William Collins, 2014.
Krakauer, John. *Into the Wild*. New York: Villard, 1996.
Lansing, Alfred. *Endurance*. New York: McGraw-Hill Book Company, Inc., 1959
Linsdau, Aaron. *Antarctic Tears*. Jackson: Sastrugi Press, 2014

SELECTED RESOURCES

Peeters, Randall L. *Journeys to the Edge*. Jackson: Sastrugi Press, 2014.

Pollan, Michael. *Food Rules: an Eater's Manual*. New York: Penguin Books, 2009.

Schimelpfenig, Tod. *NOLS Wilderness Medicine*. Maryland: Stackpole Books, 2016.

Simpson, Joe. *Touching the Void*. New York: HarperPerennial, 1998.

Steger, Will and Schurke, Paul. *North to the Pole*. St. Paul, MN: The Minnesota Historical Society Press, 1987.

Swedo, Suzanne. *Hiking the Golden Trout Wilderness*. Guilford, Connecticut: The Globe Pequot Press, 2004.

Tabor, James. *Forever on the Mountain*. New York: W. W. Norton & Company, 2007.

Thesiger, Wilfred. *Arabian Sands*. New York: Penguin Books, 1984

Twain, Mark. *Roughing It*. Layton, UT: Gibbs Smith, 2017.

United States Air Force, McCullough, Jay. *United States Air Force Survival Manual*. New York: Skyhorse Publishing, 2017.

Viesturs, Ed with Roberts, David. *No Shortcuts to the Top*. New York: Broadway Books, 2006.

Vonhoff, John. *Fixing Your Feet*. Birmingham: Wilderness Press, 6th Edition, 2016.

Magazines and Journals:

American Alpine Journal, Andy Anderson, ed. Published annually by the American Alpine Club, New York

Backpacker Magazine. El Segundo, CA: Active Interest Media.

National Geographic Magazine. New York: National Geographic Society.

National Geographic Adventure Magazine. New York: National Geographic Society.

Outside Magazine. New York: Mariah Media Inc.

Vanity Fair Magazine. New York: Condé Nast.

Internet resources:

CDC Travel website: https://wwwnc.cdc.gov/travel/

Joint Commission International website for accredited facilities: https://www.jointcommissioninternational.org/about-jci/jci-accredited-organizations/

National Outdoor Leadership School website: https://www.nols.edu

www.puncturesandpanniers.com by Clair & André

295

About the Authors

Aaron Linsdau is the second-only American to ski alone from the coast of Antarctica to the South Pole, setting a world record for surviving the longest expedition ever for that trip. He has walked across Yellowstone National Park in winter, crossed the Greenland tundra alone, has trekked through the Sahara Desert, attempted to climb Denali solo, and successfully climbed Mt. Kilimanjaro.

Aaron is an Eagle Scout and has received the Outstanding Eagle Scout Award. He holds a bachelor's degree in electrical engineering and a master's degree in computational science. Aaron wrote the book and produced the film *Antarctic Tears* and the show *World Beyond*. He also wrote guidebooks for the 2017 and 2024 total eclipses.

He is an expert at building resilience to overcome adversity. He is a motivational speaker on risk, safety, and his methods for overcoming challenges, using his stories and experiences. Book him at his website: www.ncexped.com.

Terry M. Williams, M.D. is the father of four and grandfather of nine, recently retired from a 32-year practice of Emergency Medicine in California. He is the author of several medical papers and Emergency Medicine textbook chapters. In addition to his full-time medical work in California, he has treated patients in Guatemala, Saudi Arabia, on cruise ships around the world, in Northern India, Thailand, and the highlands of Papua New Guinea. He is also a whitewater kayaker and climber with summits of Sierra 14ers, several of the Cascade volcanoes, and two of the Seven Summits (Aconcagua and Kilimanjaro).

He has served as expedition doctor on climbs, whitewater runs and in wilderness/primitive settings. He serves on the board of an international missions/humanitarian organization, Global Fellowship, and now resides in northern San Diego County with his wife of 44 years. He also serves as a medical team manager on San Diego's Urban Search and Rescue (USAR) Team, California Task Force 8. He is currently working on a new book on his adventures and career in Emergency Medicine.

Enjoy other Sastrugi Press titles

2024 Total Eclipse State Series by Aaron Linsdau
Sastrugi Press has published state-specific guides for the 2024 total eclipse crossing over the United States. Check the Sastrugi Press website for the available state eclipse books: www.sastrugipress.com/eclipse

Antarctic Tears by Aaron Linsdau
What would make someone give up a high-paying career to ski alone across Antarctica to the South Pole? This inspirational true story will make readers both cheer and cry. Fighting skin-freezing temperatures, infections, and emotional breakdown, Jackson Hole native Aaron Linsdau exposes the harsh realities of being on an expedition.

Journeys to the Edge by Randall Peeters, Ph.D.
What is it like to climb Mount Everest? It requires dreaming big and creating a personal vision to climb the mountains in your life. Randall Peeters shares his successes and failures and provides the reader with some directly applicable guidelines on how to create a life vision.

Lost at Windy Corner by Aaron Linsdau
Windy Corner on Denali has claimed lives, fingers, and toes. What would make someone brave lethal weather, crevasses, and slick ice to attempt to summit North America's highest mountain? The author shares the lessons Denali teaches on managing goals and risks. Apply the message to build resilience and overcome adversity.

Voices at Twilight by Lori Howe, Ph.D.
Voices at Twilight is a guide that takes readers on a visual tour of twelve past and present Wyoming ghost towns. Contained within are travel directions, GPS coordinates, and tips for intrepid readers.

Visit Sastrugi Press on the web at www.sastrugipress.com to purchase the above titles in bulk. They are also available from your local bookstore or online retailers in print, e-book, or audiobook form.

Thank you for choosing Sastrugi Press.
www.sastrugipress.com
"Turn the Page Loose"